Frommer's

PORTABLE
California Wine Country

4th Edition

by Erika Lenkert

D0034436

Here's what critics say about Frommer's:

"Amazingly easy to use. Very portable, very complete."

—*Booklist*

"Detailed, accurate, and easy-to-read information for all price ranges."

—*Glamour Magazine*

WILEY

Wiley Publishing, Inc.

Published by:

WILEY PUBLISHING, INC.
111 River St.
Hoboken, NJ 07030-5774

ISBN 0-7645-4444-6

Editor: Caroline Sieg
Production Editor: Tammy Ahrens
Photo Editor: Richard Fox
Cartographer: John Decamillis
Production by Wiley Indianapolis Composition Services

For information on our other products and services or to obtain technical
support, please contact our Customer Care Department within the U.S. at
800/762-2974, outside the U.S. at 317/572-3993 or fax 317/572-4002.

Wiley also publishes its books in a variety of electronic formats. Some content that appears in print may not be available in electronic formats.

Manufactured in the United States of America

5   4   3   2   1

Contents

List of Maps

ABOUT THE AUTHOR

Native San Franciscan **Erika Lenkert** fled the dot-community to find respite and great food and wine in Napa Valley. When she's not writing about dining for the *San Francisco Chronicle*, *Four Seasons Magazine*, or *InStyle*, or promoting her new book *The Last-Minute Party Girl: Fashionable, Fearless, and Foolishly Simple Entertaining*, she's in search of Wine Country pleasures to share with Frommer's readers. She also remains subservient to her owners—two Siamese cats.

In addition to this guide, Erika authors and co-authors a number of other Frommer's guides to California, including *Frommer's California*, *Frommer's San Francisco*, and *Frommer's Memorable Walks in San Francisco*.

AN INVITATION TO THE READER

In researching this book, we discovered many wonderful places—hotels, restaurants, shops, and more. We're sure you'll find others. Please tell us about them, so we can share the information with your fellow travelers in upcoming editions. If you were disappointed with a recommendation, we'd love to know that, too. Please write to:

> *Frommer's Portable California Wine Country,* 4th Edition
> Wiley Publishing, Inc. • 111 River St. • Hoboken, NJ 07030-5774

AN ADDITIONAL NOTE

Please be advised that travel information is subject to change at any time—and this is especially true of prices. We therefore suggest that you write or call ahead for confirmation when making your travel plans. The authors, editors, and publisher cannot be held responsible for the experiences of readers while traveling. Your safety is important to us, however, so we encourage you to stay alert and be aware of your surroundings. Keep a close eye on cameras, purses, and wallets, all favorite targets of thieves and pickpockets.

FROMMER'S STAR RATINGS, ICONS & ABBREVIATIONS

Every hotel, restaurant, and attraction listing in this guide has been ranked for quality, value, service, amenities, and special features using a **star-rating system.** In country, state, and regional guides, we also rate towns and regions to help you narrow down your choices and budget your time accordingly. Hotels and restaurants are rated on a scale of zero (recommended) to three stars (exceptional). Attractions, shopping, nightlife, towns, and regions are rated according to the following scale: zero stars (recommended), one star (highly recommended), two stars (very highly recommended), and three stars (must-see).

In addition to the star-rating system, we also use **seven feature icons** that point you to the great deals, in-the-know advice, and unique experiences that separate travelers from tourists. Throughout the book, look for:

Finds	Special finds—those places only insiders know about
Fun Fact	Fun facts—details that make travelers more informed and their trips more fun
Kids	Best bets for kids and advice for the whole family
Moments	Special moments—those experiences that memories are made of
Overrated	Places or experiences not worth your time or money
Tips	Insider tips—great ways to save time and money
Value	Great values—where to get the best deals

The following **abbreviations** are used for credit cards:

AE	American Express	DISC	Discover	V	Visa
DC	Diners Club	MC	MasterCard		

FROMMERS.COM

Now that you have the guidebook to a great trip, visit our website at **www.frommers.com** for travel information on more than 3,000 destinations. With features updated regularly, we give you instant access to the most current trip-planning information available. At Frommers.com, you'll also find the best prices on airfares, accommodations, and car rentals—and you can even book travel online through our travel booking partners. At Frommers.com, you'll also find the following:

- Online updates to our most popular guidebooks
- Vacation sweepstakes and contest giveaways
- Newsletter highlighting the hottest travel trends
- Online travel message boards with featured travel discussions

The Best of the Wine Country

Whether you're on a budget or blowing your annual bonus, there's no way around it: A Wine Country experience epitomizes indulgence. Literally all that's expected of you is to eat, drink, relax—and then do it all over again. The rest—wine tastings, spa treatments, hot-air balloon rides, horseback tours—is mere icing on an already idyllic cake. In fact, you don't even have to like wine to love the Wine Country; anyone who enjoys lounging in a hammock on a warm summer's day will succumb because the Wine Country is just that: the country. The verdant expanses of rolling hills patterned with grape-garnered trellises, hued with mustard and wildflowers, and dotted with farmers plowing the soil and vintners tending to their vines is country life at its picture-perfect best.

Of course, there's a whole lot more: wineries both great and small producing some of the world's finest wines, nationally renowned chefs serving exceptional cuisine, luxury resorts, and soothing mineral hot springs. Yes, the world may be falling apart elsewhere, but not here—for this eternal Eden of indulgence is where you go when you feel the need to be pampered, when it's time to whip out the charge card for that $200 dinner or bottle of cabernet sauvignon and say, "Frankly, my dear, I don't give a damn."

This is why you're holding *Frommer's Portable California Wine Country.* Consider it your personal passport to the best that Napa Valley and Sonoma Valley have to offer. Follow the suggestions herein, and you'll know why this is one of my favorite vacation spots on the planet. In time, it's bound to become one of yours, too.

1 The Best Wineries

- **Artesa** (Carneros, Napa Valley): Sure they've got a huge wine portfolio that includes a slew of tasty pinot noirs. But what makes Artesa one of my all-time favorite places to send visitors is the winery itself. Built into the Carneros hillside with stellar views of the San Pablo Bay and beyond, from the outside it seems like an underground fortress topped with super-cool fountains. From within it's an airy, modern space with plenty of elbowroom. Plainly put, it's just too darned cool. See p. 56.

- **Clos Pegase** (Calistoga, Napa Valley): Viewing the art at this temple to wine is as much the point as tasting the wines themselves. Renowned architect Michael Graves designed this incredible oasis, which integrates an impressive modern art collection—including a sculpture garden—with a state-of-the-art winemaking facility that features 20,000 square feet of aging caves. See p. 75.

- **Domaine Chandon** (Yountville, Napa Valley): Founded by Moët et Chandon, the valley's most renowned sparkling winery has all the grandeur of a world-class French champagne house. Strolling with a glass of bubbly in hand through this estate's beautifully manicured rose gardens—complete with pond and sculpture—is a quintessential Wine Country experience. If you just can't bear to leave, no worries. Just pull up a chair in their fancy French dining room or in the more casual salon or patio and relish in the pastoral splendor. See p. 60.

- **The Hess Collection** (Napa, Napa Valley): Half the fun is winding your way to this beautiful and secluded hillside winery, which is as much about contemporary art as it is about fermented grape juice. Spectacular gallery spaces show off their stunning collection and the gift shop is one of the most tasteful in the valley. It's a gorgeous place. See p. 58.

- **Joseph Phelps Vineyards** (St. Helena, Napa Valley): Intimate, comprehensive tours and knockout tastings make this one of my favorite wineries to visit. An air of seriousness hangs heavier than harvest grapes when you first arrive, but the mood lightens as your knowledgeable guide explains the ins and outs of winemaking and you begin to taste five to six varietals. These range from sauvignon blanc to what's bound to be terrific cabernet. (*Wine Spectator* regularly awards Phelps's cabernets and blended reds with scores in the high 90s, and aficionados have been known to come close to brawling over bottles of the coveted Insignia Cabernet.) Don't forget to reserve ahead; tours and tastings are by appointment only. See p. 70.

- **Schramsberg** (Calistoga, Napa Valley): Old hand-carved caves complete with cobwebs, echoes, and loads of ambience; a comprehensive walk through sparkling wine production; and a grand finale tasting around a round table in a private room make this a great stop for those looking for a little entertainment with their education. See p. 75.

- **Swanson Vineyards & Winery** (Rutherford, Napa Valley): No other winery offers such a luxurious, relaxed, and fun tasting as this sexy little reservations-only stop. Join the select few guests at a round table, taste delicious wines, and nibble on bonbons while you make new friends and learn about the famed Rutherford dust. Now that's living. See p. 63.

- **V. Sattui Winery** (St. Helena, Napa Valley): Nowhere else can you taste small-volume wines (only sold here, but not particularly noteworthy), stock up on gourmet lunch supplies (free tastes!), and join in on a huge, ongoing picnic all at the same time. It's not the wine, but the festive and family-friendly lawn party that makes this a must-stop. The crowds are mighty, but as the saying goes, "If you can't beat 'em . . . ." See p. 69.

- **The Benziger Family Winery** (Glen Ellen, Sonoma Valley): As soon as you arrive here, you'll know you're at a family-run winery—in fact, you'll feel instantly like part of the Benziger clan. This low-volume, high-quality winery offers an exceptional self-guided tour, a 40-minute tram tour through its pastoral grounds, $5 tastings, and many excellent, reasonably priced wines. See p. 137.

- **Gloria Ferrer Champagne Caves** (Carneros District, Sonoma Valley): Gloria is the grande dame of Sonoma Valley's sparkling wine producers. On a sunny day, it's impossible not to enjoy sipping a glass of brut on the terrace of this palatial estate as you take in the magnificent views of the vineyards and valley below. If you're unfamiliar with the *méthode champenoise,* make time for the 30-minute tour, which takes you past the fermenting tanks and the bustling bottling line and into the dark caves brimming with rack after rack of fermenting wine. See p. 133.

- **Gundlach Bundschu Winery** (Sonoma, Sonoma Valley): Gundlach Bundschu is the quintessential Sonoma winery: nonchalant about appearance, obsessed with wine. Oenophiles in the know covet GB's reds, particularly the zinfandels, which are remarkably inexpensive for such well-crafted wines. Tours include a trip into the 430-foot cave. GB also has the best picnic grounds in the valley. See p. 134.

- **Matanzas Creek** (Santa Rosa): It's not technically in Sonoma Valley, but if there's one winery that's worth the drive up to Bennett Valley, it's Matanzas Creek, one of the prettiest wineries in California (particularly when the lavender fields are in bloom, near the end of June). And the wines are pretty tasty, too. See p. 141.

2 The Best Winery Tours for First-Timers

- **Domaine Chandon** (Yountville, Napa Valley): Not only are the grounds sublime, but the comprehensive tour walks you through the high-tech facilities and the entire bubbly-making process, from the history of the winery to the cellars, riddling room, and bottling line. Tours are free and reservations aren't necessary, but if you want to taste, it'll cost you: $9 to $14 for a full glass (sorry, no free sips). Come during high season, though, and you can supplement your bubbly with a few appetizers and kick back on the garden-front patio. See p. 60.

- **Robert Mondavi Winery** (Oakville, Napa Valley): As one of the most prominent wineries in the valley, it's only appropriate that Robert Mondavi would offer a guided tour for every sort of wine taster. The basic 1-hour comprehensive production tour covers all aspects of the winemaking process and gives you a look at the destemmer-crusher, the tank room where fermentation is done, the bottling room, and the vineyard, all accompanied by a top-notch narrative—the guides are great at making sure you know what you're looking at. Your reward at the end? A tasting, of course. If you find yourself inspired, you can then move on to one of the other offered tours, such as the 3- to 4-hour advanced wine-growing tour, cheese and wine pairing, or "essence" tasting, which teaches you how to identify various aromas in wines. Make your reservations in advance, if possible; these tours are not offered daily and get booked up, especially in high season. See p. 61.

- **St. Supéry Winery** (Rutherford, Napa Valley): This straightforward winery is a great place for first-time tasters to learn more about oenology. The nifty self-guided tour comes complete with "SmellaVision," an interactive display that teaches you how to identify different wine aromas and attributes; there's also a demonstration vineyard that you can wander through to learn about growing techniques. See p. 64.

- **Frank Family Vineyards** (Calistoga, Napa Valley): Although this isn't a remotely comprehensive tour, it is the most unintimidating. Staff members run one of the friendliest wineries in the valley, which includes taking the time to explain *anything* you want to know about wine. They also serve you all the bubbly you want and have a back room featuring still wines. See p. 74.

- **Schramsberg** (Calistoga, Napa Valley): The label that U.S. presidents serve when toasting with dignitaries from around the globe also serves up the Wine Country's best introduction to the *méthode champenoise* process of making sparkling wine. The excellent tour at Schramsberg is comprehensive and non-threatening, and it's an experience you won't soon forget; the highlight is the visit to the 2½ miles of hand-carved champagne caves—you'll feel like you've landed in the middle of a *Tom Sawyer* adventure. And the tasting room is positively gothic. Be sure to book a spot on a tour in advance, as tours fill up quickly. See p. 75.

- **Sterling Vineyards** (Calistoga, Napa Valley): This dazzling-white, Mediterranean-style winery, perched high above the rest of the valley atop a rocky knoll (you'll arrive via aerial tram), offers one of the most comprehensive self-guided tours in the entire Wine Country. It's great for getting to know the entire winemaking process at your own pace. See p. 76.

- **The Benziger Family Winery** (Glen Ellen, Sonoma Valley): *Wine Spectator* magazine hailed this family-run winery as having "the most comprehensive tour in the wine industry." The exceptional self-guided tour, which includes a free 40-minute tram ride through the estate vineyards, is both informative and fun. Tram tickets are a hot commodity, so be sure to plan ahead for this one. See p. 137.

3 The Best Experiences Beyond the Wineries

- **Hot-Air Ballooning Over Napa's Vineyards:** Admit it: Floating over lush green pastures in a hot-air balloon is something you've always dreamed of but never gotten around to actually doing. Here's your best chance: Napa Valley is the busiest hot-air balloon "flight corridor" in the *world*—and what more romantic place to sail up, up, and away? For recommendations on the best Napa hot-air balloon companies, see "More to See & Do," in chapter 4.

- **Spreading Out Your Picnic Blanket for a Gourmet Alfresco Feast:** You've been with the crowds all day—sitting with them in traffic and sipping elbow-to-elbow in the tasting rooms. If the thought of joining the masses for a meal after all that seems about as romantic and relaxing as a New York subway ride, cancel your restaurant reservations and pack a picnic instead. Both Napa and Sonoma have some of the most spectacular picnic spots on the planet, not to mention incredible artisan food products and excellent places to fill your basket. Check out the legendary and very compact and crowded **Oakville Grocery Co.** (✆ **707/944-8802**), the West Coast outpost and flagship of New York's ultra gourmet **Dean & Deluca** (✆ **707/ 967-9980**), and the more down home **Sonoma Cheese Factory** (✆ **707/996-1000**), which offers more kinds of house-made jack cheeses than you ever imagined were possible. See "Where to Stock Up for a Picnic & Where to Enjoy It," in chapter 4 for details on picnicking in Napa, and see "Where to Stock Up for a Picnic & Where to Enjoy It," in chapter 5 for details on picnicking in Sonoma.

- **Pampering Yourself at a Spa:** The Wine Country is the perfect place to relax—so what better place to indulge in a tension-relieving massage, a purifying facial, or a rejuvenating body wrap? My favorite spots to spa it are St. Helena's **White Sulphur Springs Inn & Spa** (✆ **707/963-8588**) and **Health Spa Napa Valley** (✆ **707/967-8800**), and the **Fairmont Sonoma Mission Inn & Spa** (✆ **800/862-4945**). See chapter 4 for details on Napa spas, chapter 5 for Sonoma.

- **Horseback Riding Through the Wine Country:** If you like horses and cool, shaded forests, consider seeing the countryside from the saddle. **Triple Creek Horse Outfit** (✆ **707/933-1600**) will lead any level of rider on a leisurely ride (with the occasional trot thrown in for excitement) through beautiful Bothe-Napa Valley State Park. On the other side of the hills, they'll take you through fantastic Jack London State Historical Park. The season runs from April through October. See "More to See & Do," in chapters 4 and 5.

- **Touring Sonoma's Wineries on Two Wheels:** With quiet, gently sloping country roads and lots of bucolic scenery, Sonoma is perfect for cycling. **Goodtime Bicycle Company** (✆ **888/525-0453**) can take you on one of its organized excursions to Kenwood-area wineries or to south Sonoma's wineries; not only does Goodtime provide a gourmet lunch featuring local Sonoma foodstuffs, but it'll also carry any wine you purchase and even help with shipping it home. Goodtime will happily rent you a bike and point you to easy trails if you'd rather set out on your own. See "More to See & Do," in chapter 4 and "Touring Sonoma Valley by Bike," in chapter 5.

- **Getting Your Thrills in the Skies:** If you're the thrill-seeking type, catch a panoramic ride in an authentic 1940 Boeing-built

Stearman biplane with **Vintage Aircraft Company** (℗ 707/ **938-2444**), whose planes depart from the south end of Sonoma Valley. See "More to See & Do," in chapter 5.

- **Eating!:** Nowhere else in the country is more dedicated to celebrating the best of artisan ingredients. Add to that unparalleled access to incredible locally grown organic meats and produce, exceptionally talented chefs, and beautiful dining surroundings and trust me: You're going to have some of the best meals of your life while you're here—and are likely to eat way beyond your physical and financial means.

4 The Best Luxury Hotels & Inns

- **Auberge du Soleil** (Rutherford, Napa Valley; ℗ 800/348- **5406**): This spectacular Relais & Châteaux member is one of my absolute favorite luxury destinations on the planet. (And yes, I've seen a lot of 'em.) Quiet, indulgent, and luxuriously romantic rooms are large enough to get lost in—and you'll want to once you try out the fireplace, whirlpool tub, and private balcony overlooking the valley. Tack on an incredible spa with valley views from the hot tub and chef Richard Reddington's gorgeous food at their restaurant and it's pure heaven. If you've got the cash, this is the way to go. See p. 95.

- **Meadowood Napa Valley** (St. Helena, Napa Valley; ℗ 800/ **458-8080**): I love Meadowood, too, but it offers a more resort-like experience. Tucked away in its own private wooded valley it's a favorite retreat for Hollywood celebs and corporate CEOs who can hide out in freestanding New England–style cottages, spend days hiking the private trails or playing golf, tennis, or croquet, and follow up with a trip to the health spa and whirlpool. For those who love full-service luxury with all the fixin's, there's no better option. Indeed it's perfect anytime of year, but I find the most magical time to come is the holidays when the resort is more quiet and romantically lit with white Christmas lights. See p. 97.

- **Cottage Grove Inn** (Calistoga, Napa Valley; ℗ 800/799- **2284**): This romantic cluster of cottages is my top pick for doing the Calistoga spa scene in comfort and style. Each one-room cottage is ultra compact, but it makes a lot out of a little and comes complete with a wood-burning fireplace, homey furnishings (perfect for curling up in front of the fire), cozy quilts, and an enormous bathroom with a skylight and a deep, two-person Jacuzzi tub. But if you want the perks that come with a hotel, go for one of the suites with the outdoor hot tubs at the nearby Mount View Hotel & Spa. See p. 102.

- **Fairmont Sonoma Mission Inn & Spa** (Sonoma, Sonoma Valley; ℂ **800/862-4945**): A popular retreat for the wealthy and the well known, this multimillion-dollar resort is the last word in spa luxury. Naturally heated artesian springs are the place's coup de grace. Sauna, steam room, whirlpool, outdoor exercise pool, weight room, a whole menu of spa treatments—you can pamper yourself in myriad ways, and retire to your superluxe suite when the day is done. Alas, the rooms are über-expensive, but, hey, this is Wine Country. Get used to it. See p. 149.

- **Gaige House Inn** (Glen Ellen, Sonoma Valley; ℂ **800/935-0237**): Truth be told I've never stayed in a better B&B ever, anywhere, period. Here's what you have to look forward to: gorgeous plantation-inspired decor with tasteful worldly accents, the best robes ever designed, unbelievable nightly appetizers that inspired an invitation to the James Beard house for the chef, late-night cookie-plate raids, and professionalism associated with fine hotels. In a nutshell, it's first-class service, an abundance of amenities, luxurious rooms outfitted with top-quality goods—everything you'd expect from an outrageously expensive resort, but with a homey, tailored, and intimate atmosphere. See p. 154.

- **Kenwood Inn & Spa** (Kenwood, Sonoma Valley; ℂ **800/353-6966**): Romantics, look no further. Here, the honey-colored, Tuscan-style buildings, flower-filled flagstone courtyard, and pastoral views of vineyard-covered hills are enough to make any northern Italian homesick. The lavishly done rooms come with just about every extra you could want (except TV, which would interfere with the tranquil ambience). The full-service spa is small but to-die-for, and the staff is friendly and helpful. And those who've tried to book a room in the past, but couldn't be accommodated take note: They've added 16 brand new reasons (rooms) to pick up the phone and break out the credit card. See p. 155.

5 The Best Moderately Priced Accommodations

- **Wine Country Inn** (St. Helena, Napa Valley; ✆ 707/963-7077): This attractive wood-and-stone hideaway, complete with a French-style mansard roof and turret, offers lovingly and individually decorated rooms and copious amounts of hospitality. It's also very well priced, considering the outrageous rates usually charged in St. Helena. One of the inn's best features is its attractively landscaped outdoor pool (heated year-round); in fact, the whole charming place overlooks a pastoral landscape of Napa Valley vineyards. See p. 100.

- **Deer Run Bed & Breakfast** (St. Helena, Napa Valley; ✆ 877/333-7786): If romantic solitude and moderate prices are part of your vacation plan, this place should be on your itinerary. Each of the wood-paneled rooms looks onto innkeepers Tom and Carol Wilson's 4 acres of forest and comes outfitted with pretty antiques and a slew of amenities, not to mention all the solitude you could possibly desire. The ultimate heavenly hideaway. See p. 101.

- **White Sulphur Springs Inn & Spa** (St. Helena, Napa Valley; ✆ 800/593-8873): This woodsy escape is a short winding drive away from downtown St. Helena. Established in 1852 and set among 330 acres of creeks, waterfalls, hot springs, redwood, madrone, and fir trees, White Sulphur Springs claims to be the oldest resort in California; it's geared toward nature-nugget types, who will appreciate both the cozily rustic cabins and the pristine surroundings. A full menu of spa treatments, outdoor pool and natural hot springs, and a holistic vibe round out the relaxation. See p. 102.

- **El Dorado Hotel** (Sonoma, Sonoma Valley; ✆ 800/289-3031): Designed by the same folks who put together Napa's exclusive Auberge du Soleil, this place on Sonoma's historic square may look like a 19th-century Wild West relic from the outside, but inside, it's all 20th-century deluxe. French windows offer lovely views of the courtyard, which features a heated lap pool. See p. 150.

- **Glenelly Inn** (Glen Ellen, Sonoma Valley; ✆ 707/996-6720): With verdant views of Sonoma's oak-studded hillsides, this former 1916 railroad inn is drenched in serenity, and it has everything you'd expect from a Wine Country retreat. Bright, immaculate rooms have old-fashioned claw-foot tubs and Scandinavian down comforters, a hearty country breakfast is served beside the large cobblestone fireplace, and there's a long veranda where you can curl up in a comfy wicker chair to admire the idyllically bucolic view. See p. 155.

6 The Best Restaurants

- **Bistro Don Giovanni** (Napa, Napa Valley; © 707/224-3300): My favorite restaurant in the valley, this has a consistent combination of perfect thin-crust pizzas (margarita and the seasonal fig, prosciutto, and balsamic are spectacular), soul-satisfying pastas (anything with duck ragout!), wood-oven specialties, friendly service, and an excellent bar dining and drinking scene. Perch yourself at the bar, order a glass of wine or a cocktail from fabulous bartenders Aaron or Ben, and you're likely to strike up a jolly conversation with a local—perhaps even me! See p. 108.
- **Bistro Jeanty** (Yountville, Napa Valley; © 707/944-0103): This locals' favorite tops even my charts—after Bistro Don Giovanni, that is. The cheery and casual atmosphere and outstanding French bistro classics from long-reputed chef Phillipe Jeanty are an absolute must-try. I always have the fried smelt, pigs' feet (C'mon, try 'em!), and crème brûlée. The only downside: This bistro's tendency toward rich and heavy food may overwhelm you when it's 100 degrees outside. See p. 114.
- **The French Laundry** (Yountville, Napa Valley; © 707/944-2380): If you've got the cash, are a serious food lover, and can get a reservation, you have no choice but to dine here and find out for yourself why chef/owner Thomas Keller's restaurant continues to be hailed the best restaurant in the world. Dinner at this intimate restaurant is an all-night affair complete with truffle shavings, dramatic presentations, and swirling and sniffing. When it's finally over, you won't believe how many different delicacies found their way out of the kitchen and into your heart. See p. 113.
- **La Toque** (Rutherford, Napa Valley; © 707/963-9770): Chef Ken Frank's formal dining room and intricately constructed food is about as close to French Laundry formal as you can get in these parts without actually paying a visit to Thomas Keller's

famous restaurant. But even when the celebration is simply to honor an insatiable appetite for truly memorable French-inspired cuisine, I recommend reserving a table here—so long as you don't mind the utterly formal atmosphere. Don't forget to dress the part. This is one dining room where jeans don't cut it. See p. 117.

- **Taylor's Automatic Refresher** (St. Helena, Napa Valley; ℂ 707/963-3486): Who doesn't love a good burger? If the answer is you, no worries. This supped-up version of the old-fashioned burger stand is a gourmet fast-food Mecca where you can snack on killer burgers, fries, shakes, *and* fish tacos, salads, and wine. Order at the window, plant yourself at one of the umbrella-shaded tables, and prove Pavlov's dog right until your name is called. See p. 121.

- **Terra** (St. Helena, Napa Valley; ℂ 707/963-8931): As far as fine dining goes, Terra is my number-one choice, period. Within a historic fieldstone restaurant, James Beard Award-winning chef Hiro Sone creates incredibly sophisticated, vibrant, and refined cuisine that deftly shows his French, Italian, and Japanese culinary training as well as his appreciation for the best of local seasonal ingredients. Sone's wife—pastry chef and front-of-the-house gal Lissa Doumani—ensures each eve is delicious, from the polished service to the to-die-for desserts. Take my word for it: if you're going to splurge, Terra is a must-try. See p. 117.

- **Tra Vigne Restaurant** (St. Helena, Napa Valley; ℂ 707/963-4444): To understand heaven on earth, snag a seat in the romantic courtyard during a warm summer or autumn day, have a late lunch, and linger until the sun sets and the twinkle lights illuminate the row of trees. Order fresh heirloom tomato salad if its available, "Fritti" (fried prawns and stuff), or their famous beef short ribs with garlic soft polenta, raise a glass of wine, and now you're really living. *Note:* Inside's fine, but it's not nearly as sexy. See p. 118.

- **ZuZu** (Napa, Napa Valley; ℂ 707/224-8555): If you've had it with French and Italian fare and Wine Country–themed dining rooms race directly to this neighborhood haunt. Shockingly affordable and serving a worldly array of Mediterranean-inspired "small plates," it's a snack-lover's nirvana. I'm addicted to the single-serving paella, yummy and intriguing by-the-glass wines, and friendly attitude here. See p. 112.

- **Café La Haye** (Sonoma, Sonoma Valley; ✆ 707/935-5994): One of my personal favorites. This small, sophisticated Sonoma cafe is a must-stop on your Wine Country dining binge. You'll enjoy the simple yet savory dishes emanating from the tiny open kitchen as well as a friendly wait staff, attractive art, and absurdly reasonable prices. See p. 158.

- **Cucina Viansa** (Sonoma, Sonoma Valley; ✆ 707/935-5656): For a quick gourmet lunch in Sonoma, there's no better place to go than Cucina Viansa. This suave deli and wine bar, run by the same people responsible for the success story that is Viansa Winery, is the sexiest thing going in Sonoma. It's a visual masterpiece, with shiny black-and-white-checkered flooring, long counters of Italian marble, and an enticing display of cured meats and cheeses. See p. 163.

- **The Girl & the Fig** (Sonoma, Sonoma Valley; ✆ 707/938-3634): The cuisine at this modern, attractive cafe is nouveau-country with French nuances—and, yes, figs: They appear in such creations as the winter fig salad made with arugula, pecans, dried figs, and Laura Chenel goat cheese with a fig-and-port vinaigrette and a hearty pork chop with fig compote, roasted fennel, mashed potatoes, and pork jus. Of course there are lots of options minus the figs, too. Tourists and locals pack the place (and its lovely back patio) nightly, so reserve ahead. See p. 159.

- **Meritage** (Sonoma, Sonoma Valley; ✆ 707/938-9430): Chef Carlo Cavallo put his heart and soul into this exciting Sonoma mainstay that combines the best of Southern French and Northern Italian cuisines. What's not to like about wild boar chops in a white truffle sauce, handmade roasted pumpkin tortelloni, and napoleon of escargot in a champagne–and–wild thyme sauce—all at surprisingly reasonable prices? Check it out. See p. 161.

2

The Wine Country Experience

by John Thoreen, Wine Tutor at Meadowood Napa Valley

Over the past 20 years, John Thoreen has built an international reputation as wine lecturer and writer. Presently he is director of the Wine Center at the prestigious Meadowood Napa Valley resort. You can reach John at Meadowood at ✆ **707/967-1205.**

Seeing the Wine Country can be an enormously pleasant day trip. However, investing at least a full day in each valley will reward you with multiple hedonistic dividends—and put you near the head of the class in understanding the ultrapremium wines of California. The pages that follow give you a head start on your trip by introducing you to Napa Valley and Sonoma Valley and the exciting world of winemaking.

1 Introducing Napa Valley & Sonoma Valley

San Francisco is often seen as a charming yet congested metropolis. In contrast, the two rural valleys just an hour to the north, Sonoma and Napa, offer a delightfully calming and rustic retreat. In the Wine Country, the focus is mainly on gastronomy: adventures with wine and food, augmented by a setting of charming villages and towns, sunny afternoons, striking mountain landscapes, carefully presented works of art and architecture, and seas of the world's tidiest vineyards.

The mix of sophistication and rusticity can be peculiar: Dusty pickups park outside some of the finest restaurants in the country. Vintners clad in denim jackets carry bottles of first-growth Bordeaux Chateaux into local bistros. Barns both small and large are more likely to house wine barrels than bales of hay. Many of the homes that pepper the region, tucked back among the vines or perched on hillsides, appear in the pages of *Architectural Digest.* And these are small towns!

Although Napa and Sonoma view each other as competitors, and although you can sense a difference in attitude traveling from one valley to the other, together as the Wine Country they differ from any other region in California. This uniqueness is based on several factors: a tumultuous geology comprised of 50 or 60 perfectly poor soils; a colorful yet disjointed historical record; a climate unique to growing world-class grapes; legions of entrepreneurs who have often misunderstood the wine business; resilient farmers who once grew wheat and prunes before switching to grapes; and you, one of five million folks who visit each year. (Some years ago, a journalist claimed that Napa is second only to Disneyland as a tourist attraction—an exaggeration that has been perpetuated ever since.)

QUALITY, NOT QUANTITY   In the odd jargon of marketing, "premium" refers to wines that sell for under $7, "superpremium" wines run between $7 and $14, and "ultrapremiums" cost $15 and up. The majority of California's premium wines come not from Napa and Sonoma, but from the state's vast Central Valley. Still, most of America thinks of Napa and Sonoma as the Wine Country. In fact, the seemingly endless spread of vines in Napa and Sonoma comprise only a small part of California's total vineyard acreage. Because the yields per acre here are much lower than in the Central Valley, Sonoma produces only about 7% of the wine made in the state; Napa only around 5%. In short, the Wine Country north of San Francisco gained its fame not from quantity, but from quality.

Though the Wine Country's total acreage is small, the intensity of its winemaking activity is remarkable. Sonoma Valley claims to be home to more than 150 wine producers, Napa Valley to more than 250, which places almost *half* of California's 900-plus wine producers in just two relatively small regions. Even more remarkable is the fact that many of the hot boutique labels selling for $50 or more per bottle are housed as "tenants" in larger wineries and are not counted as wineries per se. When you combine the wineries you can visit with those that thrive as "labels," Napa and Sonoma are probably home to 60% or 70% of the ultrapremium labels in California. Thus, when you visit the Wine Country, you're sure to experience many of the very best wines that California has to offer.

THE KEY: GEOGRAPHY

Why does the Wine Country produce such a disproportionate amount of the ultrapremiums in the state? What makes the wines of Sonoma and Napa so good? Mother Nature can take most of the credit: The local climate and geology are the primary factors for the region's winemaking success. Beyond these fortuitous geographical features, the flow of history and twists of politics also come into play, though to a much lesser degree. If not for the ocean, the mountain ranges, the earthquakes, and the volcanoes, the valleys of Napa and Sonoma would never have been formed.

Heading into the Wine Country from San Francisco, you traverse a range of Mediterranean-like climates. Each differs significantly based on its distance from the ocean or San Francisco Bay, and on its proximity to the small mountain ranges that parallel the coast and block the passage of cold ocean air inland. Grapes love this particular climate, as do numerous other crops, ranging from olives, walnuts, apples, and citrus fruits to wild herbs such as fennel, bay, sage, and mustard.

The climatic differences in the Wine Country are subtle, yet significant. Although the Wine Country will never know such weather extremes as the snows of Buffalo, New York, or the humidity of Washington, D.C., everyone who lives here knows that Napa, the city, is cooler by 10 or more degrees on a warm summer day than Calistoga, 20 miles to the north. Because the south end of the Wine Country—referred to as the Carneros District—is cooled by the breeze off the bay, it works best for chardonnay and pinot noir, delicate grapes of Burgundy that cannot thrive in hot climates. Farther north, around Kenwood in Sonoma and St. Helena in Napa, the warmer climate suits Bordeaux grapes such as cabernet sauvignon, merlot, and sauvignon blanc.

THE IMPORTANCE OF PLACE: APPELLATIONS   In both Sonoma and Napa, the latest refinements occurring in the wine world involve discovering a "sense of place" for each style of wine. This critical understanding of soils and slopes happened years ago in Bordeaux, Burgundy, Chianti, and other classic wine-growing regions. Those areas' legally recognized, specific place names say, "This soil planted to this grape on this hillside makes a distinctive style of wine." The United States started such a system only recently. As a result, "Napa" was recognized as an appellation, a "named place," in 1981; the area designated "Sonoma" received its approval in 1983. Finer distinctions have sliced these larger regions into smaller pieces, each of which makes further claims to unique qualities in its wines. Today, Sonoma has 11 subappellations; Napa has 10. Thus, you might see a wine label that reads: "Kenwood Vineyards, Cabernet Sauvignon, Sonoma County, Sonoma Valley," the terms becoming increasingly more specific about the source of the grapes. In Napa it might be "Saintsbury, Pinot Noir, Napa Valley, Carneros."

Over years, players in the local wine scene have debated the merits of appellations and subappellations. One school says that the words *Napa* and *Sonoma* carry tremendous goodwill and that diluting them with numerous new terms will only confuse the consumer, who's often confused enough already about wine. The visionaries argue that as long as "Napa" and "Sonoma" appear on the label, additional specifics will only help the wine drinker. Only time will tell in this latest twist in the history and politics of the Wine Country.

A LOOK AT THE PAST

Sonoma and Napa valleys were latecomers to the California vineyard scene. Around 1780, Franciscan missionaries, establishing the first of their 21 missions in California, planted the first vineyard in the state near San Diego. The first commercial vineyards were established in Los Angeles around 1825. Around the same time, the 21st and last Franciscan mission, Mission San Francisco Solano, planted its vines near present-day Sonoma; the same vines became the first commercial vineyard in the region about 15 years later, when the missions became secularized. Napa saw its first vineyards in 1838, but it had yet to produce commercial wine until 1858, when Charles Krug made a few gallons for John Patchett.

Los Angeles continued to dominate California's wine industry until the 1870s, when Sonoma took over the leadership in total acres around 1875. In turn, Napa replaced Sonoma in acreage a decade later. Not only did Napa and Sonoma grow in size, but also tasters noticed that their wines were demonstrably superior simply because the climates of Sonoma and Napa were (and still are) distinctly cooler than those in the Los Angeles region.

Somewhat sadly, in terms of today's viticultural and winemaking successes, the delightfully colorful history of wine of early California is rather short-lived. In one sense, the wine business in California is only 40 years old. Unlike Europe and other New World wine-growing regions, which have enjoyed continuous generations of winemaking, California had a terrible break in its development—Prohibition—and had to start all over again.

Most of California's wineries shut down during Prohibition, though a few remained in operation to produce wine for sacramental and medicinal purposes. But in the years of temperance, the United States all but lost whatever palate it had acquired for dry table wines. For 35 years after Prohibition, more than half the wine consumed in this country was dessert (or "fortified") wine, so-called ports and sherries, which contain 18% to 20% alcohol and loads of sugar.

Of course, this perversion of good taste has since been reversed, but oddly so. Each wine generation has been dramatically shorter than its predecessor: The first lasted almost 100 years (1825–1919), the second (after the break for Prohibition) only 30 years (1934–65), and the third just 15 years (1966–80). From hereon, the path swerves from winemaking to growing grapes, and necessarily slows down, as the Wine Country has—albeit cautiously—hit its stride.

THE FIRST GENERATION (1825–1919)   This fascinating period in winemaking involves the entangling of a variety of ethnic groups over several generations: Spanish Fathers, Native Americans, European immigrants (the first settlers in Napa and Sonoma were mostly Germanic, followed later by Italians and French), and Chinese (the main labor force; even today you can see the miles of stone walls they built and visit caves they carved out with picks). One of the major struggles of this generation involved breaking away from the grape variety used by the missions (and therefore called *Mission*), but only a few growers possessed such vision: Count Agoston Haraszthy at Buena Vista, T. Belden Crane and Charles Krug in St. Helena, Jacob Schram at Schramsberg (a historical monument that is now making champagne), and later, Gustaf Niebaum at Inglenook (now Niebaum-Coppola).

Between 1870 and 1890, Sonoma and Napa wines won medals with some frequency in international competitions; most of the region's wines, however, were not even bottled at the wineries but rather sold in bulk to merchants, who often blended them badly. Not infrequently, they were even labeled with European names for sale on the East Coast! Regardless, these years laid a solid basis for a regional wine industry: In 1889, Sonoma could claim around 100 wineries, Napa around 140.

Unbeknownst to winemakers, however, a disaster was in the works. A plant louse the size of a pinhead, *phylloxera vastatrix,* began attacking vineyards in the 1880s. As a result, Napa lost roughly 75% of its acreage in the 1890s.

THE LOOMING SHADOW OF PROHIBITION   The business managed to hold its own after the turn of the century, only to encounter a far more formidable foe—the cries of Carrie Nation and the Temperance Movement, whose Prohibition stance had been gaining ground with the moral majority in the last decades of the 19th century. Even in Napa, the Anti-Saloon League made inroads with voters as early as 1912, 7 years before Prohibition became a national fact. During this dry era, the number of wineries dwindled from 600 to a few remaining stragglers. (Ironically, the grape acreage *exploded* to satisfy the need for home winemakers across the country who could legally make 200 gal. per household. Unfortunately, the thick-skinned grape varieties that ship well in railcars do not make fine wine.)

THE SECOND GENERATION (1934–65)   Whoopee! After years of speakeasies, bathtub gin, and phony sherry, Americans could legally drink real wine!

Well, not at first. The few hundred entrepreneurs who rushed in to make a killing in wine found that they had essentially no market and quickly went bankrupt. Americans had almost no interest in dry European-style table wines. A few producers who had made wine during the last years of Prohibition and aged it throughout the Prohibition period had some success. Growers such as Louis Martini and Cesare Mondavi had survived and flourished by shipping their grapes to home winemakers (legal during Prohibition), and were ready to start promoting their California wines in the late 1930s and early 1940s.

In trying to revive the wine business, one of the major battles was fought over varietal labeling—the labeling system we now take for granted that makes the name of the grape variety (cabernet sauvignon, chardonnay, and so on) the most important word on the label after the name of the producer. All through the 19th century and fully into the 1960s, huge volumes of wine were called Burgundy, Chablis, Chianti, Rhine wine, and such, referring wistfully to some vague growing region or type of grape, and usually delivering wine that only accidentally resembled the stated product. One grower argued vociferously against the new labeling because if the law passed, he would have to actually put some Riesling grapes in his wine labeled "Riesling." To him, Riesling was just a style or a marketing tool. Who cared if it actually tasted like Riesling?

It was a pretty grim era for American winemaking in general, and California's Wine Country wasn't faring well. In 1937 Napa had 37 wineries and Sonoma was flush with 91. Collecting accurate statistics about the era is a challenge, but apparently the number of Napa wineries decreased from 47 in 1945 to 25 in 1960. According to one source, only 12 wineries of those 25 made enough wine to sell outside Napa County; the same source reports that Sonoma's count had dwindled to 7 wineries in 1950 and grew only to 9 by 1960. If these numbers are even close to reality, it's clear that recovery from Prohibition was painfully slow, backsliding a few times along the way.

Nonetheless, a handful of well-grounded wineries sailed through this sluggish period, and a few of their wines can still be appreciated today. Most came from Napa, including Inglenook, Beaulieu, Beringer, Christian Brothers, and Louis Martini. Sonoma, in contrast, had a stronger bulk winemaking tradition and a more casual attitude about the role of wine in the good life. (Subsequently, long-winded arguments have been—and probably always will be—held about the casual Italian-Sonoma approach versus the more Northern European, image-conscious, award-bent, Napa approach.)

Ironically, in recent years, Sonoma has been touting its ability to garner more gold medals than Napa. Whatever the significance of a wall festooned with ribbons and awards, Sonoma has certainly caught up with Napa when it comes to making fine wines.

THE THIRD GENERATION (1966–80) It's impossible to draw hard lines in the flow of time, but no other single event marks the modern era of winemaking like Robert Mondavi's 1966 move away from Charles Krug, a family-owned winery since 1943, to found his own winery in Oakville. Joe Heitz had launched his own label in 1961; in Sonoma in 1959, James Zellerbach at tiny Hanzell had revived traditional Burgundian winemaking techniques. At around the same time, Peter Newton acquired the first land holdings for Sterling Vineyards. Unlike his peers in the field, Mondavi combined a push toward new winemaking technology, with an aggressive marketing flair that has grown ever since and now extends to several brands and international alliances.

Compared to previous generations of winemakers, third-generation vintners looked like grade-schoolers, a bunch of kids (many of whom were graduates of U.C. Davis or Fresno State) in playgrounds filled with new toys: stainless-steel tanks, small oak barrels, a panoply of yeast cultures to ferment their wines, new vineyards planted to the best grape varieties, and, in several senses, the freedom to play and experiment. In 1972 and 1973, a remarkable cluster of wineries came on the Napa scene: Chateau Montelena, Clos du Val, Burgess Cellars, Mt. Veeder Vineyards, Silver Oak, Caymus, Diamond Creek, Stag's Leap Wine Cellars, Carneros Creek, Franciscan, Silver Oak, Trefethen, Clos du Val, Stonegate, Joseph Phelps, and Domaine Chandon. These seasoned players now share a quarter of a century of winemaking experience—and the beginnings of a legacy.

In Sonoma Valley, Kenwood, Chateau St. Jean, and St. Francis all sprang up in the early 1970s. For these wineries, and the many that followed, the 1970s can be considered the decade when winemakers discovered their styles of wine. With all the new winemaking equipment and new vineyards, styles changed almost annually: one year a crisp, appley chardonnay with moderate oak; the next, a very fleshy, soft wine dominated by a heavy oak bouquet. In the third year, a third style. The poor consumer took a wild ride through these years, but as winemakers matured, their styles stabilized.

Napa and Sonoma had often compared their wines with international benchmarks, and favorably so. The French pooh-poohed the comparison; that is, until an English wine merchant staged a tasting in Paris in 1976. There, French wine experts on French soil gave top places in a blind tasting to the chardonnay from Château Montelena, as well as the cabernet from Stag's Leap Wine Cellars. The results shocked France and tickled the California Wine Country. At last, they were approaching the big leagues.

THE FOURTH GENERATION (1980–PRESENT)   The most recent phases of change in the Wine Country have been marked by signs of caution—both in the vineyard and in the marketplace—mingled with a few fantastic vintages. Since 1990, we have lived in a golden age of good vintages and astonishing sales, especially for more expensive wines, ranging from $50 to $150 per bottle. Throughout the 1980s and 1990s, the number of new labels has grown steadily, as if there were no problems and never will be. Wine has always created optimists.

Wine sales leveled off in the early 1980s, when both Napa and Sonoma vintners discovered that *phylloxera,* scourge louse of the 1880s and 1890s, had returned, requiring replanting of most acreage in both counties. (Actually, *phylloxera* was never really exterminated; it's permanently in the soil. Rather, the solution to fix the problem went awry.) The prospects of pulling out 70% to 80% of the vines hit growers and wineries hard, both emotionally and financially. A vineyard is a long-term investment, taking 10 to 15 years to mature and lasting 40 to 50 years—if nature, always a temperamental partner, behaves. Add to that the staggering costs—$20,000 to $25,000 per acre to plant a vineyard—and you'd best tell your banker you need another $2,000 per year per acre just to cover farming costs before you get a full crop in 4 or 5 years. Most growers worked out the financing, and by the late 1990s, more than half of the replanting had been finished. Now, with thousands of acres coming on stream, a few voices talk about overproduction. Welcome to the ever-cyclical wine business.

Although Napa and Sonoma make both white wines and red wines extremely well, the 1990s saw a breakthrough in the styling of reds, a higher-level style change than those of the 1970s and early

1980s. Using a couple techniques that you'll likely hear discussed on tours (for example, "presoaking" and "extended maceration"), wine-makers are coming up with richly flavored wines that are supple and approachable, even when young. One enthusiast of the new style, Dennis Johns, formerly at St. Clement Vineyards and now owner of White Cottage Wines, says he wants his red wines to be "sweet, round, and juicy, even in the barrel." Don't look for these wines to have true sweetness. Rather, they have a very fine grade of tannin, which in the past could make wines so puckery they went down like liquid nails. If a decade ago you were ever turned off by red wines, it's time to retaste—and hopefully, enjoy.

2 Winemaking 101

In the flush of today's golden age of California's Wine Country, one might forget that California, let alone Napa and Sonoma, did not invent wine. Credit for this discovery goes to a woman who proba-bly lived around 7,000 years ago: At least one cultural anthropolo-gist suggests that a cave-dwelling woman brought into her cave clusters of wild grapes and put them in a concavity on a rock ledge. Her child, or children, walked over them a few times (or, worse, sat on them), breaking open many berries. The busy cave keeper neg-lected the grapes for a few days. When she finally noticed the pool of juice (caves *are* dark, after all), it was frothing and giving off strange, but not unpleasant, aromas. It's hard to imagine why she would cup the juice in her hand and drink it, but she did—and it affected her most strangely. Let's assume it was pleasantly tasty, if not a little bit too sweet. In any case, she'd discovered wine—and Sonoma and Napa, as well as the rest of the world, owe her a debt of gratitude.

Amazingly, her techniques saw only a few improvements in the next millennia. First, winemakers learned that wine must be stored in sealed containers—clay amphora or wooden barrels—or it spoils, turning into vinegar. Second, cool storage also prevents spoilage, hence the use of caves and cellars. The wines of the Greeks and Romans were probably as good, or as bad, as those made by monks in the Middle Ages and only a bit improved by secular winemakers from the Renaissance to the Industrial Revolution.

The science called *oenology,* which has given the world the high-est overall quality of wine ever, was developed after Louis Pasteur's work with fermentation and bacteriology around 150 years ago. Only in the past few generations have winemakers acquired very technical training and earned PhDs in viticulture (the science of grape growing) in a concentrated effort to understand wine and vineyards.

Even with this recent development of science applied to wine, the catchphrase today for many winemakers in Sonoma and Napa is, "I want the wine to make itself." The desired image is winemaker as midwife, whose role is merely to assist the mother (grape) in a very natural process—not much different from the cave dweller and her young assistants. It sounds so simple: Harvest ripe grapes, put the juice from the grapes in a container with some yeast, watch the juice ferment into wine, clarify and age the new wine, and drink!

Obviously, making wine is much more complex than that. From arguing about the very meaning of the word *ripe* to controlling the ferment in order to affect flavors and textures of the wine, the contemporary "natural" winemaker must incorporate his or her knowledge of fermentation, microbiology, and even such vagaries as the proper barrel (French, American, or Hungarian oak) for aging. These winemakers enjoy the powerful position of being able to make wine simply, naturally, and without spoilage simply because they know, scientifically, what can go wrong. Our cave dweller didn't have a clue.

On your tours of wineries, you'll hear differing stories about the "right" way to make wine, for each vintner harbors strong opinions—almost like a creed—on his or her wine styling. Be prepared for some inconsistencies; ferreting them out can be half the fun. To help you sort through the claims, here's a brief but broad sketch of the ABCs for making white wines, red wines, and sparkling wines.

WHITE WINES   For white wines, the winemaker wants only the juice from the grapes. (For red wines, both the juice and skins of the grapes are essential; using the white winemaking technique, you can make a *white* wine from a *red-skinned grape*—white zinfandel, for example.) Grapes are picked either by hand or by machine and brought to the winery as quickly as possible. Just as a sliced apple turns brown when left on the kitchen counter, grapes oxidize—and can even start fermenting—if they are not processed quickly. At some wineries, the clusters go through a "destemmer-crusher," which pops the berries off their stems and breaks them open (not really crushing them). The resulting mixture of juices, pulp, and seeds—called *must*—is pumped to a press. At other wineries, the whole clusters are put directly into a press (a widely used technique called, logically, *whole-cluster pressing*).

Most presses these days use an inflatable membrane, like a balloon, and gently use air pressure to separate the skins from the juice, which is then pumped into fermenting vessels. In the recent past, most white wines were fermented in stainless-steel tanks fitted with cooling jackets. Cool, even cold, fermentations preserve the natural fruitiness of white grapes. More recently, many Napa and Sonoma producers have begun using small wooden barrels for fermentation of white wines, especially chardonnay. This practice reverts to old-style French winemaking techniques and is believed to capture fragrances, flavors, and textures not possible in stainless steel. Barrel fermentation is labor intensive (each barrel holds only 45–50 gal. for fermentation), and the barrels are expensive ($600–$700 each for French barrels, $250–$300 for American barrels).

After white wines are fermented, they are clarified, aged (if appropriate), and bottled, usually before the next harvest. For the simpler white wines—chenin blanc, Riesling, and some sauvignon blancs—bottling occurs in the late winter or early spring. Most sauvignon blancs and chardonnays go into the bottle during the summer after the harvest. Very few white wines, usually chardonnays, take the slow track and enjoy 15 to 18 months of aging in small barrels with prolonged aging on the *lees,* the sediments from the primary fermentation. Those treatments are unusual, but they produce chardonnays that are richly flavored, complex, and expensive.

RED WINES   The chief difference between white wines and red wines lies simply in the red pigment that's lodged in the skins of the wine grapes. So while for white wines the juice is quickly pressed away from the skins, for rosés and reds the pressing happens after the right amount of "skin contact." That can be anywhere from 6 hours—yielding a rosé or very light red—to 6 weeks, producing a red that has extracted all the pigment from the skins and additionally refined the tannin that naturally occurs in grape skins and seeds.

Almost all red wines are aged in barrels or casks for at least several months, occasionally for as long as 3 years. In the past, casks in California were usually made from redwood and were quite large (5,000–25,000 gal.). Only a few wineries still use redwood today. Most of the wooden containers—collectively called *cooperage*—are barrels now made of American or French oak, and they hold roughly 60 gallons each.

The aging of red wines plays an important role in their eventual style because several aspects of the wine change while in wood. First, the wine picks up oak fragrances and flavors. (Yes, it is possible to "overoak" a wine.) Second, the wine, which comes out of the fermenter murky with suspended yeast cells and bits of skin, clarifies as the particulate material settles to the bottom of the barrel. Third, the texture of the wine changes as the puckery tannins interact and round off, making the wine more supple. Deciding just when each wine in the cellar is ready to bottle challenges the winemaker every year. And, to make the whole process even more challenging, every year is different.

Unlike white wines, which are usually ready to drink shortly after bottling, many of the best red wines improve with aging in the bottle. Napa and Sonoma cabernet sauvignons, for example, often reach a plateau (try not to think "peak") of best drinking condition that ranges from 7 to 12 years after the vintage, the year that appears on the label. However, there are no rigid rules. Some self-proclaimed cabernet freaks prefer their reds rather rough and ready. Only by tasting, tasting, tasting will you find your own comfort zone. Such a trial!

SPARKLING WINE & CHAMPAGNE In Sonoma and Napa, sparkling wine plays the role of a serious specialty—serious enough to have drawn major investments from four of the best-known French houses from Champagne as well as two from Spain, in addition to 10 or 12 local producers.

Whether the bubbly wine in the fancily dressed bottle is called "sparkling wine" or "champagne" (it *is* legal for wineries in America to call their product "champagne," though it galls the French, pun intended), the key to the pervasive high quality of all these wineries lies in their using the *méthode champenoise* as their production technique. In Champagne, it takes the form of step-by-step regulations that, for the most part, codify practices learned by trial and error for making the best wine. Those regulations have no force in California, but the best producers follow most of them and put the words *méthode champenoise* on their labels. For quality assurance, those are the words to look for (as opposed to *bulk* or *Charmat* process).

There is no better way to understand the fascinatingly intricate "champagne method" than to see it firsthand, to walk through the process with a knowledgeable guide. The harvest begins in August in Napa and Sonoma, with the picking of pinot noir, chardonnay, pinot blanc, and pinot meunier, the grape varieties of champagne. The grapes are picked a bit underripe by "still" (nonbubbly) wine standards, both to retain crispness and to avoid excessive body and flavors. The grapes are then pressed and the juice is fermented into plain—austere, in fact—still white wines. That takes 2 weeks. By November and December, the new wines (each variety and vineyard kept as a separate lot) are clear, or "bright."

Now the winemakers *really* go to work, because they need to blend the new wines in preparation for a second fermentation—this one taking place right in the bottle, the very bottle that eventually comes to your table. That's how you get the bubbles.

The second fermentation takes 4 to 6 weeks. After that, you have primitive champagne, with 90 to 100 pounds per square inch of carbon dioxide (CO_2) in each bottle. And you also have a yeasty sediment in each bottle—a bit of a mess that must be cleaned up eventually. But for now—and perhaps for as long as 3 to 7 years—it's a benign mess. Yeast plays two virtuous roles in making sparkling wine: First, it produces the bubbles; second, as the dead yeast cells decompose over time, they release flavor products that give sparkling wines made by *méthode champenoise* their special fragrances and flavors. The amount and depth of flavor varies widely from producer to producer. Each house has its own style, light or heavy, and tries to replicate it each year. That's why people say, "I'm a Mumm drinker," or "I'm a fan of Krug."

Making fine sparkling wine, and making it well, constitutes the ultimate winemaking challenge. The general rule among winemakers is that great white wines and great red wines are derived mostly from their place of origin: the right grape planted in the right soil and right climate. Sparkling wine involves artifice and finesse at every step, making it all the more remarkable that we drink it so casually, at times even carelessly. But the producers wouldn't have it any other way—if only we would drink more of it!

GROWING GRAPES

Somehow winemaking seems much more glamorous than growing grapes. Growing grapes is farming; it's dusty and hard manual labor. In contrast, winemaking is almost ethereal (except for rolling and stacking barrels and hosing grape skins out of the press).

In truth, most winemakers in Sonoma and Napa spend more time in the vineyards than at the winery. It took 20 or 30 years to learn that quality starts, absolutely, in the vineyard, and that the winemaker can do nothing to compensate for bad fruit. There's simply so much to learn about winemaking that decisions can be revised, even reversed, annually; not so with vineyard decisions.

MODERN GROWING AS GARDENING   In the early 1980s, just as winemakers had worked their way up the learning curve for winemaking and as winery owners had turned to acquiring vineyards as the next source of quality control, everyone in the Wine Country learned that the *phylloxera vastatrix,* a soil-based plant louse, would be wiping out most of the vineyards, just as it had done a century earlier, first in Europe and then in California (for more on this, see "A Look at the Past" earlier in this chapter). The "fix" was to plant rootstocks that resisted *phylloxera* and to graft desirable grape varieties above the soil; this worked for several decades.

Unfortunately, it seems that the choice for the principal rootstock was somewhat vulnerable, or *phylloxera* mutated and developed new appetites, or perhaps a combination of both occurred. Since the mid-1980s, replanting has been a major focus, almost a preoccupation. In hindsight, *phylloxera* might be seen as a small (but enormously expensive) blessing. It has indeed refocused our attention on the soil; it's no exaggeration to say that today much of the excitement in Napa and Sonoma lies in the vineyards. And we're showing that farming there isn't agribusiness; rather, it could almost be called microfarming. Warren Winiarski, founder of Stag's Leap Wine Cellars, eloquently insists that for himself and the others in Napa, grape growing is not agriculture, it's horticulture—that is, gardening.

As you drive through Sonoma and Napa, you pass hundreds of experimental "gardens." If you look closely at the shape of the vines, the density of the planting, the height of the trellis system, and even the orientation to the compass, you'll perceive a playground in the earth just as the winemakers of the 1970s had a playground of fancy winemaking toys. It's too early to assess the results of this replanting, but the "silver lining" attitude common to farming sees higher grape quality than ever and, thus, higher wine quality.

THE CYCLE OF THE SEASONS   Because you are likely to visit the Wine Country for a day or two in one particular season, you might want to know how the Wine Country looks in other seasons. Although the climate is benign, the changes from season to season still have a drama about them. In the winter, the rainy season in Mediterranean climates, the nights can be cold, dropping to 30°F to 40°F (-1°C–4°C), but a sunny winter day sees highs in the 60s (20s Celsius)—picnic weather if you're wearing a light wool sweater.

Winter in the Wine Country also can be confused with spring elsewhere. Camellias might bloom on New Year's Day, azaleas shortly thereafter, along with the blue and yellow acacias. From

December through April, the vines are dormant, stark outlines of trunks and arms, but the valley floors and hillside are lush green with common weeds and a few seeded ground covers. One of the common weeds is mustard: In good years, you'll find acres and acres of bright-yellow mustard, celebrated each spring with the Napa Valley Mustard Festival.

The vines burst from dormancy in mid-March for the earliest varieties (chardonnay, pinot noir, gewürztraminer) and in April for the later blooming varieties (cabernet sauvignon, zinfandel). The growth is rapid—sometimes almost an inch a day. Until mid-May, there's a danger of frost. By late May and early June, the new shoots, called *canes,* have grown 3 or 4 feet in length; flower clusters start to blossom. The success of the *bloom and set,* as it's called, makes for some nervous moments: uncontrollable elements such as hot weather and rain can compromise the crop. But, especially compared with the vagaries of weather in continental Europe, the benign Mediterranean weather in the Wine Country goes sour only occasionally.

In midsummer, usually around late July, the first signs of color show up in red grape varieties, a pretty blush at first that in a couple weeks becomes a deep purple, a sure sign that the grapes are ripening. White grapes change from a lime green to a golden green as they ripen. They get delectably sweeter and sweeter, until the winemaker decides they are ripe for the picking.

From August through October, you'll probably see every available hand in the Wine Country harvesting the grapes. For a single vineyard it takes only a day—perhaps just a few hours—to pick the grapes, since they need to be as fresh and cool as possible. After the grapes are harvested, the vines hopefully have the chance to grow for a few more weeks, storing energy in the form of carbohydrates that will sustain them to the next spring.

After cold nights in November and December, the first winter rains knock and blow the vibrant-colored leaves off the vines, which then go dormant until March and April, when they start the cycle again.

THE LIFE OF THE VINE   Unless soil problems or vineyard pests intervene, a vineyard should have a commercial life of 30 to 40 years. In Sonoma, a number of producing vineyards are approaching the 100-year mark, and although the quantity of the harvest falls off in old vines, the quality seems to improve. As the Italian proverb goes, "You plant a vineyard for your son; you plant an olive grove for your grandson." Regardless of the latest technological advances in viticulture, vineyards will not be rushed—which gives much-needed consolation to grape growers, and a sense of permanence to the Wine Country.

3 How to Wine-Taste Like a Pro

Stopping at tasting rooms to sample the goods, otherwise known as *wine tasting,* ranks as one of the top rituals in Wine Country touring. It provides pleasure and a chance to learn why the wines of Sonoma and Napa rank high among the wines of the world.

Precautionary notes would say "taste moderately," for there are literally 200 or so tasting rooms, and the virtues in wine take time to notice. Most of the attendants in tasting rooms know that, generally speaking, Americans drink very little wine (10% of the population drinks more than 85% of the wine consumed). Because we're all on a very pleasant learning curve, you can discover wine at many levels. If you should encounter a winery staffer with "attitude" (unfortunately, it happens), don't buy *any* of that wine and simply move on to the next stop.

The time-honored techniques for tasting wine involve three steps: a good look, a good smell, and a good sip of each wine. You'll learn about wine most quickly if you compare them, ideally side by side. Almost any comparison will reveal features of wines you might not see by tasting one wine at a time. You might think of it as the wines talking to one another ("I'm smoother than you are"; "I'm way more puckery than all of you"). By listening to these little conversations, you can discover just how smooth or how puckery you want your wines to be. Tasting rooms in Napa and Sonoma have their own regimens, usually offering a series of wines. When it seems appropriate, and when the tasting room is not too busy, ask your host if you can do some comparisons.

THE VISUALS OF WINE

Take a moment to look at the wine for its clarity and for its hue. With just a couple glances, you'll see that red wines reveal many shades of red: ruby, garnet, purple, and variations. White wines also differ in hue, from white gold to straw to dark gold, sometimes laced with a light green. For the most part, wines ought to be clear, even brilliant, though a few unfiltered wines now bear a light haze as a badge of courage that says, "I was not heavily filtered." (Filtration for clarification is standard practice and benign if not overdone.)

Color can be a sign of a wine's condition, of its health, even of its age. White wines that show any browning might be going "over the hill" and have a musty, baked smell. Red wines that show a lot of rusty red might also be past their prime, and reds that show a lot of purple are probably young.

THE AROMAS & BOUQUETS OF WINE

Some wine professionals will tell you the olfactory aspect of wine is more important than the taste. Saner heads remind you that wine is a *beverage,* not a perfume; it comes home to rest in the mouth. It's true that our noses work better as tools of perception than our mouths. We can smell several thousand scents but can taste only four: sweet, sour, bitter, and salty. But it's also true that we smell the wine (via the retro nasal passages) when it passes through our mouths.

A decently shaped wineglass will direct a lot of aromas to your nose. Swirling the glass helps excite the fragrances. Comparing the "noses" of two or three wines can be very revealing, but possibly a bit frustrating, too: You "see" differences with your nose but might stumble when you try to describe them. The words are on the tip of your tongue, if they're there at all. What comes to mind may seem silly: "apple," "coconut," "cherries," "mushrooms," "dirt," "cheese," and the like.

If this is the case, then you've hit the Wall of Wine Tasting: vocabulary. It's not easy to describe the fragrances and flavors in wine. We are mostly reduced to similes and metaphors, to comparing wines with more familiar substances. A lot of wine writing is inadvertently humorous; some of it qualifies as bad poetry. That's neither your fault *nor* the fault of the wine. You must simply get over the inadequacies of language to describe wine—and get on with your tasting. Have fun with your verbal fantasies!

Despite all the ambiguity in wine descriptors, the words *aroma* and *bouquet* do possess widely recognized, distinct meanings (though on the street we use them almost interchangeably). **Aroma** points to the characteristic smell of the various grape varieties, which can be quite distinct. Just as you would probably not confuse a pippin apple with a golden delicious, when you are familiar with sauvignon blanc, it will not remind you of chardonnay. **Bouquet,** in the academy of wine, refers to fragrances that come from sources other than the grapes, such as the vanillalike fragrance of French oak.

During your trip to the Wine Country, you can learn the basics of aroma simply by comparing a sauvignon blanc side by side with a chardonnay. Or, in terms of bouquet, you can try a younger cabernet beside an older cabernet. Not every tasting room will be able to arrange all the comparisons, but you will find many opportunities.

THE TASTES OF WINE

Tasting wine—literally putting it through your mouth—can be seen as something quite different from *drinking* other beverages. (Of course, we can drink wine, too. Indeed, *most* of the time we should just drink wine.) Tasting, as opposed to drinking, has built-in dynamics. In fact, it helps to focus on the wine moving through the mouth: something that happens in a measured sequence, like listening to a musical phrase. It's not like taking a snapshot—"Click, I've got it."

One of the legendary tasters in California at the turn of the century, Henry Lachman, merchant and international judge of wines, wrote a monograph in which he discussed each sip of wine as having "a first taste, a second taste, and the goodbye." That's a cute way of dealing with the physiology of our mouths: In the front of the mouth, we taste for **sweetness** and feel the **body** of the wine; in the middle, we find **acidity** and the **flavors** of the grape; and in the back, we sense the **finish** or "goodbye," which can be long or short, supple or astringent. Imagine a tasting as having checkpoints in your mouth: front, middle, and back.

In the abstract, wine dynamics sound odd. With practice, however, especially as you compare the tastes of two or three wines, they become obvious, and the observational skills become quite easy to pick up. After you see how a wine can be full and lush in the front of your mouth, then turn fresh and tasty, and finally linger nicely (or fail to linger), it remains for you to decide what **shapes** you prefer in your wines. Red wines in particular show fairly clear shapes. One of the additional challenges in tasting red wines lies in knowing that the shape changes with age. Rough, puckery young red wines can age into supple, subtly flavorful, pleasing liquids.

Which red wines will age well and over what period of time is, again, something you can learn by comparison. It's best done by arranging a *vertical tasting:* several vintages of the same wine. (*Horizontal tastings* are several producers tasted from the same vintage.) Even three to five wines from vintages spread over, say, 10 years will give you a good idea of how much age you want to have on your red wines. Tasting rooms often have "reserve" wines or "library" wines that you can acquire for tasting.

Tastings of several wines—either vertical or horizontal tastings—make for marvelous evenings of gourmandizing when you return home. Have a few friends over to taste the wines blind (without labels visible). Get everyone's preference. Then sit down to dinner and finish them off, with the labels in full view. Inevitably, opinions will change, often in amusing reversals.

It's up to you to decide how seriously you want to engage the Wine Country. If it's a first visit, consider it an introduction. You can't do it all in a single visit, of course, which is all the more reason to schedule a return trip.

Finally, two important tips for a healthy day in the Wine Country: Be moderate in your wine tasting and generous in drinking water. Cheers!

3

Planning Your Trip to the Wine Country

The pages that follow tell you everything you need to know to plan your trip—how to get there, the best times to go, how much you can expect to spend, strategies for touring the region, and more.

1 Visitor Information

There's so much to see and do in the Wine Country that it's best to familiarize yourself with what's available before you start your trip. Both Napa and Sonoma offer very informative visitor guides that provide information on everything each valley has to offer.

The slick, comprehensive *Napa Valley Guide* includes listings and photos of hotels, restaurants, and hundreds of wineries, as well as hours of operation, tasting fees, and picnicking information. The **Napa Valley Conference and Visitors Bureau (NVCVB),** 1310 Napa Town Center, Napa, CA 94559 (© **707/226-7459;** www.napa valley.com), offers a $10 package that includes this guide plus a bunch of brochures, a map, a document called *Four Perfect Days in the Wine Country Itinerary,* and hot-air balloon discount coupons. If you want less to recycle, ask for just the *Napa Valley Guide,* which sells for $5.95. If you don't want to pay the bucks for the official publications, point your browser to www.napavalley.com, the NVCVB's official site, which has lots of the same information for free.

Like the town itself, the *Sonoma Valley Visitors Guide* is far less fancy—no glossy photos and far less information than Napa Valley's slick guide. But the free pocket-size booklet does offer important lodging, winery, and restaurant details, all of which is available from the **Sonoma Valley Visitors Bureau,** 453 1st St. E., Sonoma, CA 95476 (© **707/996-1090;** www.sonomavalley.com).

2 When to Go

THE SEASONS   The beauty of the Wine Country is striking at any time of the year, but it's most memorable in **September** and

October, when the grapes are being pressed and the wineries are in full production. Another great time to come is **spring,** when the mustard flowers are in full bloom and the tourist season is just starting; at this time of year, you'll find less traffic, fewer crowds at the wineries and restaurants, and better deals on hotel rooms. Although **winter** promises the best budget rates and few crowds, it often comes with chilly days and the threat of rain; the valleys, although still lovely, become less quintessentially picturesque as miles of bare vines lay dormant over the cold months. Want to visit in **summer?** Say hello to hot weather and lots of traffic.

THE CLIMATE   Although the valleys claim a year-round average temperature of 70°F (20°C), if you come with a suitcase packed with T-shirts and shorts during the winter holiday season, you're likely to shiver your way to the nearest department store to stock up on warm clothes. In summer, if you rent a car without air-conditioning, you're liable to want to make a pit stop at every hotel swimming pool you pass. And don't let that morning fog and those early cool temperatures fool you; on most days, come noon, that big ol' ball of flames in the sky sends down plenty of heat waves to bless the vineyards and your picnic spot. For the most comfortable experience no matter what time of year, dress in layers and keep in mind that the temperature can drop dramatically at night.

Average Seasonal Temperatures

	Spring (Mar–May)	Summer (June–Aug)	Fall (Sept–Nov)	Winter (Dec–Feb)
Average highs (in °F)	78	92	85	72
Average highs (in °C)	26	33	30	22
Average lows (in °F)	64	81	74	61
Average lows (in °C)	18	27	23	16

Tips **Packing Tips**

If you're visiting the Wine Country between December and March, be sure to pack an umbrella and a pair of durable walking shoes. The rainy season isn't usually fierce, but it is wet.

Wine Country fashion is part city, part country, with an emphasis on comfort. Sensible shoes are key—especially when you're wine tasting because you're likely to tromp through vineyards, gravel, and on occasion, mud. At restaurants, attire ranges from jeans and T-shirts at the more-casual eateries to jacket and tie at the few fancy stops such as The French Laundry. In general, somewhere in between is best when you're stepping out.

Festivities to Plan Your Trip Around:
The Wine Country's Best Annual Events

Napa Valley Mustard Festival kicks off tourist season starting in February with a celebration of the mustard blossoms that coat the valley and mountains in rich-yellow petals. This is 6 weeks' worth of activities ranging from a crowded, formal, and very fun gourmet gala featuring local restaurants, wineries, and artists at the CIA Greystone to a wine auction, golf benefit, recipe and photography competition, and plenty of food and wine celebrations. For information, call © **707/259-9020,** point your browser to www.mustardfestival.org, or write to P.O. Box 3603, Yountville, CA 94599.

The **Napa Valley Wine Auction,** held each June, is the area's most renowned—and exclusive—event. The annual charity affair brings close to 2,000 deep-pocketed wine aficionados to the Napa area to schmooze and spend serious cash. But don't pack your bags yet: Tickets to the event are $2,500 per couple—and they sell out every year. For information, call © **707/963-3388.**

One of my favorite festivals in Sonoma Valley is the **Heart of the Valley Barrel Tasting,** held on the third full weekend in March. This event, which gives the public a glimpse of Sonoma Valley's finest future releases and raises money for the American Heart Association, is a 2-day fiesta of finger foods, pairings, demonstrations, and all the world-class wine you can drink—all for around $30 a ticket. Buy tickets well in advance. For details, call the St. Francis Winery, at © **800/543-7713.**

Sonoma Valley's other major celebration is the **Vintage Festival,** held the last weekend in September at Sonoma's central plaza. This is a real blowout of a party, complete with live music, dancing, parades, arts-and-crafts shows, and of course, copious wine tasting. For more information, contact the **Sonoma Valley Visitors Bureau** (© **707/996-1090;** www.sonomavalley.com).

For Napa Valley happenings, contact the **Napa Valley Conference and Visitors Bureau** at © **707/226-7459** (www.napavalley.com).

3 Money Matters

WHAT THINGS COST IN THE WINE COUNTRY

One thing's for sure: Wine Country ain't cheap. Over the course of a few years, Northern California's newly wealthy poured into the region, encouraging absurdly jacked-up hotel prices and a fight to have the opportunity to pay them. Today, the pace, like the economy, has taken a turn, which is good news for the average traveler.

Hotels may still ask an average of $180 a night in Napa Valley (things aren't much cheaper in the less touristy towns of Sonoma), but there's more room for negotiation. Still, on a busy weekend, a charmless motel or a basic B&B can easily get $150 a night for a room.

But that's just the beginning. If you want to eat in any of the more renowned dining spots, you can pretty much count on shelling out at least $35 per person just for food—not including even one glass of wine. And don't even think of stepping foot in a high end haunt such as The French Laundry without at least $150 per person to burn—and we're just talking lunch. (Don't worry: I'll get to some ways around that later.)

Is that cash register ringing in your head yet? Well, keep the tab open, 'cause there's more. Although some wineries offer free wine tastings, many—particularly in Napa Valley—charge between $2 and $6; Niebaum-Coppola charges $8.50 per person. Stop by three or four in a day and—cha-ching!—they start to add up. Of course, you'll also want to buy a few bottles of your favorite vino. Cha-ching, cha-ching, cha-ching—it just keeps going. Don't let this deter you from a visit, but do expect to spend some money.

MONEY-SAVING TIPS   If you're starting to think that you just can't afford a Wine Country visit, don't despair yet: There are a few things you can do to keep your costs down and still enjoy the region to its fullest.

If you're on a budget, be sure to reserve your accommodations months in advance to secure the cheapest room; don't expect much more than a clean room and bed, and you won't be disappointed—but you're not planning to hang out in your room anyway, right? Here are some more money-saving tips:

- **Travel between December and March,** when accommodations rates are at their lowest. Stay at a place whose rates include breakfast and afternoon hors d'oeuvres, which will save you big bucks on dining out.

- **Visit wineries that don't charge to taste;** Most wineries charge to taste these days, but a few wineries are still happy to get you drunk without asking you for even one hard-earned cent.
- If you want to dine at one of the Wine Country's more expensive restaurants, **have a late lunch** there and make it the day's biggest meal. The lunch menu is often served until mid-afternoon, and main courses usually cost several dollars less than the same dishes at dinner.
- There's no better place to **picnic** than the Wine Country. Stop at a grocery or gourmet shop—each valley has lots of wonderful ones, which are recommended in the chapters that follow—and pick up the picnic fixings for breakfast, lunch, or dinner. Head to one of the fabulous picnic spots I recommend in this book, pop the cork on a bottle you've picked up in your travels, and you've got the perfect alfresco feast—for a fraction of what it would cost you to eat in a restaurant.
- **Buy wines from local wine shops,** not from the wineries. Believe it or not, prices in the shops are often better than at wineries, and they're likely to have that extra-buttery chardonnay or that perfectly balanced merlot that you fell in love with earlier in the day in stock. In Sonoma, your best bet is the **Wine Exchange,** on the plaza at 452 1st St. E. (© **707/938-1794**), which boasts more than 700 domestic wines and a remarkably savvy staff. In Napa, head to St. Helena, where both **Dean & Deluca,** 607 St. Helena Hwy. (© **707/967-9980**), and **Safeway,** 1026 Hunt Ave. (© **707/963-3833**), have enormous wine selections; Safeway tends to offer some of the best deals around.

LIVING THE HIGH LIFE   If you're not on a budget, go for broke. Reserve a room at one of Napa's or Sonoma's fabulous luxury resorts, such as Rutherford's Auberge du Soleil or the Kenwood Inn & Spa, and schedule massages twice a day; gorge yourself in gourmet fashion at The French Laundry, Terra, and Tra Vigne; and drink yourself silly. The Wine Country may be hyped, but not without justification—there may be no place in the country that's more conducive to luxurious living.

PAYING YOUR WAY

Banks throughout Napa Valley and Sonoma Valley have automated teller machines **(ATMs),** which accept cards connected to networks such as Cirrus and PLUS. For specific ATM locations, call © **800/424-7787** for the Cirrus network, and call © **800/843-7587** for the PLUS system. You also can locate Cirrus ATMs on the Web at **www.mastercard.com** and PLUS ATMs at **www.visa.com**.

Traveler's checks are still the safest way to carry currency—Visa and American Express are the kinds most widely accepted. *Remember:* You'll need identification, such as a driver's license or passport, to change a traveler's check. And be sure to record the numbers of the checks and keep that information separate from your checks in the unlikely event that they get lost or stolen. Note that there are no American Express offices in either valley.

Rather than fuss with traveler's checks, it's easier just to use **credit cards**—most notably American Express, MasterCard, and Visa—which are almost as good as cash and are accepted in most Wine Country establishments. Also, ATMs make cash advances against MasterCard and Visa cards; make sure you have your PIN (personal identification number) with you.

4 Getting There

BY PLANE

If you're arriving by plane, Wine Country is easily accessed by the Bay Area's two major airports: San Francisco International and Oakland International.

SAN FRANCISCO INTERNATIONAL AIRPORT   Almost four dozen major scheduled carriers serve **San Francisco International Airport** (© 650/821-8211; www.flysfo.com), which is 1½ to 2 hours north by car.

OAKLAND INTERNATIONAL AIRPORT   About 5 miles south of downtown Oakland and a little more than a 1-hour drive from downtown Napa, at the Hagenberger Road exit of Calif. 17 (U.S. 880), **Oakland International Airport** (© 510/577-4000; www.oaklandairport.com) is less crowded than SFO and is a very accessible airport, but it offers fewer carrier selections.

RENTING A CAR   Regardless of which airport you fly into, you should rent a car and drive to the Wine Country (see "By Car," below, for driving directions). Although for $20 you can hitch a ride to Napa Valley from SFO with **Evans Airport Service** (© 707/255-1559), and the **Sonoma Airporter** (© 707/938-4246) offers door-to-door service six times daily from SFO to hotels and inns in most areas of Sonoma ($35 for home pickup, $30 for standard downtown pickup locations), there's no useful public transportation in either valley, which makes it almost impossible to explore the region without wheels.

All the major companies have desks at the airports. Currently, you can get a compact car for about $200 a week, including all taxes and other charges (but remember that rates are always subject to change). Some of the national car-rental companies operating in San Francisco include the following: **Alamo,** 🕐 800/327-9633, www.goalamo.com; **Avis,** 🕐 800/331-1212, www.avis.com; **Budget,** 🕐 800/527-0700, www.drivebudget.com; **Enterprise,** 🕐 800/325-8007, www.pick enterprise.com; **Hertz,** 🕐 800/654-3131, www.hertz.com.

BY CAR

All these routes to the Wine Country are very well marked, with plenty of signs along the way.

TO NAPA

FROM SAN FRANCISCO   Cross the Golden Gate Bridge and go north on U.S. 101; turn east on Highway 37 (toward Vallejo), then north on Highway 29, the main road through Napa Valley. You can also take Highway 121/12 from Highway 37 and follow the signs.

FROM OAKLAND   Head eastbound on I-80 toward Sacramento; a few miles past the city of Vallejo (and after paying a $2 toll fee to cross the Carquinez Bridge), exit on Highway 12 west, which, after a few miles, intersects with Highway 29 and leads directly into Napa.

TO SONOMA

FROM SAN FRANCISCO   From San Francisco, cross the Golden Gate Bridge and stay on U.S. 101 north. Exit at Highway 37; after 10 miles, turn north onto Highway 121. After another 10 miles, turn north onto Highway 12 (Broadway), which will take you directly into the town of Sonoma.

FROM OAKLAND   Head eastbound on I-80 toward Sacramento. A few miles past the city of Vallejo (and after paying a $2 toll to cross the Carquinez Bridge), exit on Highway 12, which, after a few miles, intersects with Highway 29 at the southern foot of Napa Valley. Just before entering the city of Napa, you'll come to a major intersection, where Highway 29 meets Highway 12/121. Turn left onto Highway 12/121, which will take you directly to Sonoma Valley.

5 Getting Around

With hundreds of wineries scattered amidst Napa's 34,000 acres and Sonoma's 13,000 acres of vineyards, it's virtually impossible to explore the Wine Country without wheels. If you're arriving by air

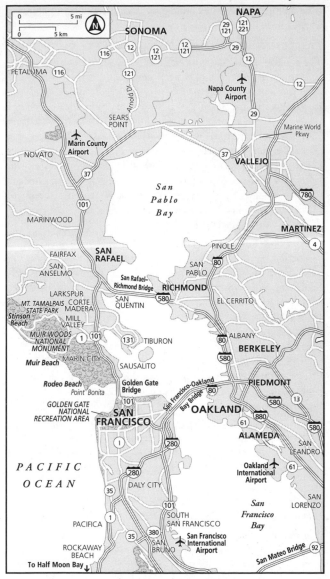

from another part of the country or abroad, see "Getting There," above, for details on renting a car.

CROSSING FROM VALLEY TO VALLEY

The easiest way to get from Napa to Sonoma and vice versa is to head to the southern end of either valley (the Carneros District) and cross over along the Sonoma Highway (Calif. 12/121). From Napa to Sonoma, the trip takes about 20 minutes, assuming that there's no traffic. Another option is to take the Oakville Grade (aka Trinity Rd.) over the Mayacamas Range, which links Oakville in Napa with Glen Ellen in Sonoma. It's an extremely steep and windy road, but it can be a real timesaver if you're headed to the northern end of either valley. There is a way to cross from Calistoga to the Sonoma Highway along Calistoga and St. Helena roads (at the northern end of Napa and Sonoma valleys), but the circuitous route takes so long that it isn't worth the effort.

DRIVING AROUND THE WINE COUNTRY   You might be wondering: Does that mean visitors are drinking and driving up here? And how. The catch is, most of the year there's so much traffic that a major high-speed collision is virtually out of the question. Meanwhile, getting totally trashed while wine tasting is the exception, and the valley has somehow avoided having a major problem with drunk-driving accidents.

Of course, we're not condoning driving under the influence. But since there's no decent public transportation (other than taxis), my best recommendation is that you take it slow, monitor the amount of wine you drink, and bring along a designated driver or take a tour (see the following section, "Strategies for Touring the Wine Country").

TAXIS   You can avoid the driving issue altogether by calling either of Napa's two main taxi services: **Napa Valley Cab** (© 707/257-6444) or **Yellow Cab** (© 707/226-3731). Sonoma is serviced by **Valley Cab** (© 707/996-6733).

Tips Napa Valley Traffic Tip

Travel the Silverado Trail as often as possible to avoid Highway 29's traffic. Avoid passing through Main Street in St. Helena during high season (May–Oct). Although a wintertime cruise from Napa to Calistoga can take 25 minutes, in summer you can expect the trek to take you closer to 50 minutes. Plan your time accordingly.

---

6 Strategies for Touring the Wine Country

I strongly suggest that you devise an itinerary before you arrive, because there's no possible way you could visit all of Napa's and Sonoma's 350-plus wineries in one visit (at least not without a few free weeks on your hands and a mid-vacation layover at the Betty Ford clinic).

Tour smarter, not harder, is the mantra you need to chant to yourself as you pore over this book in the process of planning your trip—because the less time you spend driving in circles, the more time you can spend sticking your schnozzle in wineglasses and saying silly things such as "full-bodied, yet corky."

Of course, because I don't know how long you'll be touring the Wine Country or what your level of wine knowledge is, it's impossible for me to provide you with the touring strategy that will best suit your intentions and wishes. So instead, I'll supply you with a few nuggets of Wine Country wisdom, gleaned both from experience and from picking the minds of tourist-savvy locals, and let you decide what's right for you.

NAPA VERSUS SONOMA: WHICH VALLEY IS RIGHT FOR YOU?

When it comes to comparing the two valleys, the most obvious distinction is size: Napa Valley dwarfs Sonoma Valley in population, number of wineries, and sheer volume of tourism (and traffic). Napa is also the more commercial of the two, boasting world-class wineries such as Robert Mondavi, which offer the most interesting and edifying wine tours in North America, more big-name wineries, many more spas (at cheaper rates) to choose from, and a far superior selection of fine restaurants, hotels, and quintessential Wine Country activities such as hot-air ballooning. To misquote Gertrude Stein, there's more there there. Perhaps the most important distinction between Napa and Sonoma is that Napa Valley is the undisputed cornerstone of the Wine Country. If your intention is to immerse yourself in the culture of the Wine Country, then there's no better place to start than by cruising down Napa Valley's Highway 29, the Sunset Boulevard of the Wine Country. It's along this high-rent route that all the big players in the California wine industry—Beringer, Beaulieu, Charles Krug, Niebaum-Coppola—dazzle you with their multimillion-dollar estates and pricey art collections. This is where top-notch restaurants such as The French Laundry and Tra Vigne serve world-class cuisine to casually clad diners while fresh-faced Silicon Valley millionaires play croquet at the exclusive resorts just up the hill.

As you might expect, humility isn't one of Napa's strongest attributes. So don't be surprised if you encounter a bit of snobbishness at some Napa wineries, as well as a pricey tasting fee or two.

Sonoma Valley, on the other hand, maintains a backcountry ambiance, thanks to its far lower density of wineries, restaurants, and hotels. Small, family-owned wineries are its mainstay; tastings are low-key, and they come with plenty of friendly banter with the winemakers (who often do the pouring themselves). But even though Sonoma lives in the shadow of far more famous Napa, don't let that "aw, shucks" attitude fool you—Sonomans know their stuff.

If it's serious R&R you're after, and you aren't too concerned with shopping outlets or visiting more than a handful of wineries each day, you'll probably be happier staying at one of Sonoma Valley's secluded inns and perhaps touring the valley by bicycle—most wineries are located down quiet, gently winding, woodsy roads.

Is there a friendly feud between the two valleys? You betcha, and it makes touring the entire Wine Country all the more interesting. If you have the luxury of time, don't just visit one valley: Tour them both so you can compare and contrast these two very different— and very wonderful—worlds of winemaking.

THE GOLDEN RULE OF WINE TASTING: LESS IS MORE

Yes, they all sound great. Unfortunately, it's almost impossible to hit every winery. Actually, your best plan of action is to take it slow. **Pick three or four wineries** for a single day's outing, and really get to know not only the wines but also the story behind each winery: its history, the types of wines it makes and where the grapes are grown, and the colorful people who make the wines. You can *taste* California wines just about anywhere in the world, but only by visiting the Wine Country can you learn about the painstaking, delicate, and very personal processes and years of collective experience that go into each and every bottle. Like a fine glass of wine, the Wine Country should not be rushed, but savored.

When planning your trip to the Wine Country, consider the following: Is there a specific wine you want to taste? A specific tour you'd like to take? Maybe it's the adjoining restaurant, picnic setting, or art collection that piques your interest most. Whatever your intentions might be, the best advice I can give you about visiting your chosen wineries is to **arrive early:** Most tasting rooms open at

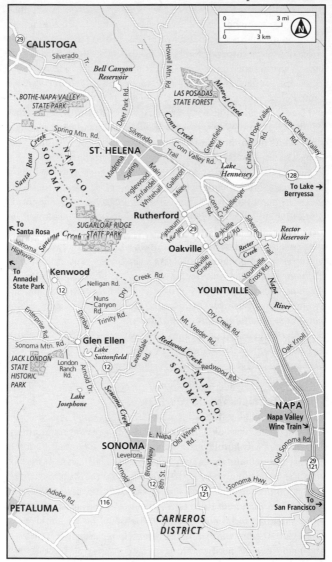

10am, and even on the busiest of weekends, most are empty that early in the morning. "What? Start drinking at 10am?" Absolutely. First of all, you're not drinking, you're tasting and learning. Second, the staff pouring the wines will have considerably more time to discuss their product. Come 1 or 2pm, the tasting room will probably be packed, and other visitors will be waiting in line simply to get a sample—while you're relaxing under an oak tree, finished with your wine-tasting rounds, enjoying a picnic lunch, and seriously contemplating an afternoon nap. Afterward, why not spend your time visiting Old Faithful in Calistoga or doing a little window-shopping while the late-birds duke it out over a sip of chardonnay?

Another consideration when wine tasting is money. It used to be that none of the wineries charged for sampling their wares, but when the popularity of the Wine Country began to soar (along with a growing intolerance for drinking and driving), wineries—particularly those in Napa—began requesting **tasting fees.** It wasn't to make additional profit, but to discourage what the winery staffs usually refer to as "recreational drinkers": visitors who, whether they're aware of it or not, prefer quantity to quality. Nowadays, the norm at Napa Valley wineries is to charge anywhere between $2 and $8 per tasting, which usually includes the tasting glass (etched with the winery's logo) and/or a refund toward a purchase.

The wineries in Sonoma Valley, however, are less likely than those in Napa Valley to charge for tasting wines. The exceptions are wineries that offer samples of their reserve wines (usually at a separate tasting area) and champagne houses.

DEALING WITH THE CROWDS

Anyone who's visited the Wine Country on a sunny August weekend knows how insane the traffic can be. Napa Valley's roads simply weren't designed to handle the influx of vehicles that can turn a 30-minute drive along Highway 29 from Napa to Calistoga into 2 hours of maddening gridlock. It's ironic, of course: People arrive for a vacation in the countryside, only to be stuck in traffic for hours.

If you want to avoid the masses altogether, the solution is simple: Either **visit during the off-season** (Nov–May) **or visit midweek.** Though the optimum time to plan your trip is during the "crush"— the grape harvest season starting in late August and continuing through October, when the grapes are harvested, sorted, crushed, and fermented—this is also the Wine Country's peak tourist season. This is a good time to schedule a midweek visit, if possible.

Tips **Some Wine-Buying Strategies**

Just because you're buying wine directly from the people who made it doesn't mean that you'll save money by purchasing bottles in the tasting room. In fact, it's usually the other way around. You'll probably end up spending a bit more at a winery than you would at superstores that buy cases in bulk and pass the per-bottle savings on to the customer. (**Safeway** in St. Helena is one of the best places to buy wine in Napa Valley.)

If you want to save money, the smart approach is to make a list of your favorite wines as you taste at the wineries, and then make your purchases when you return from your vacation. You'll not only save money on the wine, you'll save a bundle on packaging and shipping fees—but be sure to ask the winery if the release you're interested in is available in your state and where you can purchase it.

If the selection of California wines is limited where you live, see if the wine is available at one of the wine shops I recommend in the following chapters and take it to one of the shippers listed on p. 48, who can pack it up and ship it. Some wine shops, such as the **Wine Exchange** in Sonoma, will even do the shipping for you (and you might be able to sidestep the red tape that may accompany shipping wine to your home state; see the section "The Ins & Outs of Shipping Wine Home," below).

Exceptions to this strategy are wineries that offer big discounts on cases of wine and wineries that only sell their wines directly (that is, they have no distribution). *Note:* If you're able to ship your wine directly from the winery, you'll avoid having to pay sales tax; for more information, see the section "The Ins & Outs of Shipping Wine Home."

Even if your only option is to arrive on a high-season weekend, there are still ways to avoid the Napa Valley cattle drive. The smartest option is to **avoid the big wineries** such as Mondavi and Beringer and opt for the smaller, family-run places tucked into the hillsides such as Prager and Heitz. Even the wineries along the Silverado Trail, which parallels the main highway through Napa Valley, receive significantly less traffic than those on Highway 29; locals use it as their main thoroughfare during high season.

Another high-season option is to avoid Napa Valley altogether and stick to **Sonoma Valley.** Although it, too, suffers from traffic congestion, Sonoma usually gets far less saturated with visitors than Napa does.

A FEW MORE WORDS OF WINE-COUNTRY WISDOM

Here are a few final tips that should help make your visit a more pleasant experience:

- **Chart your winery tours** on a map before venturing into the countryside. It'll save you time and traffic frustration, as well as a lot of unnecessary backtracking.
- **Plan a picnic lunch** at the last winery you're going to visit for the day. (Let's face it—you'll probably be too pooped to drink more wine late in the day.) Many wineries offer free picnic facilities, and though few provide food, many wonderful gourmet shops in both Napa and Sonoma specialize in picnic items; see p. 124 and 167 for recommendations.
- Most wineries are open from 10am to 4:30 or 5pm and are closed on major holidays such as Thanksgiving, Christmas, and New Year's Day. Many also have restricted hours during the off-season, so **call ahead** if there's a winery you don't want to miss.
- Fine wine is a temperamental beast that hates to be mistreated. If you let that $60 bottle of merlot cook in the back seat of your car all day, you'll probably be surprised at the new taste it has acquired. Buy a cheap Styrofoam cooler and a couple of blue ice packs, place them in the trunk of your car, and voilà!—you have a **portable wine cellar.**
- Anyone who's ever lived in a one-road town knows that you can't avoid the law for long. **Don't speed,** and for heaven's sake, **don't drive while intoxicated.**

7 The Ins & Outs of Shipping Wine Home

Perhaps the only things more complex than that $600 case of cabernet you just purchased are the rules and regulations regarding shipping it home. Due to absurd and forever fluctuating "reciprocity laws"—which are supposedly created to protect the business of the country's wine distributors—wine shipping is limited by state regulations that vary in each of the 50 states. Shipping rules also vary from winery to winery. Hence, depending on which state you live in, sending even a single bottle of wine can be a truly Kafkaesque experience—and, other than the summertime traffic, one of the most frustrating aspects of a Wine Country vacation.

Sound confusing? Believe me, it is. Although I can't exactly outline a foolproof way to send your wine home, the following best explains what I do know about it and offers tips to help you cut through the red tape as painlessly as possible. (Note that this information was current at press time. Unfortunately, because the laws and shipping companies' procedures are ever-changing, I can't guarantee you an absolute solution; you'll have to check and see what the current situation is pertaining to your particular home state as you tour the Wine Country.)

If you happen to live in a reciprocal state and the winery you're buying from offers shipping, you're in luck. You buy, pay the postage, and the winery sends your purchase for you. It's as simple as that. If that winery doesn't ship, it will most likely be able to give you an easy shipping solution.

If you live in a nonreciprocal state, the winery may still have shipping advice for you, so definitely ask! But there's a good reason most wineries don't offer shipping to nonreciprocal states: One winery was fined big bucks (around $35,000) for breaking the law and shipping directly to a nonreciprocal state. Do be cautious of wineries that tell you they can ship to nonreciprocal states, and make sure you get a firm commitment. When one of my New York–based editors visited Napa, a winery promised her it could, in fact, ship her purchase; but when she got home they reneged, leaving her with no way to get the wine and no potable memories of the trip.

It's possible that you'll face the challenge of finding a shipping company yourself. If that's the case, bear in mind the following: According to the U.S. Postal Service, shipping alcoholic beverages is against the law. Of course, it's hard to imagine that anyone's getting arrested for sending a congratulatory bottle of bubbly to Aunt Myrna in Delaware, but if you tote a case labeled "pinot noir" into the post office, the postal clerk isn't likely to be exactly helpful. (I'm not recommending that you break the law, but if you did appear with a well-packed box, the post office would ship it, but you'd have to declare you were shipping something other than wine—and then, of course, you'd be fibbing. Not to mention it's questionable to insure your supposed case of olive oil for $600.)

All I can really tell you about shipping is to do your homework before you buy. Talk with wineries and, if necessary, shipping companies. I've listed a few below, but you also should ask the winery from which you're buying about shipping companies; because the winery wants you to buy, it's probably done more than its fair share of shipping research and resolutions, and it should be up on the latest.

Keep in mind that it's illegal to box your own wine and send it to a nonreciprocal state; the shippers could lose their license and you could lose your wine. However, if you do get stuck shipping illegally (which is done all the time), you might want to head to a post office, UPS, or other shipping company outside the Wine Country area; it's far less obvious that you're shipping wine if you're doing it from, say, Vallejo or San Francisco than it is if you're shipping from Napa Valley.

NAPA VALLEY SHIPPING COMPANIES

Ask wineries for shipping suggestions besides those listed below. They are up to date on the best ways to get your wine to any destination.

The UPS Store (formerly Mail Boxes Etc.) is at 3212 Jefferson St., in the Grape Yard Shopping Center (② **707/259-1398**). Call for rates.

The **St. Helena Mailing Center,** 1241 Adams St., Highway 29, St. Helena (② **707/963-2686**), says it will pack and ship anywhere in the United States. Rates are around $21 per case for ground delivery to Los Angeles, $66 to New York. Those who live in reciprocal states get their package insured for up to $100, but the St. Helena Mailing Center does not insure packages shipped to nonreciprocal states. However, it's no big deal; each bottle is packed in styrofoam and should make it home without a problem.

SONOMA VALLEY SHIPPING COMPANIES

The UPS Store (formerly Mail Boxes Etc.), 19229 Sonoma Hwy., at Verano Street, Sonoma (② **707/935-3438**), has experience with shipping wine. Prices vary: Call for specific rates.

The **Wine Exchange of Sonoma,** 452 1st St. E., between East Napa and East Spain streets, Sonoma (② **707/938-1794**), will ship your wine, but there's a catch: You must buy 12 bottles from the store. At press time the Wine Exchange did not ship to Utah, Kentucky, and New Hampshire, and some destinations required a case minimum. Shipping rates range from $20 to L.A. to $30 to the East Coast.

FAST FACTS: The Wine Country

For valley-specific information, also see the "Fast Facts" sections in chapters 4 and 5.

Area Code Both Napa and Sonoma counties use the **707** area code.

Banks Most banks are open Monday through Friday from 9am to 3pm; several stay open until about 5pm at least 1 day a week and offer limited hours on Saturday. **Bank of America** has several branches throughout the area, including a location at 1001 Adams St. in St. Helena (℡ **707/963-6807**). You'll also find **Wells Fargo** throughout the region, including a branch in Napa at 217 Soscol Ave., inside Raley's supermarket (℡ **707/254-8690**). The Sonoma Wells Fargo is located at 480 W. Napa St. (℡ **707/996-2360**). For a complete listing of Wells Fargo branches, call ℡ **800/869-3557**. You'll find ATMs throughout both valleys, although not as many as you'd find in a big city. For information on how to locate the nearest ATM, see "Money Matters," earlier in this chapter.

Car Rentals See "Getting Around," earlier in this chapter.

Emergencies Dial ℡ **911** for police, ambulance, or the fire department. No coins are needed from a working public phone.

Liquor Laws Liquor and grocery stores, as well as some drugstores, can sell packaged alcoholic beverages between 6am and 2am. Most restaurants, nightclubs, and bars are licensed to serve alcoholic beverages during the same hours. The legal age for purchase and consumption is 21; proof of age is required.

Safety The Wine Country still has a remarkably safe, sleepytown atmosphere. The only safety consideration you will need to heed is your own basic common sense.

Taxes A 7.5% sales tax is added at the register for all goods and services purchased in Napa Valley and Sonoma Valley. (Note that you won't have to pay sales tax if you have your purchases shipped directly from the store out of state.) Napa Valley hotel taxes range from 10% to 12%; in Sonoma Valley, the hotel tax is 10.5%.

Time The Wine Country is in the Pacific standard time zone, which is 8 hours behind Greenwich Mean Time (GMT) and 3 hours behind Eastern Standard Time (EST). For the local time, call ℡ **707/767-8900**.

Weather Though a general weather phone recording does not exist, there's an emergency number, which is in operation only during very wet weather. For information on flood conditions, contact the **Travel Advisory** at © **888/854-NAPA.**

Napa Valley

Compared to its sister valley, Sonoma, Napa is a bit farther east from San Francisco, encompasses hundreds more wineries, and has more of an overall touristy, big-business feel to it. You'll still find plenty of rolling, mustard flower–covered hills and vast stretches of vineyards, but they come hand in hand with large, upscale restaurants; designer discount outlets; rows of hotels; and in the summer, plenty of traffic. Even with hordes of visitors year-round, Napa Valley is still pretty sleepy, with a focus on daytime attractions—wine tasting, outdoor activities, and spas—and fabulous food. Nightlife is very limited, but after indulging all day, most visitors are ready to turn in early anyway.

1 Orientation & Getting Around

Napa Valley is relatively compact. Just 35 miles long, it claims more than 34,000 acres of vineyards, making Napa the most densely planted wine-growing region in the U.S. Still, it's an easy jaunt from one end to the other: You can drive it in just over half an hour—closer to an hour during high season.

Conveniently, most of the large wineries—as well as most of the hotels, shops, and restaurants—are along a single road, **Highway 29,** which starts at the mouth of the Napa River, near the north end of San Francisco Bay, and continues north to Calistoga and the top of the growing region. All of the Napa Valley coverage in this chapter—every town, winery, hotel, and restaurant—is organized below from south to north, beginning in the city of Napa, and can be reached from Highway 29.

ALONG HIGHWAY 29: NAPA'S TOWNS IN BRIEF

Although, road signs aside, it's virtually impossible to tell when you cross from one town into the next in Napa Valley, each does have its own distinct personality. The **City of Napa** serves as the commercial center of the Wine Country and the gateway to Napa Valley—hence the high-speed freeway that whips you right past it and on to the tourist towns of St. Helena and Calistoga. However, if you do veer off the highway, you'll be surprised to discover a small but burgeoning community of more than 72,000 residents with the most cosmopolitan (relatively) atmosphere in the county and some of the most affordable accommodations in the valley. It is also in the process of gentrification, thanks to (relatively) affordable housing and new restaurants and attractions like Copia: The American Center for Wine, Food & The Arts. Heading north on either Highway 29 or the Silverado Trail leads you to Napa's wineries and the more idyllic pastoral towns beyond.

Yountville, population 2,916, was founded by the first white American to settle in the valley, George Calvert Yount. Although it lacks the small-town charm of neighboring St. Helena and Calistoga—primarily because it has no rambunctious main street—it serves as a good base for exploring the valley, and it's home to a handful of excellent wineries, inns, and restaurants, including the world-renowned restaurant The French Laundry (p. 113).

Driving farther north on the St. Helena Highway (Hwy. 29) brings you to **Oakville,** most easily recognized by Oakville Cross Road and the Oakville Grocery Co. (p. 124), a great place to pick up gourmet picnic fare and one of the only indications that you've reached the small town. If you so much as blink after Oakville, you're likely to overlook **Rutherford,** the next small town, which borders on St. Helena. Each has spectacular wineries, but you won't see most of them while driving along Highway 29.

Next comes **St. Helena,** located 17 miles north of Napa on Highway 29. St. Helena is a former Seventh-Day Adventist village that manages to maintain a pseudo–Old West feel while simultaneously catering to upscale shoppers with deep pockets and its generally wealthy resident population of 5,950 and growing. This quiet, attractive little town is home to a slew of beautiful old houses, as well as great restaurants, the region's best shopping street, and many exceptional wineries.

Calistoga, the last tourist town in Napa Valley, was named by Sam Brannan, entrepreneur extraordinaire and California's first millionaire. After making a bundle supplying miners during the gold rush, he went on to take advantage of the natural geothermal springs at the north end of Napa Valley by building a hotel and spa in 1859. Flubbing up a speech in which he compared this natural California wonder to New York State's Saratoga Springs resort, he serendipitously coined the name "Calistoga" and it stuck. Today, this small, simple resort town with 5,190 residents and an old-time main street (no building along the 6-block stretch is more than two stories high) is popular with city folk who come here to unwind. Calistoga is a great place to relax and indulge in mineral waters, mud baths, Jacuzzis, massages, and, of course, wine. The vibe is more casual—and a little groovier—than you'll find in neighboring towns to the south.

VISITOR INFORMATION

Even if you plan to skip the town of Napa, you might want to stop at the **Napa Valley Conference and Visitors Bureau,** 1310 Napa Town Center (off 1st St.), Napa, CA 94559 (© **707/226-7459**), www. napavalley.com, to pick up a variety of local information and money-saving coupons.

All over Napa and Sonoma you can pick up a very informative, free weekly called the *Wine Country Review,* which provides the most up-to-date information on the area's wineries and related events.

WINE-TASTING TOURS

Driving gives you the most touring freedom, but if the whole point of this vacation is to drink too much, eat too much, and avoid all mental exertion, consider hiring one of the companies below to figure out the sightseeing and wine-tasting details.

RIDING THE NAPA VALLEY WINE TRAIN   One of the most leisurely ways to view the Wine Country is aboard the **Napa Valley Wine Train,** a rolling restaurant that makes a 3-hour, 36-mile journey through the vineyards of Napa, Yountville, Oakville, Rutherford, and St. Helena. Not for claustrophobics or anyone who enjoys hands-on adventure, this is a lazy, slow cruise through the valley on vintage-style cars finished with polished Honduran mahogany paneling and etched-glass partitions and sadly dirt-stained windows. In other words, there's nothing to do but enjoy the company you keep, peek out the window, and eat—provided you opted for a ticket that included a meal.

The staff, which serves optional "gourmet" meals complete with all the finery—damask linen, bone china, silver flatware, and etched crystal—is attentive, if not overly enthusiastic. The fixed menus consist of three to five courses of just passable fare, which might include a salmon dish or Angus beef tenderloin with cabernet sauce. Plainly put, if you're in it for the food, forget it. Go somewhere else where $75 per person will get you a memorable meal. The point here is the train ride, period.

In addition to the dining rooms, the train pulls a Wine Tasting Car, a Deli Car, and four 50-passenger lounges. Two bummers: The train doesn't stop except during one daytime ride, which includes an optional stop in Yountville and at the Grgich Winery in Rutherford for a tour followed by a tasting, and the pre-boarding wine tasting was flat-out patronizing and unpolished, which was emphasized when our instructor consistently mispronounced the grape varietal "pinot meunier" (say "*pee*-noh muh-*nyay*").

The train departs from the McKinstry Street Depot, 1275 McKinstry St. (near 1st St. and Soscol Ave.) Napa, (© **800/427-4124** or 707/253-2111; www.winetrain.com). Train fare without meals is $40 for daytime rides; fare with meals is $70 for brunch, from $65 for lunch, and $85 for dinner. To sit in the ultraswank and modern 1950s Vista Dome Car with upstairs-only seating and a glass top, you must opt for the pricier lunch or dinner served within it. Including train fare, lunch is $95 for a four-course French affair; dinner is five courses for $110. Departures are Monday through Friday at 11:30am; Saturday, Sunday, and holidays at 9am, 12:30, and 6pm. (The schedule is reduced in Jan and Feb.) *Tip:* Sit on the west side for the best views.

BICYCLING AROUND THE WINE COUNTRY **Getaway Adventures/Wine Country Bike Tours,** 1117 Lincoln Ave., Calistoga (© **800/499-BIKE** or 707/763-3040; www.getawayadventures. com) is dedicated to bicycling and adventure tours of Napa and Sonoma. Sign up for a weekend to a 6-day package, and everything's taken care of: lodging, continental breakfasts, gourmet picnic lunches, dinners at local restaurants, wine tours and tastings, and unforgettable scenery in the majestic valley, plus the bicycle, helmet, and drinking water. On weekdays, Getaway will even deliver bikes to certain hotels in the area. A 1-day tour, which includes lunch and a visit to three to five wineries, cost $105; the downhill is a good choice for people who hate to pedal. Weekend tours start at $789 per person; a 6-day trip goes for $2,199. Day rentals are $28. If you'd rather paddle than peddle, consider this: They also offer kayaking tours of the Napa-Sonoma Wilderness Marshes for $145 per person.

FAST FACTS: Napa Valley

Hospitals **Queen of the Valley Hospital,** 100 Trancas St., Napa (© **707/257-4008**), offers minor emergency care from 10am to 10pm and also has emergency-room care 'round the clock. You can also head to **St. Helena Hospital,** about 5 minutes from the town of St. Helena, at 650 Sanitarium Rd., Deer Park (© **707/963-6425**).

Information See "Visitor Information," above.

Newspapers/Magazines The *Napa Valley Register* covers the entire Napa Valley; it's available at newspaper racks on the main streets in towns throughout the county. Other local town weeklies include the *Weekly Calistogan* and the *St. Helena Star,* which are both free. Essential for all visitors is the *Napa Valley Guide,* an annual, glossy, 132-page magazine packed with valuable tourist information; it's sold in most shops and hotels and is also available at the **Napa Valley Conference and Visitors Bureau,** 1310 Napa Town Center, off 1st Street (℗ **707/226-7459**).

Pharmacies **Smith's St. Helena Pharmacy,** 1390 Railroad Ave. (at Adams St.), St. Helena (℗ **707/963-2794**), is open Monday through Friday from 9am to 6pm and Saturday from 9am to 5pm. **Vasconi Drug Store,** 1381 Main St., St. Helena (℗ **707/963-1447**), is open Monday through Friday from 11am to 7pm, Saturday from 10am to 2pm. **Raley's Pharmacy,** 217 Soscol Ave., Napa (℗ **707/224-1269**), is open Monday through Friday from 9am to 7pm and Saturday from 9am to 5pm.

Police Call ℗ **707/967-2850** or, in an emergency, ℗ **911.**

Post Offices Each town has its own post office. **Franklin Post Office,** 1351 2nd St., at Randolf Street, Napa (℗ **707/255-0621**), is open Monday through Friday from 8:30am to 5pm. **Napa Downtown,** 1625 Trancas St., at Claremont Street (℗ **707/255-0190**), is open Monday through Friday from 8:30am to 5pm. You'll find local branches in **Yountville** at 6514 Washington St. at Mulberry (℗ **707/944-2123**), open Monday through Friday from 8am to 4pm, Saturday from 9:30am to noon; in **Oakville** at 7856 St. Helena Hwy. at Oakville Cross Road (℗ **707/944-2600**), open Monday through Friday from 8am to noon and 1 to 4pm, Saturday from 8 to 11:30am; and in **Rutherford** at 1190 Rutherford Rd., at Highway 29 (℗ **707/963-7488**), operating Monday through Friday from 8am to 1pm and 2 to 4pm, Saturday from 8am to noon. The **St. Helena Post Office,** 1461 Main St., between Adams and Pine streets (℗ **707/963-2668**), is open Monday through Friday from 8:30am to 5pm and Saturday from 10am to 1pm. In **Calistoga,** head to 1013 Washington St., at Lincoln (℗ **707/942-6661**), open Monday through Friday from 9am to 4pm.

Shipping Companies See "The Ins & Outs of Shipping Wine Home," in chapter 3.

Taxi Call **Napa Valley Cab,** at ℗ **707/257-6444,** or **Yellow Cab,** at ℗ **707/226-3731.**

2 Touring the Wineries

Touring Napa Valley takes a little planning. With more than 280 wineries, each offering distinct wines, atmosphere, and experience, the best thing you can do is decide what you're most interested in and chart your path from there. (For more on this, see "Strategies for Touring the Wine Country," in chapter 3.)

The towns and wineries listed below are organized geographically, from the city of Napa in the south to Calistoga in the north. Bear in mind that because some wineries are on Highway 29 and others are on the Silverado Trail (which parallels Hwy. 29), the order in which they're listed is not necessarily the best path to follow. To save time, plan your wine tour to avoid zigzagging between the two parallel roads (see the map "Napa Valley Wineries," on p. 57 to get your bearings).

It's impossible to include a review of every valley winery, so this chapter offers a great but limited selection. For a complete list, be sure to pick up one of the free Napa Valley guides (see "Visitor Information" and "Fast Facts," above).

While you're exploring, keep in mind that some of the most memorable Wine Country experiences aren't all made on tours or in formal tasting halls, but at the mom-and-pop wineries that dot the region. These are the places where you'll discover bottles sold from the proprietor's front room and get to talk one-on-one with winemakers.

NAPA

Artesa Vineyards & Winery *(Finds*   Views, modern architecture, seclusion, and region-specific pinot noir flights are the reasons this is one of my favorite stops. Arrive on a day when the wind is blowing less than 10 mph, and the fountains are captivating; they automatically shut off with higher winds. Step into the winery, and there's plenty to do. You can wander through the very tasteful gift shop, browse a room that outlines history and details of the Carneros region, or head to the long bar for $2 tastes or $6 flights of everything from chardonnays and pinot noirs to cabernet sauvignon and zinfandel. Owned by Codorníu of Spain and previously dedicated to sparkling wine production, the winery only recently made the transition to focus on still wine. Sorry, but Artesa's permits don't allow for picnicking.

1345 Henry Rd. ⓒ **707/224-1668.** www.artesawinery.com. Daily 10am–5pm; tours daily at 11am and 2pm. From Highway 12/121, turn north on old Sonoma Rd., turn left on Dealy Lane, and turn right on Henry Rd.

Napa Valley Wineries

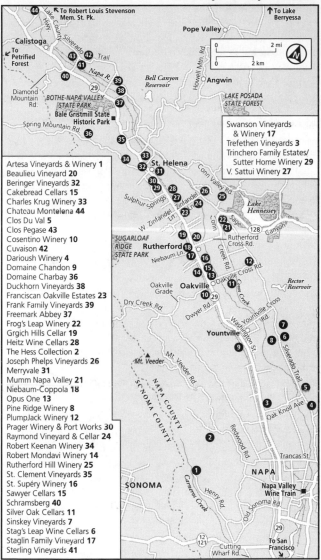

To Robert Louis Stevenson
Mem. St. Pk.

↑ To Lake Berryessa

Pope Valley

Calistoga

← To Petrified Forest

To Lake County Hwy.

Silverado Trail

Napa R.

Bell Canyon Reservoir

Howell Mtn. Rd.

Angwin

LAKE POSADA STATE FOREST

Diamond Mountain Rd.

BOTHE-NAPA VALLEY STATE PARK

Bale Gristmill State Historic Park

Spring Mountain Rd.

St. Helena

Conn Valley Rd.

Swanson Vineyards & Winery **17**
Trefethen Vineyards **3**
Trinchero Family Estates/
  Sutter Home Winery **29**
V. Sattui Winery **27**

Sulphur Springs

W. Zinfandel Ln.

Zinfandel Ln.

Conn

Lake Hennessey

Sage Canyon

128

Rutherford Cross Rd.

Conn Creek Rd.

Rector Reservoir

SUGARLOAF RIDGE STATE PARK

Rutherford

Niebaum Ln.

Oakville Grade

Oakville

Oakville Cross Rd.

Dry Creek Rd.

Dwyer Rd.

Conn Creek Rd.

Washington St.

Yountville

Silverado Trail

Mt. Veeder

NAPA COUNTY

Mt. Veeder Rd.

SONOMA COUNTY

Redwood Rd.

Oak Knoll Ave.

Trancas St.

NAPA

Napa Valley Wine Train

SONOMA

Carneros Creek

Henry Rd.

Sonoma Rd.

29

12
121

Cutting Wharf Rd.

To San Francisco ↓

0 ——— 2 mi
0 ——— 2 km

Artesa Vineyards & Winery **1**
Beaulieu Vineyard **20**
Beringer Vineyards **32**
Cakebread Cellars **15**
Charles Krug Winery **33**
Chateau Montelena **44**
Clos Du Val **5**
Clos Pegase **43**
Cosentino Winery **10**
Cuvaison **42**
Darioush Winery **4**
Domaine Chandon **9**
Domaine Charbay **36**
Duckhorn Vineyards **38**
Franciscan Oakville Estates **23**
Frank Family Vineyards **39**
Freemark Abbey **37**
Frog's Leap Winery **22**
Grgich Hills Cellar **19**
Heitz Wine Cellars **28**
The Hess Collection **2**
Joseph Phelps Vineyards **26**
Merryvale **31**
Mumm Napa Valley **21**
Niebaum-Coppola **18**
Opus One **13**
Pine Ridge Winery **8**
PlumpJack Winery **12**
Prager Winery & Port Works **30**
Raymond Vineyard & Cellar **24**
Robert Keenan Winery **34**
Robert Mondavi Winery **14**
Rutherford Hill Winery **25**
St. Clement Vineyards **35**
St. Supéry Winery **16**
Sawyer Cellars **15**
Schramsberg **40**
Silver Oak Cellars **11**
Sinskey Vineyards **7**
Stag's Leap Wine Cellars **6**
Staglin Family Vineyard **17**
Sterling Vineyards **41**

The Hess Collection (★★ (Finds   This winery brings art and wine together like no other destination in the valley. The drive itself is quintessential picturesque country splendor. But once you're at Hess, tucked in the hillside of rural Mount Veeder, you'll discover one of the region's sexiest stops. In 1978 Swiss art collector Donald Hess transformed the Christian Brothers 1903 property into a winery-cum-art gallery with gloriously lit rooms exhibiting huge, colorful works by the likes of Frank Stella and Robert Rauschenberg. A free self-guided tour leads through his collection and offers glimpses through small windows into the winemaking facilities. Equally alluring are the tranquil gardens (Come in spring when the wisteria's exploding with bloom!) and exceptionally tasteful gift shop. For $3, you can sample the current cabernet and chardonnay and one other featured wine. Prices for bottles start at $9.95 and top off around $35.

4411 Redwood Rd., Napa. ℂ 707/255-1144. www.hesscollection.com. Daily 10am–4pm. From Hwy. 29 north, exit at Redwood Rd. west and follow Redwood Rd. for 6½ miles.

Trefethen Vineyards   Listed on the National Register of Historic Places, the vineyard's main building was built in 1886 and is Napa's only wooden, gravity-flow winery. Although Trefethen is one of the valley's oldest wineries, it didn't produce its first chardonnay until 1973—but thank goodness it did. The award-winning whites and reds are a pleasure to the palate. They offer one complimentary wine daily, but if you want to sample more it'll cost you $5 to taste four current releases.

1160 Oak Knoll Ave. (east of Hwy. 29), Napa. ℂ 707/255-7700. www.trefethen. com. Daily 10am–4:30pm. Tours by appointment only.

Darioush Winery   If you want to get in on the ground floor of a winery that's sure to be a contender, visit this newbie, which opened in 2000 and was already selling out of its most coveted varietals from a double-wide trailer. The winery, once it's finished with construction—allegedly in late spring 2004—will accentuate the homeland of owner Persian-American Darioush Khaledi, who immigrated during the Islamic Revolution and found his fortune in a grocery chain. But for now you'll have to settle on $5 tastings of the likes of cabernet, shiraz, merlot, chardonnay, and viogner in the temporary tasting room. Still, Darioush does its best to make you feel at home—even offering free tastes of Persian pistachios and peeks at the plans for the stately structure and its Persian gardens.

4240 Silverado Trail (south of Oak Knoll Ave.). ℂ 707/257-2345. www.darioush. com. Daily 10:30am–5pm.

Clos Du Val A beautiful, ivy-covered building and well-manicured rose garden set the scene for a romantic and extremely friendly wine-tasting experience. Inside, the cheery small-business atmosphere completes the all-around welcoming ambience.

Bordeaux-born winemaker Bernard Portet and his younger counterpart John Clews are responsible for what ends up in the glass and have garnered a serious reputation for cabernet (which makes up 45% of the winery's production), not to mention over-the-top annual parties for cellar club members. (Seriously, the best in the valley as far as I'm concerned!) Other varietals include chardonnay, zinfandel, pinot noir, and merlot. You can try them all in the rather matter-of-fact tasting room, which is refreshingly low on merchandise. There's a $5 tasting charge (refunded with purchase) for around four wines, which may include a library selection or two.

Lovely picnic facilities offer respite in grassy nooks along the grounds. An added bonus is the extremely friendly, helpful staff, which happily offers directions to other wineries, along with a small map.

5330 Silverado Trail (north of Oak Knoll Ave.), Napa. ℂ **707/259-2200**. www.closduval.com. Daily 10am–5pm. Tours by appointment only.

Stag's Leap Wine Cellars Founded in 1972, Stag's Leap shocked the oenological world in 1976, when its 1973 cabernet won first place over French wines in a blind tasting in Paris. Visit the charmingly landscaped, unfussy winery and its very cramped tasting room, and for a whopping $10 per person, you can be the judge of five current releases (with a keepsake glass) or fork over up to $30 for estate samples. A 1-hour tour and tasting runs through everything from the vineyard and production facilities to the new, ultra-swank $5 million caves, which premiered in mid-2001.

5766 Silverado Trail, Napa. ℂ **707/944-2020**. www.cask23.com. Daily 10am–4:30pm. Tours by appointment only.

Pine Ridge Winery A pretty hillside location, less tourist traffic, good wines, and visitor-friendly touches are the reasons to visit Pine Ridge. Outside, vineyards surround the well-landscaped property, and picnickers perk up—there are a surprising number of feast-worthy tables perched on a knoll with grapes trellised along the hillside above. Across the parking lot is a demonstration vineyard, which is somewhat educational if you know something about grape growing and even more helpful if you take the tour (by appointment), which also covers the cellar and includes barrel tastings. Tastings, which are held inside a modest room, don't come cheaply, but they are refunded with the purchase of four bottles of wine. Current release tastings of chardonnay, merlot, cabernet sauvignon, and more go for $10. It's $15 for their limited-release tasting and $30 for the private reserve tasting.

5901 Silverado Trail, Napa. © **800/575-9777** or 707/253-7500. www.pineridge winery.com. Daily 11am–5pm. Tours by appointment at 11am, 1pm, and 3pm.

Sinskey Vineyards *Finds* I love this winery for myriad reasons. First, it's everything a winery should be—romantic, beautifully landscaped, friendly, and hospitable. Second, the wines are great. Robert Sinskey's varietals are made in a more sophisticated, less hit-you-over-the-head European style, which means you should be prepared to leave with the trunk full of pinot blanc, chardonnay, pinot noir, cabernet franc, merlot, and cabernet sauvignon. Finally, Robert's married to chef/cookbook author Maria Sinskey, which means they're way into tantalizing taste buds with snacks fresh from the vineyard kitchen along with their $10 flight tasting. They offer a winery production tour, wine library tour, and wine, artesian cheese, and herb garden tour, which discusses wine, cheese, and herb pairings (makes sense since tarragon chicken will pair best with a much different wine than garlic chicken, right?). All are appointment-only. They also hold killer cooking classes with famous chefs during summer that finale with memorable lunch feasts.

6320 Silverado Trail, Napa. © **707/944-9090**. www.robertsinskeyvineyards.com. Daily 10am–4:30pm. Tours by appointment only.

YOUNTVILLE

Domaine Chandon *Finds* Founded in 1973 by French champagne house Moët et Chandon, the valley's most renowned sparkling winery rises to the grand occasion with truly elegant grounds and atmosphere. Quintessentially manicured gardens showcase locally made sculpture, guests linger—their glasses fizzing with bubbly—under the patio's umbrella shade, and in the restaurant diners indulge in a formal, French-inspired meal. If you can veer away from the bubbly (sold in tastings for $9–$14 and served with complimentary bread and spread), you'll find the comprehensive tour of the facilities is interesting, very informative, and friendly. There's a shop as well as a small gallery that houses artifacts from Moët et Chandon that depict the history of champagnes. The winery also hosts art exhibits (with works available for purchase). *Note:* The restaurant tends to require reservations.

1 California Dr. (at Hwy. 29), Yountville. © **707/944-2280**. www.chandon.com. Daily 10am–6pm. Free tours 11am, 2pm, and 5pm Mon–Fri and every hour on the hour 11am–5pm Sat–Sun.

Cosentino Winery   Known for its friendly, laid-back atmosphere and vast selection of wines, Cosentino is a great stop for anyone interested in covering a lot of wine-tasting ground under one roof. Pay $5 to taste, and you'll get to keep the glass in which you try five samples of an array of wines from the Cosentino portfolio, which includes the brands Cosentino, CE2V, and Crystal Valley Cellars. With pop music playing in the background and nearly 40 different wines on sale ($12–$100), there's lots of entertainment value at the long copper-top bar. You can join the wine club to get free tastings and 25% off purchases. Keep an eye out for case discounts; during my last visit, they were up to 30% off.

7415 St. Helena Hwy/Hwy 29, Yountville. © **707/944-1220.** www.cosentinowinery. com. Daily 10am–5pm; 10am–5:30pm during daylight savings time.

OAKVILLE

Robert Mondavi Winery ☆ *Finds*   At Mission-style Mondavi, computers control almost every variable in the winemaking process—it's fascinating to watch, especially since Mondavi gives the most comprehensive tours in the valley. Basic jaunts, which take about an hour, walk through the vineyards—complete with examples of various varietals—and through the new winemaking facilities. Ask the guides anything; they know a heck of a lot. After the tour, you can taste the results of all this attention to detail in selected current wines (free). If you're really into learning more about wine, find out about more in-depth tours in advance. The "essence" tasting includes the opportunity to compare wine to the smell of fruits, spices, nuts, and more in individual glasses. An appellation tour includes a picnic lunch in the vineyards. You can also taste without taking a tour in the Appellation Room (an outdoor tasting area that is open in summer) and ToKalon Room, but it will cost you $5 for a 3-ounce taste to $30 for a rare library wine (applied toward purchase). Fridays the "Art of Wine and Food" program includes a slide presentation on the history of wine, a tour of the winery, and a three-course luncheon with wine pairing; the cost is around $65, and you must reserve in advance. The winery also offers outdoor concerts—most sell out far in advance.

7801 St. Helena Hwy. (Hwy. 29), Oakville. © **800/MONDAVI** or 707/226-1395. www. robertmondaviwinery.com. Daily 9am–5pm. Reservations recommended for guided tour; book 1 week ahead, especially for weekend tours.

Opus One   A visit to Opus One is a serious and stately affair that takes after its wine and its owners, Robert Mondavi and Baroness Philippine de Rothschild, who, after years of discussion, embarked on this state-of-the-art collaboration. Architecture buffs in particular will appreciate the tour, which takes in both the impressive Greco-Roman-meets-20th-century building and the no-holds-barred ultra-high-tech production and aging facilities.

This entire facility caters to one ultrapremium wine, which is offered here for a whopping $25 per 4-ounce taste (and a steep $150 per bottle). But wine lovers happily fork over the cash: It's a memorable red. Grab your glass and head to the redwood rooftop deck to enjoy the view.

7900 St. Helena Hwy. (Hwy. 29), Oakville. © **707/944-9442**. www.opusonewinery. com. Daily 10:30am–4pm. Tours by appointment only; in high season, book a month in advance.

Silver Oak Cellars   Colorado oil man Ray Duncan and a former Christian Brothers monk, Justin Meyer, formed a partnership and a mission to create the finest cabernet sauvignon in the world. The answer was this winery, which produces one of the valley's cabernet kings.

A narrow tree-lined road leads to the handsome Mediterranean-style winery, where roughly 40,000 cases of 100% varietal cab are produced annually. (An additional 10,000 cases are produced annually from Silver Oak's Alexander Valley winery in Geyserville.) The elegant tasting room is refreshingly quiet and soothing, adorned with redwood panels stripped from old wine tanks and warmed by a wood fire. Tastings and tours are $10, which includes a keepsake burgundy glass. No picnic facilities are available.

915 Oakville Cross Rd. (at Money Rd.), Oakville. © **707/944-8808**. www.silveroak. com. Tasting room Mon–Sat 9am–4pm. Tours Mon–Fri at 1:30pm, by appointment only.

PlumpJack Winery ⊛⊛   If most wineries are like a Brooks Brothers suit, PlumpJack stands out as the Todd Oldham of wine tasting: chic, colorful, a little wild, and popular with a young, hip crowd. Like the franchise's PlumpJack restaurant and wine shop in San Francisco and its resort in Tahoe, this playfully medieval winery is a welcome diversion from the same old same old. With Getty bucks behind what was once Villa Mt. Eden winery, the budget covers far more than just atmosphere: There's some serious winemaking going on here, too. For $5 you can sample the cabernet, sangiovese, and chardonnay—each an impressive product from a winery that's only been open to the public since mid-1997. There are no tours or picnic spots, but this refreshingly stylized, friendly facility will make you want to hang out for a while nonetheless.

620 Oakville Cross Rd. (just west of Silverado Trail), Oakville. © 707/945-1220. www.plumpjack.com. Daily 10am–4pm.

RUTHERFORD

Cakebread Cellars   This winery's moniker is actually the owners' surname, but it suits the wines produced here, where the focus is on making wine that pairs well with food. The owners have done such a good job that a large portion of their 85,000 annual cases go directly to restaurants. Here you can sample the sauvignon blanc, chardonnay, cabernet, and merlot, most of which are made from Napa Valley grapes. Prices range from $18 for a bottle of sauvignon blanc to a pricey $90 for the reserve cab, but the average bottle sells for just a little more than $30. In the tasting room, a large barnlike space, the hospitable hosts pour a $5 or $10 sampling; both include a keepsake wineglass.

8300 St. Helena Hwy. (Hwy. 29), Rutherford. © 800/588-0298 or 707/963-5221. www.cakebread.com. Daily 10am–4:30pm. Tours by appointment only.

Swanson Vineyards & Winery ★★ (Finds)   The valley's most posh and unique wine tasting is yours with a reservation and $25 to $45 fee at Swanson. Here wine tasting is more like a private party, which they call a "SA-lon." You and up to seven other guests sit at a centerpiece round table in a vibrant coral parlor adorned with huge paintings, sea shells, and a fireplace, and take in the uncommonly refined yet whimsical atmosphere. The table's set more for a dinner party than a tasting, with Reidel stemware, slivers of a fine cheese or two, crackers, and one superb chocolate Alexis ganache-filled bonbon, which you will be glad to know can be purchased on the premises. Over the course of the hour-or-more snack-and-sip event, a winery host pours four wines and discusses the history and fine points of each. You're likely to be in store for a bright pinot grigio, old vine syrah, and hearty Alexis, Swanson's signature cab-syrah blend. But just as important to the experience is the everyday conversation and making of new friends, which almost invariably occurs because the experience puts everyone in such a festive mood. This is definitely a must-do for those who don't mind spending the money. And you'll surely part with more since they sell what they pour.

1271 Manley Lane (off Hwy. 29), Rutherford. © 707/967-3500. www.swanson vineyards.com. Appointments available. Wed–Sun 10am–4pm.

Staglin Family Vineyard   This, one of the area's prestige wineries, was never open to the public until winter 2001, when Staglin debuted its new wine caves and private tours. Now you can turn off

Highway 29, through a quiet residential area, to beautifully trellised vineyards and the daily private wine tasting with no more than 10 guests. During the visit they'll tell you about the winery history and the famed "Rutherford dust" and taste you through four wines— two chardonnays and two cabernet sauvignons under two labels, Staglin Family and their secondary brand Salus. Wines range from $35 to $100 and are served at a sit-down tasting in the caves. At $20 a pop and with little in the way of bells and whistles (other than the wine, of course), this excursion is best for those who want a more intimate understanding of Staglin rather than winemaking in general and for those who want to purchase some of Staglin's product.

P.O. Box 680, Rutherford. ℂ 707/944-0477. www.staglinfamily.com. One tasting daily, by appointment.

Sawyer Cellars ⟨ₖ⟩ ⟨Finds⟩   The most attractive thing about Sawyer, aside from its clean and tasty wines, is its ability to embody a dedication to extremely high quality and maintain a humble, accommodating attitude. Step one foot into the simple, restored 1920s barn to see what I mean. Whatever you ask, the tasting room host will answer. Whatever your request, Sawyer does its best to accommodate. Want to picnic on the back patio overlooking the vineyards? Be Sawyer's guest. Like to participate in the crush? Come on over and get your hands dirty. Want to reserve the charming wine library for a private luncheon? Pay a minimal fee and make yourself at home. Here you can tour the property on a little tram or learn more about winemaker Brad Warner, who spent 30 years at Mondavi before embarking on this exclusive endeavor. Or simply drop in and spend $5 to taste delicious estate-made wines: sauvignon blanc, merlot, cabernet sauvignon, and meritage. The wines run from $18 to $38 per bottle for current releases, and some argue they are worth twice the price. With a total production of only 3,500 cases and a friendly attitude, this is a rare treat.

8350 St. Helena Hwy. (Hwy. 29), Rutherford. ℂ 707/963-1980. www.sawyercellars. com. Mon and Wed–Sat 10am–5pm; Sun and Tues by appointment. Tours by appointment.

St. Supéry Winery ⟨ₖ⟩ ⟨Kids⟩   The outside looks like a modern corporate office building, but inside you'll find a functional, welcoming winery that encourages first-time tasters to learn more about oenology. On the self-guided tour, you can wander through the demonstration vineyard, where you'll learn about growing techniques. Inside, "SmellaVision," an interactive display, teaches you how to identify different wine characteristics. Adjoining is the

Atkinson House, which chronicles more than 100 years of wine-making history. For $5, you'll get lifetime tasting privileges. Because some are not nationally distributed, you're likely to sample something new here, from sauvignon blanc, semillon, and chardonnay to cabernet, cabernet franc, syrah, and merlot. Prices start at $16 per bottle, many wines hover around $20, and the highest price tag goes to their Dollarhide Ranch cab at $70. In the tasting room, a large barnlike space, the hospitable hosts pour a $5 or $10 sampling. In late 2003 they launched a "grafting seminar" ($99), which allows guests to graft their own bud to rootstock, take it home, and grow their own vine.

8440 St. Helena Hwy. (Hwy. 29), Rutherford. (ℂ) **800/942-0809** or 707/963-4507. www.stsupery.com. Daily 10am–4:30pm. Guided tours daily at 1pm and 3pm.

Niebaum-Coppola Hollywood meets Napa Valley at Francis Ford Coppola's historic Inglenook Vineyards, now known as Niebaum-Coppola (pronounced *nee*-bomb *coh*-pa-la). From the outside, the spectacular, ivy-draped, 1880s stone winery and grounds are historic grandeur. On the inside it's one big and impressive retail center promoting Coppola's products and, more subtly, his films. On display are Academy Awards and memorabilia from *The Godfather* and *Bram Stoker's Dracula;* the Centennial Museum chronicles the history of the estate and its winemaking as well as Coppola's filmmaking. Wine, food, and gift items dominate the cavernous tasting area where an array of wines such as an estate-grown blend, cabernet franc, merlot, chardonnay, zinfandel, and others made from organically grown grapes, can be sampled for $8.50 (plus a souvenir glass). Bottles range from around $10 to more than $80. The château and garden tour is one of the most expensive in the valley, at $20 a pop; the 1½-hour journey includes a private tasting and a souvenir glass. *Tip:* Drop by, snoop around on your own, and spend the cash saved on one more bottle for your vacation collection. You're welcome to picnic at any of the designated garden sites.

1991 St. Helena Hwy. (Hwy. 29), Rutherford. (ℂ) **707/968-1100.** www.niebaum-coppola.com. Daily 10am–5pm (until 6pm Memorial Day to Labor Day). Tours daily at 10:30am, 12:30pm, and 2:30pm.

Beaulieu Vineyard Bordeaux native Georges de Latour founded the third-oldest continuously operating winery in Napa Valley in 1900. With the help of legendary oenologist André Tchelistcheff, he has produced world-class, award-winning wines that have been served by every president of the United States since Franklin D.

Fun Fact **Tasting a Flight**

A *flight* is an array of wines of the same varietal, with each showing different characteristics ranging from the origin of the grapes used and production methods to the year the wine was produced and the producer itself. Tasting a flight allows you to get a sense of how influences such as age, production, origins, year of harvest, and winemaker styles can affect the bouquet and flavor. It's a great way to become more familiar with a particular varietal.

Roosevelt. The brick-and-redwood tasting room isn't much to look at, but with the stellar reputation of Beaulieu (pronounced *bowl-you*), it has no need to visually impress. Tastings cost $5, and a variety of bottles sell for under $20. The Private Reserve Tasting Room offers a flight of five reserve wines to taste for $25, but if you want to take a bottle to go, it may cost as much as $130. A free tour explains the winemaking process and the vineyard's history.

1960 St. Helena Hwy. (Hwy. 29), Rutherford. © 707/967-5230. www.bvwine.com. Daily 10am–5pm. Tours daily 11am–4pm.

Grgich Hills Cellar   Yugoslavian émigré Miljenko (Mike) Grgich (pronounced *grr*-gitch) made his presence known to the world when his Château Montelena chardonnay bested the top French white burgundies at the famous 1976 Paris tasting. Since then, the master vintner has teamed up with Austin Hills (of the Hills Brothers coffee fortune) and started this extremely successful and respected winery.

The ivy-covered stucco building isn't much to behold, and the tasting room is even less appealing, but people don't come here for the scenery: As you might expect, Grgich's chardonnays are legendary—and priced accordingly. The smart buys are the outstanding zinfandel and cabernet sauvignon, which cost around $23 and $50, respectively. The winery also produces a fantastic fumé blanc for as little as $18 a bottle. Before you leave, be sure to poke your head into the barrel-aging room and inhale the divine aroma. Tastings cost $5 (which includes the glass) on weekends. No picnic facilities are available.

1829 St. Helena Hwy. (Hwy. 29, north of Rutherford Cross Rd.), Rutherford. © 707/963-2784. www.grgich.com. Daily 9:30am–4:30pm. Free tours by appointment only, Mon–Fri 11am and 2pm, Sat–Sun 11am and 1:30pm.

Mumm Napa Valley   At first glance, Mumm, housed in a big redwood barn, looks almost humble. But once you're in the front door, you'll know that they mean business—big business. Just beyond the extensive gift shop (which is filled with all sorts of namesake mementos) is the tasting room, where you can purchase sparkling wine by the glass ($5–$8), 3-wine flights ($8–$25), or bottles ($16–$70), and appreciate breathtaking vineyard and mountain views. Unfortunately, there's no food or picnicking here, but during warm weather, out on the open patio with a glass of champagne in hand, you'll forget all about nibbling. Mumm also offers a 45-minute educational tour and is worth visiting if only to take a gander at its impressive art gallery, which features a permanent Ansel Adams collection and an ever-changing photography exhibit.

8445 Silverado Trail (just north of Rutherford Cross Rd.), Rutherford. © 800/ 686-6272 or 707/942-3434. www.mummcuveenapa.com. Daily 10am–5pm. Tours offered every hour daily 10am–3pm.

Frog's Leap Winery   One of the valley's leaders in organic farming, Frog's Leap is known for its killer zinfandels (but its sauvignon blancs, merlots, cabernets, and chardonnays are nothing to sneeze at). The entrance is confusing, but bear in mind that the beautifully restored 1884 big red barn is where the action takes place; the small gift shop behind the barn on the left is the best place to locate an employee if you don't find someone immediately. In the gift shop you'll find trinkets featuring the winery's motto—"Time's fun when you're having flies"—and where you'll start your tour. The 45-minute expedition gives "a scintillating history" of how Frog's Leap began, a tour of the barn, and wine tasting—and the wine may even be poured directly from the tanks. If there's action on the vines, you might get to pick and eat fresh grapes.

Considering that Frog's Leap is a favorite on restaurant wine lists and has a small annual production of 50,000 cases, the wine is well priced. A 2001 zin goes for $23 a bottle; the 2002 sauvignon blanc, $17. The only current releases are the cab ($35) and merlot ($30).

8815 Conn Creek Rd. (west of Silverado Trail), Rutherford. © 800/959-4704 or 707/963-4704. www.frogsleap.com. Mon–Sat 10am–4pm. Tastings and tours by appointment only. From Hwy. 29, take Rutherford Cross Rd. and turn left at the fork.

Rutherford Hill Winery   Rutherford Hill Winery isn't particularly well known for its wine, although it does produce a wide array—chardonnay, cabernet, zinfandel port, sangiovese, cabernet sauvignon, and merlot, which makes up around 80% of its entire wine production. But it does have lots of reasons to pay a visit. For example, thanks to massive drilling machinery imported from England, nearly a mile has been carved into the limestone slopes behind the winery, where more than 8,000 barrels of wine are stored in a naturally tem-perature-controlled environment. Half-hour tours include a trip through the caves and take you into the bowels of the immense wooden structure that houses the fermentation tanks and tasting room. A tour costs $10 and includes a wineglass for current-release tasting; for $15 you get the tour, the glass, and a reserve tasting.

Perched high above the valley, Rutherford Hill is also the Wine Country's premier picnicking site, offering the same superb views of the valley that guests of Auberge du Soleil (see "Where to Stay," later in this chapter) pay big bucks for. Prices for current wines range from $14 for the gewürztraminer to $32 for cabernet sauvignon.

200 Rutherford Hill Rd. (off Silverado Trail), Rutherford. (Ⓒ 800/MERLOT-1 or 707/963-7194. www.rutherfordhill.com. Daily 10am–5pm. Tours daily at 11:30am, 1:30, and 3:30pm.

Franciscan Oakville Estates   Franciscan's tasting room is Pot-tery Barn chic with its slick zinc centerpiece bar, dark wood shelv-ing, high ceilings, and suave displays. But the point of a visit is less superficial. Here it's $5 for the entry-level tasting of current releases and reserve wines for $10. For an even more in-depth experience, book a space in one of the private educational tastings, which range from an "essence" tasting (how to identify sensory elements in wine) to wine and cheese pairing. Each class is around an hour long and is held in the posh, wood-paneled, librarylike private section of the new building. The private tasting/educational classes cost $10 to $20 and should be reserved in advance.

1178 Galleron Rd (east of Hwy. 29), Rutherford. (Ⓒ 800-529-WINE or 707/963-7111. www.franciscan.com. Daily 10am–5pm; closed major holidays. Reservations suggested for classes.

ST. HELENA

Raymond Vineyard & Cellar   As fourth-generation vintners from Napa Valley and relations of the Beringers, brothers Walter and Roy Raymond have had plenty of time to develop terrific wines—and an excellent wine-tasting experience. The short drive through vineyards to reach the friendly, unintimidating cellar is a case in point: Passing the heavy-hanging grapes (in summer) makes you feel like you're really in the thick of things before you even get in the door. The spa-cious, warm room, complete with dining table and chairs, is a perfect setting for sampling the four tiers of wines. Most are free for the tast-ing and well priced to appeal to all levels of wine drinkers: The Amber Hill label starts at $8 a bottle for chardonnay and $11 for cab; the reserves are priced in the low $30s, and the Generations cab costs $65.

Along with the overall experience, there's a great gift selection, which includes barbecue sauces, mustards, chocolate wine syrup, and gooey hazelnut merlot fudge sauce. Private reserve tastings cost $5. Sorry, there are no picnic facilities.

849 Zinfandel Lane (off Hwy. 29 or Silverado Trail), St. Helena. (🄫 **800/525-2659** or 707/963-3141. www.raymondwine.com. Daily 10am–4pm. Tours by appointment only.

V. Sattui Winery 🌟🌟 *Finds* *Kids* So what if it's touristy and crowded? This enormous winery is a fun picnic party stop, thanks to its huge gourmet deli and grassy expanse. It's especially great for families because you can fill up on wine, pâté, and cheese samples without ever reaching for your pocketbook, while the kids romp over the grounds. The gourmet store stocks more than 200 cheeses, sandwich meats, pâtés, breads, exotic salads, and desserts such as white-chocolate cheesecake. (It would be an easy place to graze, were it not for the continuous mob scene at the counter.) Meanwhile, the wine flows at the long wine bar in the back, which offers chardonnay, sauvignon blanc, Riesling, cabernet, and zinfandel to Madeira and muscat. V. Sattui wines aren't distributed, so if you taste something you simply must have, buy it. (If you buy a case, ask to talk with a manager, who'll give you access to the less crowded, more exclusive private tasting room.) Wine prices start at around $9, with many in the $13 neighborhood; reserves top out at around $75. *Note:* To use the picnic area, you must buy food and wine here.

1111 White Lane (at Hwy. 29), St. Helena. (🄫 **707/963-7774.** www.vsattui.com. Winter daily 9am–5pm; summer daily 9am–6pm.

Heitz Wine Cellars If you're looking for a big wine-tasting hullabaloo, don't come here. At Heitz's tiny, modest tasting room, the point is the wine and the wine alone. Joe Heitz, who passed away in December 2000, launched his winery in 1961, when there were fewer than 20 wineries in the valley. Today, his son David oversees the production of 40,000 cases per year, and although his reputation was built on cabernets (such as the Martha's Vineyard cab, which will set you back $110–$150 depending on the vintage), he's also produced a Napa Valley chardonnay ($15–$30) as well as less costly cabs, zins, more unusual offerings such as the Grignolino rosé (a mere $10), and two ports. Tastings are complimentary, but if you want to take home the fruits of Heitz's labors, count on spending upwards of $20 per bottle.

436 St. Helena Hwy. (Hwy. 29), St. Helena. (🄫 **707/963-3542.** www.heitzcellar. com. Daily 11am–4:30pm. Tours Mon–Fri by appointment only.

Merryvale   Merryvale may be approachable and low-key, but not because it's yet to be discovered. Wines here have received plenty of attention from the likes of *Wine Spectator* and *Wine & Spirits*—especially in recent years. Actually, the winery has a much longer history. It was originally built around the time of Prohibition. And allegedly, Peter and Robert Mondavi started their winemaking careers at this site. The property's current identity (Merryvale was founded in 1983 and was previously Sunny St. Helena) celebrates its history with a tasting room and the Cask Room, complete with century-old 2,000-gallon casks. As for the wine, a $5 tasting fee gets you access to current releases; it's $7 for reserve selections, and $12 for the Classic Reserve Prestige Selection. Varietals include sauvignon blanc, chardonnays, semillon, merlot, pinot noir, cabernet sauvignon, and antigua (a muscat dessert wine). Current releases begin at $13 for semillon and top off at $90 for the delicious Profile (a proprietary bourdeaux varietal blend).

Every weekend morning at 10:30am there's a 2-hour $15 seminar (reserve in advance); three Saturdays of the month you can make a reservation for a wine component–tasting seminar and the fourth Saturday of the month you can sign up for the Food and Wine in Balance seminar. Another fun reason to stop by is the barrel tastings, which happen every second Saturday of every month from 1 to 5pm; for $3 you can sample wine aging in the barrel. Also worth noting: While most wineries close around 5pm, this one keeps on pouring until dinnertime!

1000 Main St. (Hwy. 29), St. Helena. (℃) **707/963-7777**. www.merryvale.com. Daily 10am–6:30pm.

Joseph Phelps Vineyards 🍷🍷   Visitors interested in intimate, comprehensive tours and a knockout tasting should schedule a tour at this winery. A quick turn off the Silverado Trail in Spring Valley (there's no sign—watch for Taplin Rd., or you'll blast right by), Joseph Phelps was founded in 1973 and is a major player in both the region and the worldwide wine market. Phelps himself accomplished a long list of valley firsts, including launching the syrah varietal in the valley and extending the 1970s Berkeley food revolution (led by Alice Waters) to the Wine Country at his store, the Oakville Grocery (p. 124).

A favorite stop for serious wine lovers, this modern, state-of-the-art winery and big-city vibe are proof that Phelps's annual 100,000 cases prove fruitful in more ways than one. When you pass through the wisteria-covered trellis to the entrance of the redwood building, you'll encounter an air of seriousness that hangs heavier than harvest grapes. Fortunately, the mood lightens as the well-educated tour guide explains the details of what you're tasting while pouring samples of five to six wines, which may include Riesling, sauvignon blanc, gewürztraminer, syrah, merlot, zin, and cab. (Unfortunately, some wines are so popular that they sell out quickly; come late in the season, and you may not be able to taste or buy them.) Tastings run $5 for a sample or $10 for a 2-ounce pour of Insignia. The three excellently located picnic tables, on the terrace overlooking the valley, are available by reservation.

Taplin Rd. (just west of Silverado Trail), P.O. Box 1031, St. Helena. (C) 800/707-5789. www.jpvwines.com. Mon–Sat 9am–5pm; Sun 9am–4pm. Tours and tastings by appointment only.

Prager Winery & Port Works ✿   If you want a real down-home, off-the-beaten-track experience, Prager can't be beat. When you pull open the creaky, old wooden door to this shack of a wine-tasting room, you'll begin to wonder if you're in the right spot, but don't turn back! Pass the oak barrels, and you'll quickly come upon the clapboard tasting room, made homey with a big Oriental rug, a cat, and during winter, a small space heater. Most days, your host will be Jim Prager himself, a sort of modern Santa Claus in both looks and demeanor. But you won't have to sit on his lap for your wish to come true: Fork over $10 (with complimentary glass), and he'll pour you samples of his late-harvest Riesling, and the recently released 10-year-old port (which costs $45 per bottle and has won various awards). Also available is Prager Chocolate Drizzle, a chocolate liqueur that tops ice creams and other desserts. If you're looking for a special gift, see Jim's daughter, who custom-etches bottles for around $75 in the design of your choice, plus the cost of the wine.

1281 Lewelling Lane (just west of Hwy. 29, behind Trinchero Family Estates/Sutter Home Winery), St. Helena. (C) 800/969-7678 or 707/963-7678. www.pragerport.com. Daily 10:30am–4:30pm.

Trinchero Family Estates/Sutter Home Winery   This winery's been around since 1874, but its widespread reputation stems from the early 1980s, when its introduction of white zinfandel to the mass market made pink the prominent color in America's wineglasses. Although wine-drinking trends have evolved, Sutter Home's department store–like tasting room is a fair indication that this winery is still pouring for the people. In the friendly, bustling room, visitors surround the enormous U-shaped bar to sample a slew of Sutter Home wines, with chardonnay, cabernet, zin, and other varietals topping out at $8 a bottle. (Alcohol-free wines are as low as $4; Trinchero Reserve cab is $45.) Along the periphery of the room is an endless selection of food products, ranging from mustard and barbecue to pasta and chocolate sauces, as well as a Sutter Home wardrobe line, featuring everything from boxers to baseball-style jackets.

Tastings range from free to $7 for reserves (plus a souvenir glass). No tours are offered, but you're invited to take a self-guided walk through the surrounding Victorian gardens.

277 St. Helena Hwy. (at Thomann Lane), St. Helena. © 707/963-3104. www.sutter home.com. Daily 10am–5pm, except major holidays.

Robert Keenan Winery *Finds*   It's a winding, uphill drive to reach secluded Robert Keenan, but this far off the tourist track, you're guaranteed more elbow room at the tasting bar and a quieter, less commercial experience. When you drive in, you'll pass a few modest homes with kids' bikes out front, and you'll wonder whether one of the buildings is the family winery. It's not. Keep driving (slowly— kids and dogs at play) and you'll know when you get to the main building and its redwood tasting room.

The 10,000 cases produced here per year are the result of a fast-paced professional who left his business behind and headed for the hills. In this case, it's native San Franciscan Robert Keenan, who ran his own insurance agency for 20 years. When he merged with another firm and was bought out in 1981, he had already purchased his "retirement property," the winery's 176 acres, and he soon turned his fascination with winemaking into a second career. The renovated stone building has a much older history, dating back to the old Conradi Winery, which was founded in 1890.

Today, Robert Keenan Winery is known for its big, full-bodied reds, such as the Mountain cab and merlot. Chardonnay, cabernet franc, and zin sold exclusively at the winery range from $20 to $34 per bottle. Older vintages, which you won't find elsewhere, are for sale here as well. Take the tour to learn about their vineyards, production facilities, and winemaking in general. Those looking for a pastoral picnic spot should consider spreading their blankets out here. The three tables, situated right outside the winery and surrounded by vineyards, offer stunning views sans tourist trample.

3660 Spring Mountain Rd. (west of Hwy. 29), St. Helena. © 707/963-9177. www. keenanwinery.com. Tours and tastings weekends 11am–4pm; call for weekday hours.

Domaine Charbay Winery & Distillery   After you finally reach this mountaintop hideaway, affectionately called "the Still on the

Hill," you immediately get the sense that something special is going on here. Miles Karakasevic, the owner of this family operation, considers himself more of a perfume maker than the 12th-generation master distiller he is, and it's easy to see why. The tiny distillery is crammed with bottles of his latest fragrant projects-in-the-making, such as brandy, whole-fruit-flavor-infused vodkas, grappa, and pastis. He's also become known in the valley for other elixirs: black walnut liqueur, apple brandy, a line of ports, several cabernet sauvignons, and the charter product—Charbay (pronounced shar-*bay*)— a brandy liqueur blended with chardonnay.

The tour—which costs $20 per person and is a private and exclusive visit—centers around a small, 25-gallon copper alambic still; you'll be lovingly guided through an explanation of the distilling process by either daughter Laura, gregarious sons Miles, and Marko, or his wife Susan. Alas, there's no tasting other than cabernet and port due to legal limitations, but your fee is applied toward any purchase. It's all very low-key and laughter-filled at Domaine Charbay, one of the most unique and interesting places to visit in the Wine Country. Sadly, there are no picnic facilities. *Note:* Do not show up without an appointment; you'll be turned away.

4001 Spring Mountain Rd. (5 miles west of Hwy. 29), St. Helena. ⓒ 800/634-7845 or 707/963-9327. www.charbay.com. Mon–Sat (except holidays) by appointment only.

Beringer Vineyards ⚸ *Finds*   Follow the line of cars just north of St. Helena's business district to Beringer Vineyards, where everyone stops at the remarkable Rhine House to taste wine and view the hand-dug tunnels carved into the mountainside. Founded in 1876 by brothers Jacob and Frederick, this is the oldest continuously operating winery in Napa Valley—it was open even during Prohibition, when Beringer stayed afloat by making sacramental wines. White zinfandel is the winery's most popular nationwide seller, but plenty of other varietals are available to enjoy. Tastings of current vintages ($5) are conducted in new facilities, where there's also a large selection of bottles for less than $20. Reserve wines are available on the second floor of the Rhine House, for a fee of $2 to $10 per taste.

2000 Main St. (Hwy. 29), St. Helena. ⓒ 707/963-7115. www.beringervineyards. com. Off-season daily 9:30am–5pm (last tour 4pm, last tasting 4:30pm); summer 9:30am–6pm (last tour 5pm, last tasting 5:30pm). $5 45-min. tours every 30 min. (free for anyone under 21 and accompanied by an adult).

Charles Krug Winery   Founded in 1861, Krug was the first winery built in the valley. The family of Peter Mondavi (yes, Robert is his brother) owns it today. It's worth paying your respects here.

Unfortunately, ongoing retrofitting means you can't tour the red-wood Italianate wine cellar, built in 1874. But you can drop $5 to sip current releases, $8 to sample reserves. Or kick it at one of the umbrella-shaded picnic tables overlooking vineyards or the wine cellar. At press time, tours were not being given due to renovations, so call to confirm before arriving for a tour.

2800 St. Helena Hwy (just north of the tunnel of trees at the northern end of St. Helena), St. Helena. ℂ **707/963-5057**. www.charleskrugwinery.com. Daily 10:30am–5pm.

Duckhorn Vineyards With quintessential pastoral surroundings, brand new digs, and a unique wine-tasting program, Duckhorn Vineyards has much to offer for visitors interested in spending a little money and time to relax and taste. The airy Victorian farmhouse is very welcoming; you can stand on the veranda and look out on the surrounding meadow, and the interior affords equally bucolic views. If you're going to taste wine in the surprisingly modern tasting room, complete with cafe tables and a centerpiece bar, you need to make a reservation and pay $10 for current release tasting. The fee may sound steep, but this not your run-of-the-mill drink-and-dash. You get plenty of attention and information on their sauvignon blanc, merlot, and cabernet sauvignon. Wanna really ante up? Drop $25 for the estate wine tasting.

1000 Lodi Lane (at Silverado Trail), St. Helena. ℂ **707/963-7108**. www.duckhorn.com. Open daily 10am–4pm. Tastings by appointment only.

Freemark Abbey Set in a low-key shopping mall, Freemark Abbey's friendly tasting room has a hunting-lodge feel. The huge space features open-beamed ceilings, a roaring fire (in winter), and comfy couches. There's a $5 charge for a keepsake wineglass in which you might sample chardonnay and cabernet (three types of each), and merlot (ranging from $19–$65 per bottle). They also pour cabernet franc, petite sirah, viognier, and sangiovese, which are only available here. During summer, you can take your taste out onto the lovely outdoor terrace. The half-hour appointment-only tour covers the history of the winery, its viticulture, and its wine cellars. No picnic facilities are available.

3022 St. Helena Hwy. N. (Hwy. 29, at Lodi Lane), St. Helena. ℂ **800/963-9698**. www.freemarkabbey.com. Daily 10am–5pm; summer 10am–6pm. Tour by appointment only.

CALISTOGA

Frank Family Vineyards ⦵ *Finds* "Wine dudes" Bob, Dennis, and Rich will do practically anything to maintain their rightfully self-proclaimed reputation as the "friendliest winery in the valley." The name may have changed from Kornell Champagne Cellars to Frank-Rombauer to Frank Family, but the vibe's remained constant; it's all about down-home, friendly fun. No muss, no fuss, no intimidation factor. At Frank Family, you're part of their family—no joke. They'll greet you like a long-lost relative and serve you all the bubbly you want (four to six varieties: brut, blanc de blanc, blanc de noir, and extra-dry reserve, $20–$70 a bottle). Still-wine lovers can slip into the equally casual back room to sample chardonnay and a very well received cabernet sauvignon. Be sure to embark on the tour of the oldest champagne cellar in the region and ask about Marie Antoinette's relationship with glassware. Behind the tasting room is a choice picnic area, situated under the oaks and overlooking the vineyards.

1091 Larkmead Lane (just west of Silverado Trail), Calistoga. © **707/942-0859.** Daily 10am–5pm; tours by appointment.

Schramsberg ★★ *Finds*   This 200-acre champagne estate, a landmark once frequented by Robert Louis Stevenson, has a wonderful Old World feel that is one of the valley's all-time best places to explore. Schramsberg is the label that presidents serve when toasting dignitaries from around the globe, and there's plenty of historic memorabilia in the front room to prove it. But the real mystique begins when you enter the champagne caves, which wind 2½ miles (reputedly the longest in North America) and were partly hand-carved by Chinese laborers in the 1800s. The caves have an authentic *Tom Sawyer* ambience, complete with dangling cobwebs and seemingly endless passageways; you can't help but feel you're on an adventure. The comprehensive, unintimidating tour ends in a charming tasting room, where you sit around a big table and sample several surprisingly varied selections of bubbly. Tastings are a bit dear ($20 for three current releases), but it's money well spent. *Note:* Tastings are offered only to those who take the free tour, and you must reserve in advance.

1400 Schramsberg Rd. (west of Hwy. 29), Calistoga. © **707/942-2414.** www.schramsberg.com. Daily 10am–4pm. Tours and tastings by appointment only.

Clos Pegase ★★ *Finds*   What happens when a man falls in love with art and winemaking, purchases more than 450 acres of prime growing property, and sponsors a competition commissioned by the San Francisco Museum of Modern Art to create a "temple to wine"? You'll find out when you visit this magnificent winery. Renowned architect Michael Graves designed this incredible oasis, which integrates art, 20,000 square feet of aging caves, and a luxurious hill-top private home. Viewing the art is as much the point as tasting the wines—which, by the way, don't come cheap: Prices range from $13 for the Vin Gris merlot to as much as $80 for the Hommage Artist Series Reserve, an extremely limited blend of the winery's finest lots of cabernet sauvignon and merlot. Tasting current releases costs $7.50 for samples of three premium wines. The grounds at Clos Pegase (pronounced clo pey-*goss*) feature an impressive sculpture garden as well as scenic picnic spots.

1060 Dunaweal Lane (between Hwy. 29 and Silverado Trail), Calistoga. © 707/942-4981. www.clospegase.com. Daily 10:30am–5pm. Tours daily at 11am and 2pm.

Sterling Vineyards ⓡ *(Finds* *(Kids*   No, you don't need climbing shoes to reach this dazzling-white, Mediterranean-style winery, perched 300 feet up on a rocky knoll. Just fork over $10 and take the aerial tram, which offers dazzling bucolic views along the way. (As a bonus, you get free tastings for your tram fare.) If you've been here before, you'll notice major changes even before embarking due to a complete renovation in 2001. Once you're back on land, follow the self-guided tour (one of the most comprehensive in the Wine Country) of the winemaking process. Currently owned by the Sea-gram company, the winery produces more than 500,000 cases per year. If you're not into taking the tram or you have kids in tow, visit anyway; there's an elevator that can take you to the tasting room, and kids get a goodie bag and a hearty welcome (a rarity at wineries). Samples at the panoramic tasting room cost $10 (but free if you've already paid for the tram ride). Expect to pay anywhere from $14 to $100 for a souvenir bottle ($20 is the average).

1111 Dunaweal Lane (between Hwy. 29 and Silverado Trail), Calistoga. © 800/726-6136 or 707/942-3344. www.sterlingvineyards.com. Daily 10:30am–4:30pm.

Cuvaison   In 1969, Silicon Valley engineers Thomas Cottrell and Thomas Parkhill began Cuvaison (pronounced koo-vay-*sawn,* a French term for the fermentation of wine on the skins) with a 27-acre vineyard of cabernet. Today, that same vineyard has expanded to 400 acres, producing 63,000 cases of premium wines every year. Known mainly for chardonnays, winemaker Steven Rogstad also produces a limited amount of merlot, pinot noir, cabernet sauvignon, and zin-fandel within the handsome Spanish mission-style structure.

Tastings are $8 and $10, which include a glass. Wine prices range from $22 for a chardonnay to as much as $40 for a cabernet sauvi-gnon. Beautiful picnic grounds are situated amidst 350-year-old moss-covered oak trees.

4550 Silverado Trail (just south of Dunaweal Lane), Calistoga. © **707/942-6266.** www.cuvaison.com. Daily 10am–5pm. Tours at 10:30am daily.

Chateau Montelena   Perhaps you've heard of the California chardonnay that revolutionized the world of wine when it won the legendary Paris tasting test of 1976, beating out France's top white burgundies? That wine was a Chateau Montelena 1973 chardonnay, the product of Mike Grgich's (who now owns his own winery, Grgich Hills) second vintage as winemaker for Chateau Montelena. Though the tasting room is rather plain, the winery itself—housed in a replica of the great châteaux of Bordeaux—is a feast for the eyes, as are the Chinese-inspired lake and gardens behind the château. Tastings are $10 and bottle prices are on the steep side, ranging from $18 for a Riesling to $125 for the Montelena Estate cabernet sauvignon. After sampling the winery's superb chardonnay, cabernet, and Napa Valley cabernet sauvignon (a blend of cabernet sauvignon and merlot), wander around back to marvel at this classic French castle and picturesque grounds, replete with wild fowl, lush foliage, and romantic walkways. Unfortunately, picnicking is not an option here. Reservation-only tours are a hefty $25, but include a 2-hour tour and sit-down tasting.

1429 Tubbs Lane (off Hwy. 29, just past the Old Faithful Geyser), Calistoga. © **707/ 942-5105.** www.montelena.com. Daily 10am–4pm. Guided tours by appointment only, at 9:30am and 1:30pm and cost $25 per person.

3 More to See & Do

I'm not going to lie to you: If days filled with wine tasting, dining on fancy food, and just lounging around in the country excite you about as much as a trip to the DMV, buy a *TV Guide* and make yourself real cozy—it's going to be one helluva long stay in the Wine Country.

However, there are a few daytime attractions—such as golf, spectacular spas, a few wonderful shops, and museums—that will perk up anyone who simply can't take one more glass of wine.

NAPA

If you have plenty of time and a penchant for Victorian architecture, check out the **Napa Valley Conference and Visitors Bureau,** 1310 Napa Town Center, off 1st Street (© **707/226-7459;** www.napavalley. com), which offers self-guided walking tours of the town's historic buildings.

Anyone with an appreciation for art absolutely must visit the **di Rosa Preserve** ✿, which until recently was closed to the public.

Rene and Veronica di Rosa, who have been collecting contemporary American art for more than 40 years, converted their 215 acres of prime Wine Country property into a monument to northern California's regional art and nature. Their world-renowned collection features 1,800 works in all media by more than 700 greater Bay Area artists. Their treasures are displayed practically everywhere, from along the shores of their 30-acre lake to each nook and cranny of their 143-year-old winery-turned-residence. With hundreds of surrounding acres of rolling hills protected under the Napa County Land Trust, this place is truly a must-see for both art and nature lovers. It's at 5200 Sonoma Hwy. (Hwy. 121/12)—look for the blue gate. Visits are by appointment only, and a maximum of 25 guests are guided through the preserve. Each tour lasts 2 to 2½ hours and costs $12 per person. Call © 707/226-5991 for reservations, and go to www.dirosapreserve.org for more information.

Shopaholics should head to the **Napa Premium Outlets.** I've never been much of a fan of discount malls, but the occasional treasures I've found at Barney's New York inspire even a jaded local to take the 1st Street exit off Highway 29 and brave the crowds. (Unfortunately, they've only carried cheap Barney's brand outlet store stuff lately, but on occasion I've scooped up Prada shoes at a third of the price.) Along with the aforementioned Barney's, you'll find multiple places to part with your money, including my favorite, the Tse cashmere outlet, Nine West, Jones New York, BCBG, a few kitchenware shops, a food court, and a decent sushi restaurant. The shops are open Monday through Saturday from 10am to 8pm and Sunday 10am to 6pm. Call © 707/226-9876 for more information.

The biggest new attraction in Napa Valley, **Copia: American Center for Wine, Food & the Arts** ⭐, 500 1st St. (© 888/51-COPIA or 707/259-1600; www.copia.org), opened at the end of 2001, with a mission to explore how wine and food influence U.S. culture. This

---

Tips Exercising in Napa

If you crave a place to work off those extra calories you're taking in, head to downtown Napa's **Exertec,** 1500 1st St. (© 707/226-1842). A $15 day pass gets you access to classes ranging from yoga, tai chi, and aerobics to spinning and cardio-kick; a heated swimming pool; and a sea of exercise machines and weights. Reward yourself with one of a dozen variations of massage.

Moments Up, Up & Away . . .

Admit it: Floating across lush green pastures in a hot-air balloon is something you've always dreamed of but never gotten around to actually doing. Well, here's your best chance, because believe it or not, Napa Valley is the busiest hot-air balloon "flight corridor" in the *world*. Northern California's temperate weather allows for ballooning year-round, and on clear summer weekends in the valley, it's a rare day when you don't see at least one of the colorful airships floating above the vineyards.

Trips usually depart early in the morning, when the air is cooler and the balloons have better lift. Flight paths vary with the direction and speed of the changing breezes, so "chase" crews on the ground must follow the balloons to their undetermined destinations. Most excursions last between 1 and 3 hours and end with a traditional champagne celebration and breakfast. Reservations are required and should be made as far in advance as possible. Prices, which often include shuttle service from your local hotel, run close to $200 per person; wedding, wine-tasting, picnic, and lodging packages are also available. *Warning:* When the valley is fogged in, companies drive passengers outside the valley to nearby areas to balloon. Though they cannot guarantee the flight path until hours before liftoff, they should refund your money if you decide not to partake. For more information or reservations, call Napa's **Bonaventura Balloon Company** (© **800/FLY-NAPA;** www.bonaventura balloons.com), a highly reputable organization owned and operated by master pilot Joyce Bowen. Another good choice is **Napa Valley Aloft** (© **800/944-4408** or 707/944-4408; www.nvaloft.com), Napa Valley's oldest hot-air-balloon company.

$50 million multifaceted facility, which was spearheaded and is chaired by Robert Mondavi, tackles the topic in myriad ways, including visual arts a la rotating exhibits, vast vegetable and herb gardens, culinary demonstrations, basic wine classes, concerts, and opportunities to dine and drink on the premises. Programs are geared toward all types of visitors. Kids get a kick out of identifying candy bars through pictures, and connoisseurs might slip into a lecture or cooking class by Rocco DiSpirito, Ming Tsai, or other famous chefs. Day passes include entrance into the building and gardens, exhibitions, tours, and free 30-minute introductory classes. More advanced food, wine, garden, and art classes cost extra. All the food exploration might get you hankering for a snack, so a cafe offers gourmet picnic items, and the adjoining restaurant, Julia's Kitchen, which is named after Chef Child, is a French-California affair.

If you're around in summer or fall definitely check out the Monday night outdoor concert series (usually around $20 per ticket). I often grab a lawn chair and head to the amphitheater for spectacular vocal and dance performances under Napa's soothing night sky. It's Napa at its best.

Prices of admission are as follows: adult $13; students and seniors 65 and over $10; children 6 to 12 $7.50; children under 6 free. The center is open Wednesday through Monday from 10am to 5pm.

SHOPPING   If you're looking for a trinket but don't quite know what you want, plan to spend at least an hour strolling the **Red Hen Antiques** co-op collection of antiques. You'll find everything from baseball cards to living-room sets, and prices are remarkably affordable. You can't miss this enormous red barn–style building at 5091 St. Helena Hwy., on Highway 29 at Oak Knoll Avenue West (© 707/257-0822). It's open daily from 10am to 5:30pm. During winter, bring a scarf and mittens as there's little in the way of indoor heating.

HITTING THE LINKS   South of downtown Napa, 1⅓ miles east of Highway 29 on Calif. 12, is the **Chardonnay Club** (© 707/257-8950), a challenging 36-hole land-links golf complex with first-class service. You pay just one fee, which makes you a member for the day. Privileges include the use of a golf cart, the practice range (including a bucket of balls), and services usually found only at a private club (such as roving snack carts and complimentary clubs cleaning). The course ambles through and around 325 acres of vineyards, hills, creeks, canyons, and rock ridges. There are three nines of similar challenge, all starting at the clubhouse so that you can play the 18 of your choice. Five sets of tees provide you with a course measuring from 5,300 yards to a healthy 7,100. Starting times can be reserved up to 2 weeks in advance. Greens fees (including mandatory cart and practice balls) from March 16 through November are $70 on weekdays (with a 2pm twilight for $45) and $90 on weekends (with a 2pm twilight for $55). Rates are discounted in winter. Other spots to swing your clubs include the city's public course, **Napa Municipal Golf Course,** at Kennedy Park (2295 Streblow Dr., off Silverado Trail; ℂ **707/255-4333**). At $31 for nonresidents on weekdays, and $41 on weekends, it's a bargain for travelers who would prefer to save their extracurricular funds for food and wine splurges. The optional cart is an additional $13.

RUTHERFORD
Want to bring home an unusual and beautiful handcrafted decoration for your home or yard? Seek out **Napa Valley Grapevine Wreath Company,** Hwy. 128/Rutherford Crossroad, P.O. Box 67, Rutherford, CA 94573 (ℂ **707/963-8893**), which weaves big and small indoor or outdoor sculptures made out of little more than cabernet grapevines. Call for directions, as this tiny shack of a shop is hidden on a side road among Rutherford's vineyards. Hours vary during winter, but are generally Thursday through Monday from 10:30am to 5:30pm.

ST. HELENA
Literature buffs and other romantics will want to visit the **Silverado Museum,** 1490 Library Lane (ℂ **707/963-3757**), which is devoted to the life and works of Robert Louis Stevenson, who honeymooned here in 1880 in an abandoned Silverado Mine bunkhouse. The collection of more than 8,000 items includes original manuscripts, letters, photographs, and portraits, plus the desk he used in Samoa. Hours are Tuesday through Sunday from noon to 4pm; admission is free.

SPAS   If the Wine Country's slow pace and tranquil vistas aren't soothing enough for you, St. Helena's diverse selection of spas can massage, bathe, wrap, and steam you into an overly pampered pulp.

If you're a fitness freak, **Health Spa Napa Valley** 𝒜, 1030 Main St. (Hwy. 29; ℂ **707/967-8800**), is a mandatory stop after a few days of inevitable overindulgence. Here you can treadmill or Stair-Master yourself silly then reward yourself with spa treatments: Immerse yourself in Wine Country ways with a grape-seed mud wrap ($95), or go all out with a Abhyanga treatment ($160), in which two massage therapists get out the knots with synchronized motion. These are the newest facilities around and the local favorite for fitness. Memberships are $25 per day Monday through Thursday, $40 per day Friday through Sunday, and free for guests of The Inn at Southbridge (see "Where to Stay," below).

SHOPPING   St. Helena's Main Street is the best place to go if you're suffering serious retail withdrawal. Though you'll find only a few blocks of stores that are credit-card worthy, a lot of damage can still be done. Take, for example, **Vanderbilt and Company** ⚔, 1429 Main St., between Adams and Pine streets (© **707/963-1010**), which offers the crème de la crème of cookware, hand-painted Italian dishware, linens, and everything else you could possibly convince yourself you need for your gourmet kitchen and dining room. Open daily from 9:30am to 5:30pm.

Another great gift shop is **Olivier,** 1375 Main St. (© **707/967-8777**). This shop claims to be the number-one supplier for Williams-Sonoma, and it's named for everything related to delicious Napa Valley olives. Taste and pour your own oil from huge copper tanks or grab a beautifully prepackaged bottle along with other food products galore.

I also have no bones to pick with **Fideaux,** 1312 Main St. (© **707/967-9935**), a wonderfully charming boutique that's like an Eddie Bauer for dogs and cats. Hand-painted feeders, beautiful ceramic water bowls, custom-designed scratching posts, silk-screened dog and cat pillows, rhinestone collars, unique toys, and gourmet dog treats are just a few pet must-haves you'll find here. The ultimate way to bring the Wine Country home to Spot? Try a wine-barrel doghouse. Hours are 9:30am to 5:30pm daily.

Shopaholics won't be able to avoid at least one sharp turn off Highway 29 for a stop at the **St. Helena Premium Outlets,** 2 miles north of downtown St. Helena (© **707/963-7282**). Featured designers include Donna Karan, Coach, Movado, and London Fog. The stores are open daily from 10am to 6pm.

Napa's best deals on wine are found not in the wineries, but in a couple St. Helena stores. **Dean & Deluca,** 607 S. Main St. (Hwy. 29; © **707/967-9980**), and—believe it or not—**Safeway,** 1026 Hunt Ave. (© **707/963-3833**), have enormous wine selections.

One last favorite stop: **Napa Valley Olive Oil Manufacturing Company,** 835 Charter Oak Ave., at the end of the road behind Tra Vigne restaurant (© **707/963-4173**), a tiny market that presses and bottles its own oils and sells them at a fraction of the price you'd pay elsewhere. It also has an extensive selection of Italian cooking ingredients, imported snacks, and the best deals on dried mushrooms. You'll love the age-old method for totaling the bill, which you simply must find out for yourself. It's open daily 8am to 5pm.

BICYCLING The quieter northern end of the valley is an ideal place to rent a bicycle and ride the Silverado Trail. **St. Helena Cyclery,**

1156 Main St. (© 707/963-7736; www.sthelenacyclery.com), rents bikes for $7 per hour or $30 a day, including rear rack and picnic bag.

NIGHTLIFE   The whole valley has little in the way of after-dinner entertainment, which leaves revelers with little choice but to turn to **1351 Lounge,** 1351 Main St. (© **707/963-1969**), a gussied-up, stone-walled former bank, complete with a shiny vault. Here locals and visitors settle around cocktail tables or at the old mahogany bar for cocktails and music, ranging from open-mike night to a DJ or live rock, blues, or funk. If a swank but more low-key scene is what you're seeking and you're in downtown Napa, check out **The Bounty Hunter,** a wine bar, at 975 First St. (© **707/255-0622;** www.bounty hunterwine.com). Surrounded by dark woods, wine bottles, fun wines by the glass, and excellent sculpted gourmet appetizers such as seared salmon perched atop a cube of sticky rice with wasabi cream, it's downtown's sexiest place to sip and snack—and it stays open late-night on Thursday through Saturday. The Yountville option is the bar at Thomas Keller's restaurant **Bouchon,** 6534 Washington St. (© **707/944-8037**) where locals hang and nosh until the wee hours.

CALISTOGA

Calistoga Depot, 1458 Lincoln Ave. (on the site of Calistoga's original 1868 railroad station) has a variety of shops, some of which are housed in six restored passenger cars dating from 1916.

NATURAL WONDERS   Old Faithful Geyser of California, 1299 Tubbs Lane (© **707/942-6463**), is one of only three "old faithful" geysers in the world. It's been blowing off steam at regular intervals for as long as anyone can remember. The 350°F (180°C) water spews at a height of about 60 feet every 40 minutes, day and night. The performance lasts about a minute, and you can bring along a picnic lunch to munch on between spews. An exhibit hall, a gift shop, and a snack bar are open every day. Admission is $8 for adults, $7 for seniors, $3 for children 6 to 12, and free for children under 6. Open daily from 9am to 6pm (to 5pm in winter). To get there, follow the signs from downtown Calistoga; it's between Calif. 29 and Calif. 128.

You won't see thousands of trees turned into stone, but you'll still find many interesting petrified specimens at the **Petrified Forest,** 4100 Petrified Forest Rd. (© **707/942-6667;** www.petrifiedforest. org). Volcanic ash blanketed this area after the eruption of Mount St. Helena 3 million years ago. As a result, you'll find redwoods that have turned to rock through the slow infiltration of silicas and other minerals, as well as petrified seashells, clams, and marine life, indicating that water covered this area before the redwood forest appeared. Admission is $5 for adults, $4 for seniors and youths 12 to 17, $2 for children 4 to 11, free for children under 4. Open daily 9am to 6pm (to 5pm in winter). Heading north from Calistoga on Calif. 128, turn left onto Petrified Forest Road, just past Lincoln Street.

BICYCLING   See "Bicycling Around the Wine Country," p. 54.

HORSEBACK RIDES   If you like horses and venturing through cool, misty forests, then $50 will seem like a bargain for a 1½-hour ride with a friendly tour guide from **Triple Creek Horse Outfit** (© **707/933-1600**). You'll be led on a leisurely stroll, with the occasional trot thrown in for excitement. The ride goes through beautiful Bothe-Napa Valley State Park, off Highway 29 near Calistoga.

MUD BATHS   One thing you should do while you're in Calistoga is what people have been doing here for the past 150 years: Take a **mud bath** ⚑. The natural baths are composed of local volcanic ash, imported peat, and naturally boiling mineral hot-springs water, all mulled together to produce a thick mud that simmers at a temperature of about 104°F (40°C). It's a Creature-from-the-Black-Lagoon experience for sure—some people love it and some can't get far enough away from it—but one thing's for sure: You've got to try it out.

After you've overcome the hurdle of deciding how best to maneuver your naked body into the tub filled with steamy-hot and clumpy mud, the rest is pure relaxation, as you soak with surprising buoyancy for about 10 to 12 minutes. A warm mineral-water shower, a mineral-water whirlpool bath, and a mineral-water steam-room visit follow. Afterward, a blanket wrap slowly cools down your body, and then—for a little extra cash—you get a half-hour muscle-melting massage. The outcome is a rejuvenated, revitalized, squeaky-clean you. **Note:** Mud baths aren't recommended for those who are pregnant or have high blood pressure.

The spas also offer a variety of other treatments, such as hand and foot massages, herbal wraps, acupressure face-lifts, skin rubs, and herbal facials. Prices for treatments range from $35 to $150, and appointments are necessary for all services; call at least a week in advance, and as far in advance as possible during the busy summer season.

Indulge yourself at any of these Calistoga spas: **Dr. Wilkinson's Hot Springs,** 1507 Lincoln Ave. (© 707/942-4102); **Golden Haven Hot Springs Spa,** 1713 Lake St. (© 707/942-6793); **Calistoga Spa**

Hot Springs, 1006 Washington St. (© 707/942-6269); **Calistoga Village Inn & Spa,** 1880 Lincoln Ave. (© 707/942-0991); **Indian Springs Resort,** 1712 Lincoln Ave. (© 707/942-4913); **Nance's Hot Springs,** 1614 Lincoln Ave. (© 707/942-6211); or **Roman Spa Motel,** 1300 Washington St. (© 707/942-4441).

4 Where to Stay

With more than 2,200 hotel rooms available throughout Napa County, you'd think it'd be a snap to secure a room. Unfortunately, choosing and reserving accommodations—especially from April through November—can be a challenge. Adding to the frustration is that ever-burdening 2-night minimum.

Because Napa Valley is so small, it really doesn't much matter which town you base yourself in; everything's within a 30- or 45-minute drive from everything else (traffic permitting). There are, however, a number of other things you should think about when deciding where to stay. Consider whether you want to be in a modern hotel with all the expected conveniences or a quaint, Victorian B&B; surrounded by acres of vineyards or closer to the highway; in the company of the more conservative wealthy or those leading alternative lifestyles. Accommodations here run the gamut—from motels and B&Bs to world-class luxury retreats—and all are easily accessible from the main highway. Although I recommend shacking up in the more romantically pastoral areas such as Yountville, Rutherford, or St. Helena, there's no question you're going to find better deals in the towns of Napa or laid-back Calistoga. As always, the primary determining factor will come down to one question: How much are you willing to spend?

The accommodations listed below are arranged first by area and then by price, using the following categories: **Very Expensive,** more than $250 per night; **Expensive,** $200 to $250 per night; **Moderate,** $150 to $200 per night; and **Inexpensive,** less than $150 per night. (Sorry—the reality is that anything less than $150 a night qualifies as inexpensive 'round these parts.)

When planning your trip, keep in mind that during the high season—between June and November—most hotels charge peak rates and sell out completely on weekends; many have a 2-night minimum. Always ask about discounts. During the off-season, you have far better bargaining power and may be able to get a room at almost half the summer rate.

RESERVATIONS SERVICES A number of companies offer help with hotel and B&B reservations at no charge. **Accommodation Referral Bed & Breakfast Exchange** (✆ **800/240-8466,** 800/499-8466 in CA, or 707/965-3400), which also represents hotels and inns, asks you for dates, a price range, and what kind of accommodations you're looking for before coming up with recommendations. **Bed & Breakfast Inns of Napa Valley** (✆ **707/944-4444**), an association of B&Bs, provides descriptions and makes reservations. **Napa Valley Reservations Unlimited** (✆ **800/251-NAPA** or 707/252-1985) is a source for everything from accommodations to hot-air balloon and glider rides to wine-tasting tours by limousine.

NAPA

Wherever tourist dollars are to be had, you're sure to find big hotels with familiar names, catering to independent vacationers, business travelers, and groups. **Embassy Suites,** 1075 California Blvd., Napa, CA 94559 (✆ **800/362-2779** or 707/253-9540; www. embassysuites.com), offers 205 two-room suites, each of which includes a kitchenette, a coffeemaker, modem capabilities, and two TVs; extras include a complimentary cooked-to-order breakfast, indoor and outdoor pools, and a restaurant; rates range from $169 to $280. The 191-room **Napa Valley Marriott Hotel and Spa,** 3425 Solano Ave., Napa, CA 94558 (✆ **800/228-9290** or 707/253-7433; www.marriott.com), offers lighted tennis courts, an exercise room, a heated outdoor pool and spa, and two restaurants; rates range from $154 to $320. **Best Western Inn Napa Valley,** 100 Soscol Ave., Napa, CA 94559 (✆ **800/528-1234** or 707/257-1930), is a last-resort option, promising little more than 68 basic air-conditioned units in industrial surroundings. But at $89 to $255 per night, it's hard to complain.

VERY EXPENSIVE

Milliken Creek Inn ⭐⭐ This riverfront retreat just north of downtown Napa captures the essence of upscale boutique hotel accommodation and country living. Part of its allure is due to a change of hands and $1 million renovation in 2001. The rest is the great taste and location. Right on Silverado Trail and surrounded by tranquil gardens, oaks, and redwoods, the 10 spacious and refined rooms are located in three neighboring buildings (including the restored 1857 Coach House) and are luxuriously appointed. Soothing shades of brown and beige, greens, and yellows become even warmer and more welcoming when the fireplace is in action. King-size beds are firm and draped in Italian linens, tubs are the whirlpool variety,

Napa Valley Accommodations

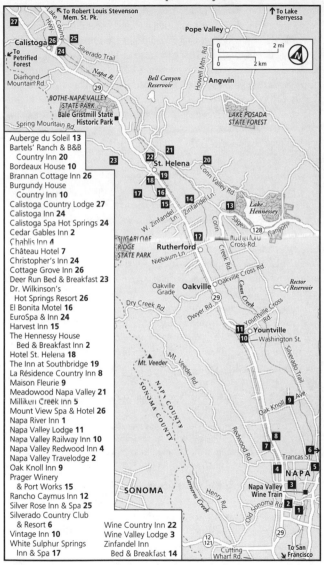

Auberge du Soleil **13**
Bartels' Ranch & B&B
  Country Inn **20**
Bordeaux House **10**
Brannan Cottage Inn **26**
Burgundy House
  Country Inn **10**
Calistoga Country Lodge **27**
Calistoga Inn **24**
Calistoga Spa Hot Springs **24**
Cedar Gables Inn **2**
Chablis Inn **4**
Château Hotel **7**
Christopher's Inn **24**
Cottage Grove Inn **26**
Deer Run Bed & Breakfast **23**
Dr. Wilkinson's
  Hot Springs Resort **26**
El Bonita Motel **16**
EuroSpa & Inn **24**
Harvest Inn **15**
The Hennessy House
  Bed & Breakfast Inn **2**
Hotel St. Helena **18**
The Inn at Southbridge **19**
La Résidence Country Inn **8**
Maison Fleurie **9**
Meadowood Napa Valley **21**
Milliken Creek Inn **5**
Mount View Spa & Hotel **26**
Napa River Inn **1**
Napa Valley Lodge **11**
Napa Valley Railway Inn **10**
Napa Valley Redwood Inn **4**
Napa Valley Travelodge **2**
Oak Knoll Inn **9**
Prager Winery
  & Port Works **15**
Rancho Caymus Inn **12**
Silver Rose Inn & Spa **25**
Silverado Country Club
  & Resort **6**
Vintage Inn **10**
White Sulphur Springs
  Inn & Spa **17**

Wine Country Inn **22**
Wine Valley Lodge **3**
Zinfandel Inn
  Bed & Breakfast **14**

and fluffy robes await. Delicious perks include a picnic breakfast delivered to your door and a nightly wine and cheese tasting, which is served in the sophisticated parlor and often accompanied by live jazz piano. No doubt this is the best new hotel to open in 2001 and Napa's finest choice, unless you prefer the larger-hotel benefits of downtown's Napa River Inn, the resort facilities of Silverado Country Club & Resort, or the more country-chic atmosphere of La Residence.

1815 Silverado Trail, Napa, CA 94558. ℭ 888/622-5775 or 707/255-1197. Fax 707/ 255-3112. www.millikencreekinn.com. 12 units. $295–$625 double. AE, DC, DISC, MC, V. **Amenities:** Yoga gazebo; in-room massage. *In room:* A/C, TV/DVD, CD player, high speed dataport, minibar, hair dryer, iron on request.

Oak Knoll Inn ✿✿✿   If you've got the bucks and want an extremely intimate luxury escape you can't do much better than this four-room French country–style B&B surrounded by 600 acres of vineyards. Each of the enormous stone-walled rooms are tastefully decorated in florals and have vaulted ceilings, working fireplaces, king-size beds, private entrances, and plenty of elbow room. But no doubt you'll want to spend most of your time in the common areas, such as the vineyard-front back deck where arguably the best private tastings are held nightly and are hosted by the winemaker or a winery representative, and accompanied by an amazing appetizer spread that could easily substitute for dinner. The pool and whirlpool spa also beckon, as does the small sitting area complete with crackling fire in the fireplace during winter and the charming dining room where a fantastic full gourmet breakfast is served daily by Shirley, once a San Francisco restaurant chef and now this inn's friendly keeper. Take my word for it: If you plan to hang around your hotel, this spot is definitely worth a splurge.

2200 E. Oak Knoll Ave. (between the Silverado Trail and Hwy. 29), Napa, CA 94558. ℭ 707/255-2200. www.oakknollinn.com. 4 units. $250–$450. Rates include breakfast, wine and appetizers. MC, V. **Amenities:** Unheated pool; Jacuzzi. *In room:* AC, TV on request, phone on request, hair dryer, iron.

Silverado Country Club & Resort ✿   If you long for the opulence of an East Coast country club, bring your racquet and golf clubs to this 1,200-acre resort in the Napa foothills, where the focus is on the sporting life. Two cleverly designed golf courses by Robert Trent Jones Jr. are the focal point; the 6,500-yard South Course has a dozen water crossings, and the 6,700-yard North Course is somewhat longer but a bit more forgiving. A staff of pros is on hand, and greens fees are $150 for 18 holes on either course (off-season is discounted), including a mandatory cart. The spacious, individually owned accommodations range from very large studios with king-size bed, kitchenette, and a roomy, well-appointed bathroom to one-, two-, or three-bedroom cottage suites. Each has a wood-burning fireplace. Cottage suites are in private, low-rise groupings tucked away in shared courtyards along peaceful walkways. All rooms are individually decorated with country home–style furnishings, and manage to offer a sense of privacy despite the resort's size.

Though they've got restaurants on property, I'd recommend dining elsewhere. But when it comes to spa facilities, they've definitely got the goods.

1600 Atlas Peak Rd., Napa, CA 94558. ⓒ **800/532-0500** or 707/257-0200. Fax 707/257-2867. www.silveradoresort.com. 280 suites. $275 junior suite; $355 1-bedroom suite; $455–$555 2- or 3-bedroom suite. Golf and spa promotional packages available. AE, DC, DISC, MC, V. Drive north on Hwy. 29 to Trancas St.; turn east to Atlas Peak Rd. **Amenities:** 2 restaurants (steak/seafood, bar and grill); bar; heated outdoor pool; 9 unheated pools; 2 18-hole golf courses; 17 tennis courts; exercise room; full-service spa; tour desk; business center; limited room service; in-room massage. *In room:* A/C, TV, dataport, kitchenette in some units, minibar, coffeemaker in some units, hair dryer, iron.

EXPENSIVE

La Résidence Country Inn 🐾   If you consider a B&B too homespun and a luxury hotel too impersonal, La Residence is a good alternative. Set on 2 acres on Highway 29, the inn's rooms are in either the late-18th-century revival-style main house or the newer French barn–style building. Rooms are individually decorated with wall-to-wall carpeting, period antiques, armoires, designer fabrics, fireplaces (in most), CD players, and patios or verandas. The pool area and large spa are secluded and well manicured. A full breakfast is served in the attractive dining room, which is often warmed by a roaring fire on chilly mornings; in the afternoon, wine and hors d'oeuvres are offered. If a recent four-star rating isn't enough encouragement to book a room, neighboring delicious Bistro Don Giovanni should be.

4066 St. Helena Hwy., Napa, CA 94558. ⓒ **707/253-0337.** Fax 707/253-0382. www.laresidence.com. 23 units. $225–$350 double; lower rates Dec–Mar. AE, DC, MC, V. **Amenities:** Heated outdoor pool; Jacuzzi; concierge. *In room:* A/C, TV in some units, CD player, fridge in some units, hair dryer, iron available.

Napa River Inn 🐾🐾   Downtown Napa's newest and most luxurious hotel manages an old-world boutique feel through most of its three buildings, which house 66 rooms. The main building, part of the newly renovated Napa Mill and Hatt Market, is an 1884 historic landmark. Each of the fantastically appointed rooms is exceedingly

romantic, with burgundy-colored walls, original brick, wood furnishings, plush fabrics, and seats in front of the gas fireplace. A gilded claw-foot tub beckons in the luxurious bathroom. The newest addition is a brand-new building with bright and airy accommodations overlooking the Napa River. Less luxurious but equally well-appointed are the mustard-and-brown rooms that also overlook the riverfront but have a nautical theme and less daylight. Extra perks abound and include complimentary vouchers to a full breakfast and evening cocktails at one of the adjoining restaurants. A small but excellent spa is located in the hotel's parking lot.

500 Main St., Napa, CA 94559. ℂ **877/251-8500** or 707/251-8500. Fax 707/251-8504. www.napariverinn.com. 66 units. $179–$499 double. Rates include vouchers to a full breakfast and evening cocktails at one of the adjoining restaurants. AE, DC, DISC, MC, V. **Amenities:** Restaurant; concierge; business services; same-day laundry service and dry cleaning. *In room:* A/C, TV, dataport, coffeemaker, hair dryer, iron, safe, CD clock radio, fridge.

MODERATE

Cedar Gables Inn *Finds* Innkeepers Margaret and Craig Snasdell have developed quite a following with their grand, romantic B&B in Old Town Napa. The Victorian was built in 1892, and rooms reflect the era, with rich tapestries and stunning gilded antiques. Five rooms have fireplaces, five have whirlpool tubs, and all feature queen-size brass, wood, or iron beds. Guests meet each evening in front of the roaring fireplace in the family room for wine and cheese. At other times, the family room is a perfect place to cuddle up and watch the large-screen TV. Added bonuses include a full breakfast each morning, port in every room, and VIP treatment at many local wineries.

486 Coombs St., Napa, CA 94559. ℂ **800/309-7969** or 707/224-7969. Fax 707/224-4838. www.cedargablesinn.com. 9 units. $179–$309 double; winter specials available. Rates include full breakfast, evening wine and cheese, and port. AE, DISC, MC, V. From Hwy. 29 north, exit onto First St. and follow signs to downtown; turn right onto Coombs St.; the house is at the corner of Oak St. *In room:* A/C, dataport, hair dryer, iron.

INEXPENSIVE

Chablis Inn There's no way around it: If you want to sleep cheaply in a town where the *average* room rate tops $200 per night in high season, you're destined for a motel. But look on the bright side: Because your room is likely to be little more than a crash pad after a day of eating and drinking, a clean bed and a remote control are all you'll really need anyway. And Chablis offers much more than that. Each of the superclean motel-style rooms here has a newish

mattress, and some even boast kitchenettes, whirlpool tubs, or both. Guests have access to an outdoor heated pool and hot tub, plus a very basic continental breakfast.

3360 Solano Ave., Napa, CA 94558. ⓒ **707/257-1944.** Fax 707/226-6862. www. chablisinn.com. 34 units. May to mid-Nov $125–$235 double; mid-Nov to Apr $70–$120 double. AE, DC, DISC, MC, V. **Amenities:** Heated outdoor pool; hot tub. *In room:* A/C, TV, dataports in some rooms, kitchenettes in some rooms, fridge, coffeemaker, hair dryer.

Château Hotel   This contemporary two-story motel complex tries to evoke the aura of a French country inn, but it isn't fooling anybody—a basic motel's a basic motel. However, the plain-Jane rooms are C-H-E-A-P and bathrooms are spacious, and have separate vanity/dressing areas. Some units have refrigerators and ten rooms are specially designed for guests with disabilities. If you're used to a daily swim, you'll be glad to know that the Château also has a heated pool and spa. Bargain travelers, be sure to ask about discounts; some special rates will knock the price down by $20.

4195 Solano Ave., Napa, CA 94558. ⓒ **800/253-6272** in CA or 707/253-9300. Fax 707/253-0906. 115 units. Apr–Oct $119–$169 double; Nov–Mar $99 double. Continental breakfast included. AAA, government, corporate, senior, and other discounts available. AE, DC, MC, V. From Hwy. 29 north, turn left just past Trower Ave., at the entrance to the Napa Valley wine region. **Amenities:** Restaurant; heated outdoor pool; hot tub. *In room:* A/C, TV.

The Hennessy House Bed & Breakfast Inn   This Eastlake-style Queen Anne Victorian may be old enough to be on the National Register of Historic Places, but its antiquity is contrasted by the fresh hospitality of owners Alex and Gilda Feit. Since the couple took over the B&B in late 1997, they've been on a mission to satisfy each and every guest. Their genuine concern makes a stay here very personable. Rooms in the main house are quaint, with a combination of antique furnishings, queen-size bed, fireplace, and/or a claw-foot bathtub or patios. Carriage-house accommodations, located just off the main house, are larger but less ornate and feature whirlpool tubs (a bummer to climb into if you're not agile); all have fireplaces. Because walls are thin throughout both structures, TVs are out of the question (except in a few rooms, where additional insulation was recently added), and if your neighbor's a snorer, you'll know it firsthand. But it'll make for fun conversation over breakfast, when guests meet in the dining room for an impressive full meal. The adjoining living room allows TV junkies to stay tuned. The small garden is a nice spot for a bit of morning sun.

1727 Main St. (between Lincoln and 1st sts.), Napa, CA 94559. ℂ **707/226-3774.** Fax 707/226-2975. www.hennessyhouse.com. 10 units. Mid-Mar to mid-Nov $140–$279 double; mid-Nov to mid-Mar $129–$259 double. Rates include full breakfast, afternoon tea and cookies, and nightly wine-and-cheese hour. AE, DC, DISC, MC, V. **Amenities:** Sauna. *In room:* A/C.

Napa Valley Redwood Inn   This no-frills lodging (read: seriously basic) has an excellent location and simple, clean, comfortable rooms. Local calls are free, and guests can enjoy the complimentary coffee in the lobby and the small pool on the premises (heated in summer only).

3380 Solano Ave., Napa, CA 94558. ℂ **707/257-6111.** Fax 707/252-2702. www.napavalleyredwoodinn.com. 58 units, all with bathroom (shower only). May–Oct from $83 double weekday and from $150 on weekends; Nov–Apr from $67 double weekday and $90 on weekends. Rates include continental breakfast. AE, DC, DISC, MC, V. **Amenities:** Small seasonally heated pool. *In room:* A/C, TV, high-speed Internet dataport.

Napa Valley Travelodge (*Value*   In these parts, rarely does so much come so cheaply. This Travelodge has been around for a while, but in early 1998, the owners gutted the entire place with the intent of turning it into a "New Orleans–style" motel (including a cobblestone center courtyard/parking area). Although there are no wild partyers hanging over the balconies throwing beads, there's still plenty to celebrate. Every room has a VCR, a 36-inch TV, and a coffeemaker, some feature a Jacuzzi tub, and all of them are in a great part of downtown Napa—within walking distance of the city's best dining. If you're lucky enough to secure a room, you will have gotten one of the best deals around. Ask about discounts for AAA and other clubs.

853 Coombs St., Napa, CA 94559. ℂ **800/578-7878** or 707/226-1871. Fax 707/226-1707. 45 units. $109–$189 double. DC, DISC, MC, V. **Amenities:** Heated outdoor pool; access to nearby fitness center (fee); video library; coin-operated laundry. *In room:* A/C, TV/VCR, hair dryer, iron.

Wine Valley Lodge 🐾 (*Value*   Dollar for dollar, the Wine Valley Lodge offers the most for the least in all the Wine Country. At the south end of town, in a quiet residential neighborhood, the Mission-style motel is extremely well kept and accessible, just a short drive from Highway 29 and the wineries to the north. The reasonably priced deluxe rooms, which hold two bedrooms connected by a bathroom, are great for families.

200 S. Coombs St. (between 1st and Imola sts.), Napa, CA 94559. ℂ **800/696-7911** or 707/224-7911. www.winevalleylodge.com. 54 units. $79–$119 double; $130–$165 deluxe. AE, DC, DISC, MC, V. **Amenities:** Heated outdoor pool; continental breakfast included. *In room:* A/C, TV.

YOUNTVILLE
EXPENSIVE

Vintage Inn ☆☆ This contemporary, French-country hotel is situated on an old 23-acre winery estate in the heart of Yountville. The complex feels far more corporate than the name "inn" suggests, but its big-business appearance does have perks, such as a very professional staff and rooms that are bright and cozy with a fireplace and private veranda, oversized beds, Jacuzzi tubs, plush bathrobes, and a welcome bottle of wine. You can rent a bike, reserve one of the two tennis courts, or take a dip in the 60-foot swimming pool or outdoor whirlpool, both of which are heated year-round. An champagne breakfast buffet and afternoon tea are served daily in the lobby. If they're booked, ask about their sister property, the spa-centric Villagio Inn & Spa, a sexy Tuscan-style hotel complex just down the road.

6541 Washington St. (between Humboldt St. and Webber Ave.), Yountville, CA 94599. ℂ 800/351-1133 or 707/944-1112. Fax 707/944-1617. www.vintageinn.com. 80 units. $210–$400 double; $300–$400 minisuites and villas. Rates include champagne breakfast buffet, complimentary wine upon arrival and afternoon tea. AE, DC, MC, V. Free parking. From Hwy. 29 north, take the Yountville exit and turn left onto Washington St. Pets $30. **Amenities:** Concierge; business center; secretarial services; room service; in-room massage; laundry service; dry cleaning. *In room:* A/C, TV/VCR with a movie library, dataport, fridge, coffeemaker, hair dryer, iron.

MODERATE *very pretty*

Maison Fleurie ☆☆ Maison Fleurie, one of the prettiest hotels in the Wine Country, is a trio of beautiful 1873 brick-and-field-stone buildings overlaid with ivy. The main house—a charming Provençal replica with thick brick walls, terra-cotta tile, and paned windows—holds seven rooms; the rest are in the old bakery building and the carriage house. Some units feature private balconies, patios, sitting areas, Jacuzzi tubs, and fireplaces. Breakfast is served in the quaint little dining room; afterward, you're welcome to wander the landscaped grounds or hit the wine-tasting trail, returning in time for afternoon hors d'oeuvres. It's impossible not to enjoy your stay at Maison Fleurie.

6529 Yount St. (between Washington St. and Yountville Cross Rd.), Yountville, CA 94599. ℂ 800/788-0369 or 707/944-2056. Fax 707/944-9342. www.foursisters. com. 13 units. $115–$275 double. Rates include full breakfast and afternoon hors d'oeuvres. AE, DC, MC, V. **Amenities:** Heated outdoor pool; Jacuzzi; free bikes. *In room:* A/C, TV, dataport, hair dryer, iron.

Napa Valley Lodge ☆☆ *Finds* Many frequent visitors compare this contemporary hotel to the nearby, upscale Vintage Inn, noting that it's even more personable and accommodating. The lodge is just off Highway 29, beyond a wall that does a good job of disguising the road. Guest rooms, which were upgraded in 2001, are large, ultraclean, and better appointed than many others in the area. Many have vaulted ceilings, and 33 have fireplaces. Each has a king- or queen-size bed, wicker furnishings, robes, and a private balcony or a patio. In 1997, all the bathrooms were upgraded to include a vanity area and nice tile work. The least expensive units, at ground level, are smaller and get less sunlight than those on the second floor. Extras include concierge, afternoon tea and cookies in the lobby, Friday-evening wine tasting in the library, and a full champagne breakfast. With all this, it's no wonder AAA gave the Napa Valley Lodge the four-diamond award for excellence. Ask about winter discounts, which can be as high as 30%.

2230 Madison St., Yountville, CA 94599. (℃ 800/368-2468 or 707/944-2468. Fax 707/944-9362. www.napavalleylodge.com. 55 units. $252–$495 double. Rates include champagne breakfast buffet, afternoon tea and cookies, and Friday-evening wine tasting. AE, DC, DISC, MC, V. **Amenities:** Heated outdoor pool; small exercise room; Jacuzzi; redwood sauna. *In room:* A/C, TV w/pay movies, dataport, minibar, coffeemaker, hair dryer, iron.

INEXPENSIVE

Bordeaux House   Considering the name, I was expecting this centrally located hotel on a quiet Yountville street to be some kind of romantic, antique French–style structure. I was way off. How far? Try 1980 two-story brick. Nonetheless, there are eight ultratidy and simple rooms here, each renting for what in this neck of the woods is a very reasonable price. Each has a private entrance; six have fireplaces and private patios, and while interiors border on motel-bland (especially the small bathrooms), the few furnishings do have a homier, more stylish quality than most motels. Added bonuses include complimentary port, brandy, sherry, and homemade treats served in the common area and proximity to The French Laundry, just down the block.

6600 Washington St., Yountville, CA 94599. (℃ 800/677-6370 or 707/944-2855. Fax 707/945-0471. www.bordeauxhouse.com. 8 units. Sun–Thurs $145 double, Fri–Sat $175 double. Additional person $25 extra. 2-night minimum during high season. Rates include full breakfast and complimentary port and sherry. MC, V. *In room:* Central A/C, TV, dataport, hair dryer, iron.

Burgundy House Country Inn   This distinctly French country inn, built of local fieldstone and river rock in the early 1890s as a brandy distillery, is tiny but atmospheric. The interior features thick stone walls and hand-hewn post and lintel beams, enhanced today by antique country furnishings. The six cozy guest rooms (all untra-ditionally French in their no-smoking status) have colorful quilted spreads and comfortable beds, along with very small bathrooms. Sweet touches include fresh flowers in each of the units, a full break-fast, and complimentary port and sherry in the common area. Breakfast can be eaten inside or out in the pretty garden.

6711 Washington St. (P.O. Box 3156), Yountville, CA 94599. © 707/944-0889. www.burgundyhouse.com. 6 units, all with bathroom (shower only). $125–$175 double. MC, V. From Hwy. 29 north, take the Yountville exit and turn left onto Wash-ington St. *In room:* A/C, no phone.

Napa Valley Railway Inn ⟨ƒ⟩ This is one of my favorite places to stay in the Wine Country. Why? Because it's inexpensive and it's cute as all get-out. Looking hokey as heck from the outside, the Railway Inn consists of two rows of sun-bleached cabooses and rail cars sitting on a stretch of Yountville's original track and connected by a covered wooden walkway. Things get considerably better when you enter your private caboose or car. They're sumptuously appointed, with comfy love seats, queen-size brass beds, and tiled baths. The coups de grâce are the bay windows and skylights, which let in plenty of California sunshine. The cars are all suites, so if you're looking to save your pennies, opt for a caboose. Adjacent to the inn is Yountville's main shopping complex.

6503 Washington St., Yountville, CA 94599. © 707/944-2000. 9 units. $100–$200 double. AE, MC, V. *In room:* A/C, TV (no cable), coffeemaker, hair dryer upon request.

OAKVILLE & RUTHERFORD
VERY EXPENSIVE

Auberge du Soleil ⟨ƒ⟩⟨ƒ⟩⟨ƒ⟩ *(Moments)* This spectacular Relais & Châteaux member is the kind of place you'd imagine movie stars fre-quenting for clandestine affairs or weekend retreats. Set high above Napa Valley in a 33-acre olive grove, it's quiet, indulgent, and luxu-riously romantic. The Mediterranean-style rooms are large enough to get lost in, and you might want to once you discover all the amenities. The bathtub alone—an enormous hot tub with a skylight overhead—will entice you to grab a glass of California red and set-tle in for awhile. Oversized, cushy furniture surrounds a wood-burning fireplace—the ideal place to relax and listen to CDs. (The stereo comes with a few selections, and there's also a VCR.) Fresh flowers, original art, terra-cotta floors, and wood and leather fur-nishings whisk you out of the Wine Country and into the South-west. Each sun-washed private deck has views of the valley that are nothing less than spectacular. Those with money to burn should opt for the $2,250-per-night cottage suite; the 1,800-square-foot hide-away has two fireplaces, two full baths, a den, and a patio Jacuzzi. Now that's living.

Guests have access to a celestial swimming pool, exercise room, and the most fabulous spa in the Wine Country, which opened in 2001. Only guests can use the spa, but if you want to get all the romantic grandeur of Auberge without staying here, have lunch on the patio at the wonderful restaurant overlooking the valley (see "Where to Dine," later in this chapter, for more information). Over-all, this is one of my favorite Wine Country places. *Parents take note:* This is not the kind of place you take the kids.

180 Rutherford Hill Rd., Rutherford, CA 94573. ℂ **800/348-5406** or 707/963-1211. Fax 707/963-8764. www.aubergedusoleil.com. 50 units. $400–$750 double, $675-$1275 suites. AE, DC, DISC, MC, V. From Hwy. 29 in Rutherford, turn right on California 128 and go 3 miles to the Silverado Trail; turn left and head north about 200 yd. to Rutherford Hill Rd.; turn right. **Amenities:** Restaurant; 3 outdoor pools ranging from hot to cold; 3 tennis courts; health club and full-service spa; sauna; steam; bikes; concierge; secretarial services; salon; 24-hr. room service; massage; same-day laundry service and dry cleaning. *In room:* A/C, TV/DVD w/pay movies, dataport, kitchenette, minibar, fridge, coffeemaker, hair dryer, iron.

MODERATE

Rancho Caymus Inn ℛ   This Spanish-style hacienda, with two floors opening onto wisteria-covered balconies, was the creation of sculptor Mary Tilden Morton (of Morton Salt). Morton wanted each room in the hacienda to be a work of art, and she hired the most-skilled craftspeople she could find. She designed the adobe fireplaces herself, and she wandered through Mexico and South America, purchasing artifacts for the property, which was completed in 1985.

Guest rooms surround a whimsical garden courtyard with an enormous outdoor fireplace. The mix-and-match decor is on the funky side, with overly varnished dark-wood furnishings and braided rugs. The inn is cozy, however, and rooms are decent-sized, split-level suites with queen beds, wet bars, sofa beds in the sitting areas, and small private patios. Most of the suites have fireplaces, and five have kitchenettes and whirlpool tubs. Breakfast, which includes fresh fruit, granola, orange juice, and breads, is served in the inn's dining room. Since chef Ken Frank's La Toque opened here, this funky inn has also become a dining destination (see "Where to Dine," later in this chapter, for complete details).

1140 Rutherford Rd., P.O. Box 78, Rutherford, CA 94573. ℂ **800/845-1777** or 707/963-1777. Fax 707/963-5387. www.ranchocaymus.com. 26 suites. $195–$255 double; from $305 master suite; $385 2-bedroom suite. Rates include continental breakfast. AE, MC, V. From Hwy. 29 north, turn right onto Rutherford Rd./Calif. 128 east; the hotel is on your left. **Amenities:** Restaurant. *In room:* A/C, TV, dataport, kitchenette in some rooms, minibar, fridge, hair dryer, iron in some rooms.

ST. HELENA
VERY EXPENSIVE

The Inn at Southbridge 🌟🌟   Eschewing the lace-and-lattice-work theme that plagues most Wine Country inns, the Inn at Southbridge takes an unswervingly modern, pragmatic approach. Instead of stuffed teddy bears, you'll find terry robes, fireplaces, bathroom skylights, down comforters, private balconies, and a host of other little luxuries. The decor is upscale Pottery Barn trendy, and for some it's a welcome departure from quaintly traditional hotel-style stuff. One notable bummer: The inn is along the highway, so it lacks that reclusive feel many other upscale hotels offer. The hotel is not ideal for families (especially considering the high price tag), but the adjoining casual and cheap Italian restaurant, which has games, TV, and pizzas, is ideal for the wee ones.

1020 Main St., St. Helena, CA 94574. ℂ 800/520-6800 or 707/967-9400. Fax 707/967-9486. 21 units. $235–$590 double. AE, DC, MC, V. **Amenities:** Restaurant; large heated outdoor pool; excellent health club and full-service spa; Jacuzzi; concierge; limited room service; massage; same-day laundry service and dry cleaning. *In room:* A/C, TV, dataport, minibar, coffeemaker, hair dryer, iron.

Meadowood Napa Valley 🌟🌟🌟 *Finds*   This ultraluxurious resort, tucked away on 256 acres of pristine mountainside in a forest of madrone and oak trees, is quiet and secluded enough to make you forget that the busy wineries are just 10 minutes away. Originally a private country club for Napa's well-to-do families, Meadowood is one of California's top-ranked privately owned resorts, a favorite retreat for celebrities, CEOs, and, well, me. Rooms, which vary in size tremendously depending on the price, are furnished with American country classics and have beamed ceilings, private patios, stone fireplaces, and views of the forest. Many are individual suite-lodges so far removed from the common areas that you must drive to get to them. Lazier folks can opt for more centrally located accommodations.

The resort offers a wealth of activities: golf on a challenging nine-hole course, tennis on seven championship courts, and croquet (yes, croquet) on two international regulation lawns. There are also private hiking trails, a health spa, heated pools, and a whirlpool. Those who might actually want to leave and do some wine tasting can check in with John Thoreen, the hotel's wine tutor, whose sole purpose is to help guests better understand and enjoy Napa Valley wines. Alas, the restaurants never quite settle into greatness, but their more casual dining room does offer one of the best breakfasts up-valley and their fancier joint has a killer fireplace in the bar that's perfect for winter snuggling and wine sipping.

900 Meadowood Lane, St. Helena, CA 94574. (©) 800/458-8080 or 707/963-3646. Fax 707/963-3532. www.meadowood.com. 85 units. $375–$790 double; 1-bedroom suite from $760; 2-bedroom from $1270; 3-bedroom from $1780; 4-bedroom from $3585. Ask about promotional offers and off-season rates. 2-night minimum stay on weekends. AE, DC, DISC, MC, V. **Amenities:** 2 restaurants; 2 large heated outdoor pools; golf course; 7 tennis courts; 2 croquet lawns; health club and full-service spa; Jacuzzi; sauna; concierge; secretarial services; room service; same-day laundry service and dry cleaning. *In room:* A/C, TV, dataport, kitchenette in some rooms, minibar, coffeemaker, hair dryer, iron.

EXPENSIVE

Bartels' Ranch & B&B Country Inn ✿

Perched on 60 acres of rolling meadows studded with fig trees, cypress, old oaks, and a vineyard, this whimsical, completely unique retreat is run by ebullient innkeeper Jami Bartels, who also designed and decorated the 7,000-square-foot stone ranch house. More like a B&B than a hotel, here a select few guests have reason to linger in the house teeming with knickknacks. The four individually decorated rooms boast all the creature comforts, including fireplaces and patios. A couple rooms even have their own huge Jacuzzis. My personal favorite is the Heart of the Valley Suite, with a custom king adjustable bed (all the beds are new as of 2001) and blue, heart-shaped Jacuzzi tub. There's a communal sundeck around the outdoor unheated pool, as well as a book-filled game room with pool and Ping-Pong tables. The bountiful breakfasts are served on the patio on warm mornings; complimentary wine, fruit, and cheese are served each afternoon. Other treats include evening dessert, and coffee, tea, and cookies are always on hand. Forever aiming to please, Jami provides her guests with picnic supplies and bicycles, and she will arrange as much or as little of your vacation as you wish; she's also the ultimate source regarding the valley. With a bocce ball court, croquet lawns, and access to horseback riding, tennis, and custom-made VIP itineraries, Jami ensures that there's never a dull Wine Country moment.

1200 Conn Valley Rd., St. Helena, CA 94574. (©) **707/963-4001.** Fax 707/963-5100. www.bartelsranch.com. 4 units. $235–$455 double. AE, DC, DISC, MC, V. Rates include breakfast and sherry and snacks. From downtown St. Helena, turn east on Pope St., cross Silverado Trail, and continue onto Howell Mountain Rd.; bear right onto Conn Valley Rd.; the inn is 2 miles ahead on the left. **Amenities:** Large unheated outdoor pool; croquet lawns; bocce ball court; bikes; concierge. *In room:* A/C, TV/VCR (with video library), CD player, voice mail, dataport, coffeemaker, hair dryer, iron.

Harvest Inn ⟨★⟩ *(Kids)*   Ornate brick walkways lead through beautifully landscaped grounds to pools and freestanding accommodations at this sprawling Tudor-style resort. Each of the immaculate rooms is furnished with dark-oak beds and dressers, brown leather chairs, and antique furnishings; most have brick fireplaces, wet bars, refrigerators, CD players, feather beds, down comforters, and a 25-inch TV with VCR. (Videos are for rent on the property.) With four-diamond ratings from AAA and all the big-hotel bells and whistles it's not surprising this spot is on the wedding and conference circuit.

1 Main St., St. Helena, CA 94575. © **800/950-8466** or 707/963-9463. Fax 707/963-4402. www.harvestinn.com. 54 units. $255–$535 double; $645–$675 suite. AE, DC, DISC, MC, V. **Amenities:** Wine and beer bar; 2 outdoor heated pools; 2 outdoor Jacuzzis; concierge; business center. *In room:* A/C, TV/VCR, CD player, dataport, minibar, fridge, coffeemaker, hair dryer, iron.

MODERATE

Hotel St. Helena   This downtown hotel occupies a historic 1881 building, the oldest wooden structure in St. Helena. The hotel keepers celebrated the building's 100th birthday with a much-needed renovation; now it's more comfortable than ever. The hallways are cluttered with stuffed animals, wicker strollers, and other memorabilia. Most of the rooms have been decorated with brass beds, wall-to-wall burgundy carpeting, and oak or maple furnishings. There's a garden patio and a wine and coffee bar. Perhaps most enjoyable is the hotel's downtown location, front-and-center to the area's best shopping and restaurants. Smoking is discouraged.

1309 Main St., St. Helena, CA 94574. © **888/478-4355** or 707/963-4388. www.hotelsthelena.com. 18 units, 14 with private bathroom. $125–$165 double without bathroom; $185–$275 double with bathroom. Rates discounted up to 30% in winter. Rates include continental breakfast. AE, DC, MC, V. *In room:* A/C, TV.

Prager Winery & Port Works   The two suites at Prager Winery are one of the best-kept secrets in the valley. Their incognito location—on a residential side street behind Trinchero Family Estates/Sutter Home Winery—gives no indication of the affordable accommodations within. The smaller "Winery" suite, which is still huge, is perched above the winery (see "Touring the Wineries," earlier in this chapter), up a flight of stairs. It boasts a bedroom with a queen bed, living room with fireplace, fridge, coffeemaker, and a lovely private sundeck. The garden cottage, or "Vineyard Suite," is also enormous and immaculate, and has a bedroom, living room with piano, TV/VCR, fireplace, and private garden. Both are homey, sleep up to four, and come with a full, delivered breakfast and unlimited wine tastings; the Pragers don't rent for about 3 days around Christmas so they can accommodate their large and festive family.

1281 Lewelling Lane, St. Helena, CA 94574. © **707/963-3720**. Fax 707/963-7679. www.pragerport.com. 2 units. $225–$325 double. Rates include a full breakfast en suite and unlimited tastings in the tasting room. MC, V. *In room:* A/C.

Wine Country Inn ⭐⭐   Just off the highway behind Freemark Abbey vineyard, this attractive wood-and-stone inn, complete with a French-style mansard roof and turret, overlooks a pastoral landscape of vineyards. The individually decorated rooms contain iron or brass beds, antique furnishings, and handmade quilts; most have fireplaces and private terraces overlooking the valley, and some have private hot tubs. One of the inn's best features (besides the absence of TVs) is the heated outdoor pool, which is attractively landscaped into the hillside. Another favorite is the selection of suites, which have stereos, plenty of space, and lots of privacy. The newest addition, two 800-square-foot luxury cottages added in 2002, boast hardwood floors, a fireplace, wet bar, fridge, coffeemaker, stereo, two-person tub, walk-in shower, heated bathroom floors, and a deck or patio. The family that runs this place puts personal touches everywhere and makes every guest feel welcome. They serve wine and plenty of appetizers nightly, along with a big dash of hotel-staff hospitality in the inviting living room. A full buffet breakfast is served there, too.

1152 Lodi Lane, St. Helena, CA 94574. © **707/963-7077**. Fax 707/963-9018. www.wine-country-inn.com. 26 units (12 with shower only). $130–$345 double. Rates include breakfast and appetizers. MC, V. **Amenities:** Heated outdoor pool; Jacuzzi; concierge. *In room:* A/C, stereo, hair dryer.

Zinfandel Inn Bed & Breakfast   Frilly romantics, get ready to break out your credit cards. Within the walls of this English Tudor are three rooms guaranteed to charm anyone into lace and old-world elegance. The Chardonnay Room has a rock-work fireplace. The very romantic Zinfandel Suite includes a Jacuzzi and king-size four-poster bed with huge private deck, an enormous bathroom (with a window overlooking the deck), and a double shower and sink. The Chablis Room, styled in French Victorian fashion, is hardly bigger than a shoe box but has just enough room to fit a queen bed, a gas fireplace, and a private bath.

Sun worshipers will appreciate the manicured, grassy, and secluded backyard—a peaceful and expansive spot with a large aviary, small unheated pool, gazebo, and canopied new hot tub.

Rates also include a delicious, full-service breakfast and liqueurs. *Note:* Although this place is sweet, it is a bit overpriced.

800 Zinfandel Lane (east of Hwy. 29), St. Helena, CA 94574. (℃) **707/963-3512.** Fax 707/963-5310. www.zinfandelinn.com. 3 units. Mar–Nov $250–$330 double; call for off-season rates. Rates include full breakfast, plus champagne and truffles on arrival. MC, V. **Amenities:** Unheated outdoor pool; Jacuzzi. *In room:* A/C; TV; hairdryers, robes.

INEXPENSIVE

Deer Run Bed & Breakfast 🐾 If romantic solitude is a big part of your vacation plan, Deer Run should be on your itinerary. Situated 4½ miles (10 min. by car) from downtown St. Helena along a winding mountain road, this four-room B&B is a heavenly hideaway. Each of the wood-paneled rooms looks onto owners Tom and Carol Wilson's 4 acres of forest, and each features gorgeous antiques, a feather bed, a private entrance, a deck, a decanter of brandy, fridge, coffee and tea, robes, and access to hiking trails. One unit adjoins the cedar-shingled main house and boasts a king bed, Laura Ashley textiles, a wood-burning fireplace, and an open-beam ceiling. The Carriage House Suite offers an antique queen bed, Spanish tile floors, a gas stove, and a huge bathroom. The Studio Bungalow is fashioned in Ralph Lauren style, with Spanish tile, a cathedral ceiling, and whitewashed cedar. Deer meander by the Honeymoon Suite (the most secluded), a sweet split-level cottage with a separate bedroom and gas fireplace; its price includes a full breakfast prepared and delivered to your door. Outside, Cody, the resident chocolate Lab, hangs out by the small pool.

3995 Spring Mountain Rd. (P.O. Box 311), St. Helena, CA 94574. (℃) **877/333-7786** or 707/963-3794. Fax 707/963-9026. 4 units, all with bathroom (shower only). $160–$195 double. AE, MC, V. Rates include full breakfast (in-room for Honeymoon Suite guests only). **Amenities:** Small outdoor unheated pool. *In room:* A/C, TV, hair dryer.

El Bonita Motel 🐾 *Value* *Kids* This 1930s Art Deco motel is a bit too close to Highway 29 for comfort, but the 2½ acres of beautifully landscaped gardens behind the building (away from the road) help even the score. The rooms, while small and nothing fancy, are spotlessly clean (and sometimes smell strongly of air freshener). They are decorated with newish furnishings, and some have kitchens or whirlpool baths. Many families, attracted to the larger bungalows with kitchenettes, consider El Bonita one of the best values in Napa Valley—especially considering the pool, Jacuzzi, sauna, and new massage facility.

195 Main St. (at El Bonita Ave.), St. Helena, CA 94574. ℂ 800/541-3284 or 707/963-3216. Fax 707/963-8838. www.elbonita.com. 41 units. $89–$259 double. Rates include continental breakfast. AE, DC, DISC, MC, V. **Amenities:** Heated outdoor pool; spa; Jacuzzi. *In room:* A/C, TV, fridge, coffeemaker, microwave, hair dryer, iron.

White Sulphur Springs Inn & Spa 🐟

If your idea of the ultimate vacation is a cozy cabin on 45 acres, paradise is a short, winding drive away from downtown St. Helena. Established in 1852, Sulphur Springs claims to be the oldest resort in California. The property holds creeks, waterfalls, one naturally heated sulfur hot spring, and redwood, madrone, and fir trees. Guests stay in small and large creekside cabins (which were renovated in 1998 and 1999), the inn, and the carriage house. The cabins are decorated with simple but homey furnishings; Cabin 9 has two queen beds and a kitchenette. While you're here you can take a dip in the natural hot sulfur spring; lounge by the large outdoor unheated pool; sit under a tree and watch for deer, foxes, raccoons, spotted owls, or woodpeckers; or schedule a day of fantastic massage, aromatherapy, and other spa treatments in the understated Zen-like spa, which was completed in early 2001. *Note:* No RVs are allowed without advance notice. Smoking is not allowed in the rooms. Call well in advance; the resort is often rented by large groups.

3100 White Sulphur Springs Rd., St. Helena, CA 94574. ℂ 800/593-8873 in CA, or 707/963-8588. Fax 707/963-2890. www.whitesulphursprings.com. 37 units, including 14 with shared bathroom and 9 cottages. Carriage House (shared bathroom) $85–$100 double; inn $115–$140 double; creekside cottages $150–$195. Rates include continental breakfast. Off-season and midweek discounts available. 2-night minimum stay on weekends Apr–Oct and all holidays. MC, V. **Amenities:** Heated outdoor pool; full-service spa; Jacuzzi; soaking pool; Internet hook-up in hospitality room. *In room:* A/C in some rooms, TV, hair dryer on request.

CALISTOGA
EXPENSIVE

Cottage Grove Inn 🐟🐟   Standing in two parallel rows at the end of the main strip in Calistoga is this strip of cottages that, though on a residential street (with a paved road running between two rows of accommodations), seem removed from the action once you've stepped across the threshold. Each compact guesthouse has a woodburning fireplace, homey furnishings, cozy quilts, and an enormous bathroom with a skylight and a deep, two-person Jacuzzi tub. Guests enjoy such niceties as gourmet coffee and a wet bar, but unfortunately have no common public areas other than the room adjoining the office. Still, several major spas are within walking distance so if you want to do the Calistoga spa scene in comfort and style you can hoof it from here and return to Calistoga's most contemporary accommodations at the end of the day. Smoking is allowed only on the small front porch.

1711 Lincoln Ave., Calistoga, CA 94515. © **800/799-2284** or 707/942-8400. Fax 707/942-2653. www.cottagegrove.com. 16 cottages. $235–$295 double. Rates include continental breakfast and evening wine and cheese. AE, DC, DISC, MC, V. *In room:* A/C, TV/VCR, dataport, fridge, coffeemaker, hair dryer.

MODERATE

Christopher's Inn 🐾

A cluster of five buildings make up one of Calistoga's most attractive accommodation options. Ten years of renovations and expansions by architect/owner Christopher Layton have turned sweet old homes at the entrance to downtown into hotel rooms with a little pizzazz. Options range from somewhat simple, tasteful rooms with colorful and impressive antiques and small bathrooms to huge, lavish abodes with four-poster beds, rich fabrics and brocades, and sunken Jacuzzi tubs facing gas fireplaces. Room Number 3 impresses with its commanding 9-foot-tall blackwood carved Oriental panels. Most have gas fireplaces, and some have quirks such as small, older TVs (with cable). Outstanding bouquets attest that the management goes the distance on the details. Those who prefer homey accommodations will feel comfortable here; the property doesn't have corporate polish or big-business blandness. The two rather plain but very functional two-bedroom homes are ideal for families, provided that they're not expecting the Ritz. An extended continental breakfast is delivered to your room daily.

1010 Foothill Blvd., Calistoga, CA 94515. © **707/942-5755.** Fax 707/942-6895. www.christophersinn.com. 22 units. $175–$425 double; $330–$350 house sleeping 5. Rates include continental breakfast. AE, V. *In room:* TV, dataport.

EuroSpa & Inn 🐾🐾

In a quiet residential section of Calistoga, this small European-style inn and spa provides a level of solitude and privacy that few other spas can match. The horseshoe-shaped inn consists of a dozen stucco bungalows, a spa center, and an outdoor patio, where a light breakfast and snacks are served. The rooms, although small, are pleasantly decorated in Pottery Barn–style decor that was implemented in 2000; a few have whirlpool tubs. Spa treatments range from clay baths and foot reflexology to mini-facials.

1202 Pine St. (at Myrtle), Calistoga, CA 94515. © **707/942-6829.** Fax 707/942-1138. www.eurospa.com. 13 units. $129–$229 double. Rates include continental breakfast. Weekend packages $369; off-season and midweek package discounts available. AE, DC, DISC, MC, V. **Amenities:** Outdoor heated pool; Jacuzzi. *In room:* A/C, TV, dataport, fridge, hair dryer, iron, microwave.

Mount View Hotel & Spa ⌾   Located on the main road in the middle of downtown Calistoga, this National Historical Landmark is the best hotel in town. Rooms within the main building and cottages are cheerily decorated in either Victorian or Art Deco–style and trimmed with beautiful hand-painted accents. Some units are small, but they are well appointed, considering most of the area's funkier options. The three self-contained cottages are fab for romantics; each cozy nest has a queen-size bed (including featherbed and down duvet), a wet bar, a private deck, and a secluded fenced-in outdoor hot tub. Almost everything in town is within walking distance, although once you settle in, you might not want to leave the quiet, sunny swimming-pool area or spa.

1457 Lincoln Ave. (on Calif. 29, near Fairway St.), Calistoga, CA 94515. ⌾ **800/ 816-6877** or 707/942-6877. Fax 707/942-6904. www.mountviewhotel.com. 32 units, including 3 cottages. $125–$205 double; $175–$275 suite; $250–$300 cottage. Rates include continental breakfast. Packages available. 2-night minimum on weekends. AE, DISC, MC, V. **Amenities:** Large heated outdoor pool; full-service spa; hot tub. *In room:* A/C, TV, VCR and fridge in some units, coffeemaker, hair dryer, iron, robes.

Silver Rose Inn & Spa ⌾   If you're idea of living is a contemporary ranch-style spread complete with themed accommodations, a large wine bottle-shaped heated pool, and a smaller unheated pool, two hot tubs, dual tennis courts, and even a chipping and putting green, then you'll love the Silver Rose Inn & Spa. Situated on a small oak-covered knoll overlooking the upper Napa Valley, the inn, which is known for its polished hospitality, offers so many amenities that you'll have a tough time searching for reasons to leave (other than to eat dinner, which is not available on-site). Each spacious guest room is individually—and whimsically—decorated, in themes ranging from the peach-colored Peach Delight, to the Oriental Room, complete with shoji screens and Oriental rugs, to the Mardi Gras Room, which is adorned with colorful masks. Several rooms have fireplaces, whirlpool baths, and private balconies or terraces. Guests are offered access to the full-service spa, as well as an afternoon hospitality hour of wine, cheese, and crackers. Their on-premises winery offers free samples ($5 for outside guests) as well as daily 11am barrel tastings.

351 Rosedale Rd. (off the Silverado Trail), Calistoga, CA 94515. ⌾ **800/995-9381** or 707/942-9581. www.silverrose.com. 20 units. $165–$255 double weekdays; $195–$300 double weekends. Rates include continental breakfast. AE, DISC, MC, V. **Amenities:** 2 pools; spa; 2 hot tubs. *In room:* A/C.

INEXPENSIVE

Brannan Cottage Inn   This cute little 1860 cottage, complete with the requisite white picket fence, sits on a quiet side street. One of Sam Brannan's original resort cottages, the inn was restored through a community effort to salvage an important piece of Calistoga's heritage; it's now on the National Register of Historic Places. The six spacious rooms are decorated with down comforters and white lace curtains; each room also has a ceiling fan, private bathroom, and its own entrance; two rooms have four-poster beds. There's a comfortable parlor and a pleasant brick terrace, furnished with umbrella tables.

109 Wapoo Ave. (at Lincoln Ave.; P.O. Box 81), Calistoga, CA 94515. (℃) 707/ 942-4200. www.brannancottageinn.com. 6 units. $125–$160 double. Extra person $15. Rates include full buffet breakfast. Off-season discounts available. MC, V. *In room:* A/C, TV in some units, fridge.

Calistoga Country Lodge ⟨⟩ *Value*   This rustic, secluded inn in the western foothills of Calistoga is one of the best bargains in the Wine Country. Where else can you get a spacious, attractively furnished room with a king or queen bed, fireplace, sitting chairs, and verdant views for as little as $130 a night? Innkeeper Jennifer Biskind runs this 1915 farmhouse, which she snared in mid-2002 and gussied up with her own art collection, bleached pine and lodgepole furniture, and American antiques. It's all very tastefully done. In winter, the two rooms with fireplaces are the way to go (although these are the same two rooms that share a hallway bathroom). In summer, the private deck in the attic-level Lookout Room offers bucolic views of the surrounding century-old oak groves. Just in case you're still not convinced, there's always the newly renovated giant pool, heated April through November, and the 24-hour hot tub, which is heated year-round. A full buffet breakfast—perhaps including quiches with vegetables from Jennifer's garden—is served from 7 to 10am, and wine and cheese are served in the evening.

2883 Foothill Blvd. (1 mile north of Lincoln Ave.), Calistoga, CA 94515. (℃) 707/ 942-5555. Fax 707/942-5864. www.countrylodge.com. 6 units, 2 with shared bathroom. $130–$215 double. Rates include full breakfast and wine and cheese in the evening. AE, MC, V. **Amenities:** Seasonally heated outdoor pool; hot tub. *In room:* A/C, no phone.

Calistoga Inn   Would the fact that the Calistoga Inn has its own brewery influence my decision to recommend it? You betcha. Here's the deal: You're probably in town for the spa treatments, but unfortunately, the guest rooms at almost every spa are lacking in the personality and warmth department. A better bet for the budget traveler is to book a room at this homey inn, then walk a few blocks up the street for a mud bath and massage. You'll have to share the bathrooms, and the rooms above the inn's restaurant can be noisy, but otherwise, you get a cozy little room with a queen-size bed, washbasin, and continental breakfast, for a weekend rate that's half the average in these parts. What's more, there's no minimum stay, and the best beer in town is served downstairs. *Tip:* Request a room as far from the bar/restaurant as possible.

1250 Lincoln Ave. (at Cedar St.), Calistoga, CA 94515. ℂ **707/942-4101.** Fax 707/ 942-4914. www.calistogainn.com. 18 units, none with bathroom. $65–$90 double. Rates include continental breakfast. AE, MC, V.

Calistoga Spa Hot Springs 🔆 *Value* *Kids*   Very few hotels in the Wine Country cater specifically to families with children, but I recommend Calistoga Spa Hot Springs if you're bringing the little ones. Even if you don't have kids, this is a great bargain, offering unpretentious yet comfortable rooms, as well as a plethora of spa facilities. All of Calistoga's best shops and restaurants are within easy walking distance, and you can even whip up your own grub at the barbecues near the large pool and patio area.

1006 Washington St. (at Gerrard St.), Calistoga, CA 94515. ℂ **707/942-6269.** www.calistogaspa.com. 57 units, 1 family unit. Winter $99 double, $154 family unit; summer $121 double, $176 family unit. MC, V. **Amenities:** 3 heated outdoor pools; kids' wading pool; exercise room; spa. *In room:* A/C, TV, kitchenette, fridge, coffeemaker, hair dryer on request, iron.

Dr. Wilkinson's Hot Springs Resort 🔆 *Value*   This spa "resort," located in the heart of Calistoga, is one of the best deals in Napa Valley. The rooms range from attractive Victorian-style accommodations with sundecks and garden patios to modern, cozy, newly renovated guest rooms in the main fun-funky 1950s-style motel. All rooms are spiffier than most motel options in the area, with surprisingly tasteful textiles and basic motel-style accouterments. Larger rooms have refrigerators and/or kitchens. The facilities include three mineral-water pools (two outdoor and one indoor), a Jacuzzi, a steam room, and mud baths. Facials and all kinds of body treatments are available in the salon, and spa service is excellent. Be sure to inquire about the excellent midweek packages.

1507 Lincoln Ave. (Calif. 29, between Fairway and Stevenson aves.), Calistoga, CA 94515. ℂ **707/942-4102.** www.drwilkinson.com. 42 units. Winter $109–$139 double; summer $149–$189 double. Weekly discounts and packages available. AE, MC, V. **Amenities:** 2 outdoor mineral-water pools; indoor mineral-water pool; spa, Jacuzzi; steam room. *In room:* A/C, TV; coffeemaker; hair dryer; iron on request.

5 Where to Dine

Napa Valley's restaurants draw as much attention to the valley as its award-winning wineries. Nowhere else in the state are kitchens as deft at mixing fresh seasonal, local, organic produce into edible magic, which means that menus change constantly to reflect the best available ingredients. Add that to a great bottle of wine and stunning views, and you have one heck of an eating experience.

To best enjoy the valley's restaurant scene, keep one thing in mind: Reserve—especially if you want a seat in a famous room. Beyond that, expect to spend some money! Aside from taco stands and great little Mexican joints tucked throughout the valley quality doesn't come cheaply in these parts.

The restaurants listed below are classified first by town, then by price, using the following categories: **Expensive,** dinner from $50 per person; **Moderate,** dinner from $35 to $50 per person; and **Inexpensive,** dinner less than $35 per person. These categories reflect prices for an appetizer, a main course, and a dessert.

NAPA
MODERATE

Angèle ☞ COUNTRY FRENCH   A family affair by Claude Rouas (founder of Auberge du Soleil) and daughters Bettina and Claudia, this new riverside spot incited a stampede of restaurateurs and winemakers when it opened at the end of 2002. The draw? Its cozy combo of raw wood beams, taupe-tinted concrete-block, concrete slab floors, bright yellow leather bar stools, candlelight, and a menu that tips its toque to country French classics. Sure-things include rich oxtail and lentil salad perked with elegantly acidic "ravigote" dressing ($10), giant white bowls of steamed mussels in a light braised fennel broth ($12), and braised chicken with chestnuts, celery root, and foie gras butter ($18). Perks include a citrus-tree-flanked, heater-warmed patio above the Napa River (weather permitting), a festive full bar, and hobnobbing with restaurateurs and winemakers.

Tips Dining Out Wisely

In the Wine Country, food is usually served in large portions and washed down with copious amounts of wine. Therefore, you might want to plan to have one big meal per day at a restaurant and picnic or snack the rest of the day.

---

540 Main St. (in the Hatt Building). ℂ 707-252-8115. Reservations recommended. Main courses $16–$22. AE, MC, V. Daily 11:30am–10pm.

Bistro Don Giovanni ⭐⭐⭐ *Value* REGIONAL ITALIAN Donna and Giovanni Scala own this bright, bustling, and cheery Italian restaurant, which also happens to be one of my favorite dining destinations in Napa Valley. Fare prepared with quality ingredients and California flair never disappoints, especially when it comes to the thin-crust pizzas and house-made pastas. Every time I grab a menu, I can't get past the beet and haricots verte salad and pasta with duck Bolognese. On the rare occasion that I do, I am equally smitten with outstanding classic pizza Margarita, fresh from the wood-burning oven, seared salmon filet perched atop a tower of buttermilk mashed potatoes, and steak frites. Even though portions are generous, there's always room for tiramisu! Alfresco dining in the vineyards is available—and highly recommended on a warm, sunny day. Midwinter, I'm a fan of ordering a bottle of wine and dining at the bar where friendly bartenders Aaron and Ben make sure everyone's well taken care of.

4110 St. Helena Hwy. (Hwy. 29, just north of Salvador Ave.), Napa. ℂ 707/224-3300. Reservations recommended. Main courses $12–$24. AE, DC, DISC, MC, V. Sun–Thurs 11:30am–10pm; Fri–Sat 11:30am–11pm.

Pearl CALIFORNIA ECLECTIC   If you prefer to skip the destination restaurants and head for a casual but quality meal among the locals, pull up a chair in Pearl's warm, friendly dining room or on the lovely enclosed patio. The limited menu includes a nice selection of salads such as a whole-leaf Caesar and Asian noodle and vegetables. Main courses include sandwiches such as the grilled ahi with pickled onions and house-made tartar sauce on a potato bun and grilled New York steak with grilled onion on house focaccia. Also recommended are the soft polenta with sautéed seasonal veggies and the double-thick pork chops with mashed potatoes and vegetables. I always go for the grilled items and love the summer special of grilled corn bathed in sour cream with chili powder and sprinkled with manchego cheese. Downsides? Service can be woefully slow and they're beer-and-wine only. Live music fans take note: They often have an acoustic duo playing in the courtyard during summer weekend eves.

1339 Pearl St., no. 104 (at the convergence of Franklin, Clay, and Pearl sts.). ℂ 707/224-9161. Reservations recommended. Main courses $10–$22. MC, V. Tues–Thurs 11:30am–2pm and 5:30–9pm, Fri–Sat 11:30am–2pm and 5:30–9:30pm, Sun–Mon closed.

Napa Valley Dining

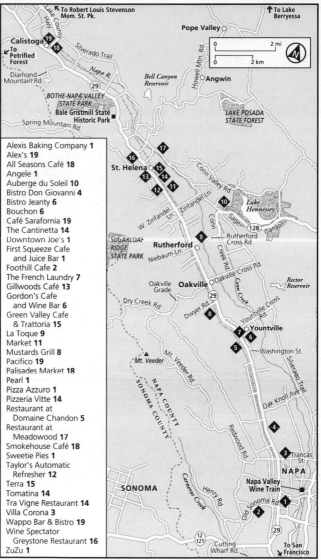

To Robert Louis Stevenson Mem. St. Pk.

To Lake Berryessa

Pope Valley

Calistoga 19
18

To Petrified Forest

Silverado Trail

Diamond Mountain Rd.

Napa R.

Bell Canyon Reservoir

Angwin

Howell Mtn. Rd.

29

BOTHE-NAPA VALLEY STATE PARK

LAKE POSADA STATE FOREST

Bale Gristmill State Historic Park

Spring Mountain Rd.

17

Alexis Baking Company 1
Alex's 19
All Seasons Café 18
Angele 1
Auberge du Soleil 10
Bistro Don Giovanni 4
Bistro Jeanty 6
Bouchon 6
Café Sarafornia 19
The Cantinetta 14
Downtown Joe's 1
First Squeeze Cafe and Juice Bar 1
Foothill Cafe 2
The French Laundry 7
Gillwoods Café 13
Gordon's Cafe and Wine Bar 6
Green Valley Cafe & Trattoria 15
La Toque 9
Market 11
Mustards Grill 8
Pacifico 19
Palisades Market 18
Pearl 1
Pizza Azzuro 1
Pizzeria Vitte 14
Restaurant at Domaine Chandon 5
Restaurant at Meadowood 17
Smokehouse Café 18
Sweetie Pies 1
Taylor's Automatic Refresher 12
Terra 15
Tomatina 14
Tra Vigne Restaurant 14
Villa Corona 3
Wappo Bar & Bistro 19
Wine Spectator Greystone Restaurant 16
ZuZu 1

16
St. Helena 15
13 14
12 11

Conn Valley Rd.

Lake Hennessey

10

128

Sage Canyon

SUGARLOAF RIDGE STATE PARK

W. Zinfandel Ln.

Zinfandel Ln.

9

Rutherford

Rutherford Cross Rd.

Conn Creek Rd.

Niebaum Ln.

Oakville Grade

Oakville

Oakville Cross Rd.

Conn Creek

Rector Reservoir

Dry Creek Rd.

29

Dwyer Rd.

8

Yountville Cross Rd.

7 Yountville
6

5

Washington St.

Mt. Veeder

Mt. Veeder Rd.

Silverado Trail

NAPA COUNTY

SONOMA COUNTY

Oak Knoll Ave.

Redwood Rd.

4

3 Trancas St.

NAPA

Carneros Creek

SONOMA

Henry Rd.

Napa Valley Wine Train

Old Sonoma Rd.

1

2

12 121

Cutting Wharf Rd.

29

To San Francisco

INEXPENSIVE

Alexis Baking Company 👥👥 BAKERY/CAFE   Alexis (aka ABC) is a quaint, casual stop for residents and in-the-know tourists. On weekend mornings—especially Sundays, which is the only time you can get their out-of-this-world huevos rancheros—the line stretches out the door. But once you order (from the counter during the week and at the table on weekends) and find a seat in the sunny room, you can relax, enjoy the coffeehouse atmosphere, and start your day with spectacular pastries, coffee drinks, and breakfast goodies like pumpkin pancakes with sautéed pears. Lunch also bustles with locals who come for simple, fresh fare like grilled hamburgers with gorgonzola; grilled-chicken Caesar salad; roast lamb sandwich with minted mayo and roasted shallots on rosemary bread; and lentil bulgur orzo salad. Desserts run the gamut; during the holidays, they include a moist and magical steamed persimmon pudding. Oh, and the pastry counter's cookies and cakes beg you take something for the road.

1517 Third St. (between Main and Jefferson), Napa. © **707/258-1827.** Main courses $4.25–$10 at breakfast, $7–$10 at lunch, Mon–Fri 6:30am–4pm; Sat 7:30am–3pm; Sun 8am–2pm.

Downtown Joe's AMERICAN BISTRO   Foodies will want to steer clear, but those looking for a good hangover breakfast, a down-home atmosphere, lots of beer on tap, and grooving tunes will appreciate this well-priced restaurant. The menu is all over the place, offering everything from porterhouse steaks to omelets, pasta, and seafood specials. The beers, such as the tart Golden Ribbon American beer, are made in-house, as are the some of the breads and desserts. If the sun's out, request a table on the outside patio, adjacent to the park. Thursday through Sunday nights, rock, jazz, and blues bands draw in the locals.

Another reason to visit Joe's are their happy hours, which are Monday through Friday and feature changing daily specials such as $2.75 pints and free appetizers (certain days) plus a drawing every hour to win free stuff.

902 Main St. (at 2nd St.), Napa. © **707/258-2337.** Main courses $6–$10 breakfast, $9–$18 lunch and dinner. AE, DC, DISC, MC, V. Mon–Thurs 10:30am–10:30pm (lunch and dinner), Fri 10:30–midnight, Sat 8:30am–2pm (brunch) and 2–midnight (dinner), Sun 8:30am–10:30pm.

First Squeeze Cafe and Juice Bar DELI/JUICE   Stay in town long enough, and you're bound to crave simple, wholesome, healthy fare, and First Squeeze is just the place to find it. I drop by for fresh smoothies such as a protein-powder shake with wheat grass, spirulina, ginseng, bee pollen, and brewer's yeast. But you can also order at the counter, settle amidst spartan furnishings (and decor to match), and dig into a full breakfast or a big, bulky sandwich.

1126 1st St. (in Clocktower Plaza), Napa. ℂ **707/224-6762**. Deli items $3–$7. AE, DC, MC, V. Mon–Fri 7am–3pm, Sat–Sun 8am–3pm.

Foothill Café ⟨⟨ AMERICAN Unpretentious, not fancy, astounding value, and creative good-quality food are the name of the game at this hidden local favorite in a tiny mall. With a mere 42 seats and a serious following the east-Napa neighborhood joint is always crowded, but the feeling is still intimate and casual. Chef/owner Jerry Shaffer's menu trots the backyard and the globe with items such as Thai salad, crab cakes, his famed oak-roasted baby back ribs, and duck breast with huckleberry sauce, garlic mashed potatoes, and sautéed vegetables. Sometimes dishes are complete winners, other times they're very good. In both cases they're served by a friendly staff and accompanied by affordable wines, making this stop a great choice for anyone interested in a fine Napa Valley meal without the fanfare or price tag of fine dining rooms.

2766 Old Sonoma Rd. (at Foothill Blvd.). ℂ **707/252-6178.** Reservations recommended. Main courses $14–$18. AE, MC, V. Wed–Sun 4:30–9:30pm.

Pizza Azzurro ⟨ ITALIAN This casual, cheery, family-friendly restaurant serves the best fancy thin-crust pies in downtown Napa. Unlike many Valley dining rooms, the place has an authentic neighborhood feel thanks to a very low-key atmosphere, and the continual presence of chef/owner Michael Gyetvan who spent 10 years in the kitchens of Tra Vigne, One Market, and Lark Creek Inn. While killer thin-crust pizzas—such as the incredible *Salsiccia* (tangy tomato sauce, rustic Sonoma-made fennel pork sausage, crunchy red onion, and mozzarella) star here, they've got great salads, too. Try the respectable Caesar or the marinated chickpea salad, a giant serving of chopped romaine, garbanzos, and canned albacore, cucumber, red pear tomatoes, and olives tossed in a lightly acidic citrus dressing that can easily serve four. Pastas, such as rigatoni in red sauce with hot Italian sausage and mushrooms, play it safe, while *manciatas*—soft, lightly cooked pizza dough meant to be folded and eaten like a soft taco—are very satisfying. (Try the B.B.L.T. version.) Although Bistro Don Giovanni is king of fancy pasta and pizza fixes, Azzurro is cheaper and far better if you've got the kids in tow or want to have a low-key or fast dinner. *Note:* There's no dessert here, but Ben & Jerry's is a quick stroll away.

400 Second St. (at Franklin St.). © **707/255-5552**. No reservations. Main courses $9.95–$12. AE, MC, V. Mon–Fri 11:30am–9pm, Sat 5pm–9pm. Closed Sun.

Sweetie Pies ★ *Finds* CAFE/BAKERY

Simple breakfasts of granola, egg-and-cheese croissant sandwiches, quiche, and coffee are a perfect and light way to kick off each decadent day at this very adorable and aptly named country bakery. But yummy pastries, decadent individual cakes, huge cookies, and lunchtime edibles like ham and fontina panini and pizzettas with mixed green salads are equal reason to stop by and linger at one of the few tables. Got a sweet tooth? You can't go wrong with the dark chocolate and caramel ganache fudge cake or tiramisu cheesecake.

520 Main St., at the south end, Napa. © **707/257-7280**. Breakfast snacks $2.75–$3.50; pastries $1.60–$2; cake $5; sandwiches $5.50. MC, V. Mon–Wed 6:30am–6pm, Thurs 6:30am–7pm, Fri–Sat 6:30am–10pm, Sun 7am–5pm.

Villa Corona ★ MEXICAN

The best Mexican food in town is served in this bright, funky, and colorful box of a restaurant hidden in the southwest corner of a strip mall behind an unmemorable sports bar and restaurant. The winning plan here is simple. Order and pay at the counter, sit at either a plastic-covered table or at one of the few sidewalk seats, and wait for the huge burritos, enchiladas, and chimichangas to be delivered to your table. Those with pork preferences shouldn't miss the carnitas, which is abundantly flavorful and juicy. My personal favorites are chicken enchiladas, with its light savory red sauce and generous side of beans and rice and hard shell tacos. Don't expect to wash down your menudo, or anything else for that matter, with a margarita. The place is beer and wine only. Don't hesitate to come for a hearty breakfast, too. Excellent chilaquiles (eggs scrambled with salsa and tortilla) and huevos rancheros are part of the package.

3614 Bel Aire Plaza (on Trancas St.), Napa. © **707/257-8685**. Breakfast $4.50–$6.75; lunch/dinner $3.75–$9.75. MC, V. Tues–Fri 9am–9pm, Sat 8am–9pm, Sun 8am–8pm.

ZuZu ★★ TAPAS

The most exciting Napa restaurant opening of 2002 wasn't a big fancy dining room, but rather this tiny downtown spot serving delicious affordable small plates of Spanish fare ($2–$11!). A local place to the core, no reservations are taken here, and diners crowd into the cramped wine and beer bar until they can be seated. The comfortable, warm, and not remotely corporate atmosphere extends from the environment to the food, which is seriously good. Chef Charles Weber presides over the tiny kitchen cranking out sizzling skillets of tangy and fantastic paella, fresh and clean corn soup, addictive sizzling prawns with requisite bread-dipping sauce, light and delicate sea scallop ceviche salad, and Moroccan barbecued lamb chops with a sweet-and-spicy sauce guaranteed to make you swoon. Desserts aren't as fab, but with a bottle of wine and many more tasty plates than you can possibly devour, who cares? Stop here and I promise you'll be saying to yourself that you wish there was a ZuZu in your neighborhood.

829 Main St., Napa. ℰ **707/224-8555.** Reservations not accepted. Tapas $2–$10. AE, MC, V. Mon–Thurs 11:30am–10pm; Fri 11:30am–midnight; Sat 4pm–midnight; Sun 4–9pm.

YOUNTVILLE
EXPENSIVE

The French Laundry ✮✮✮ CLASSIC AMERICAN/FRENCH It's almost futile to include this restaurant, because you're about as likely to secure a reservation—or get through on the reservation line, for that matter—as you are to drive Highway 29 without passing a winery. Several years after renowned chef-owner Thomas Keller bought the place and caught the attention of epicureans worldwide (including the judges of the James Beard Awards, who named him "Chef of the Nation" in 1997), the discreet restaurant is the hottest dinner ticket *in the world.*

Plainly put, the French Laundry is unlike any other dining experience, period. Part of it has to do with the intricate preparations, often finished tableside and always presented with uncommon artistry and detail from the food itself to the surface it's delivered on. Other factors are the service (superfluous, formal, and attentive) and the sheer length of time it takes to ride chef Keller's culinary magic carpet. The atmosphere, which is as serious as the diners who quietly swoon over the ongoing parade of bite-size delights, ranges from downstairs and upstairs to garden seating (seasonal). Technically, the prix-fixe menu offers a choice of five or nine courses (including a vegetarian menu), but after a slew of cameo appearances from the kitchen, everyone loses count. Signature dishes include Keller's "tongue in cheek" (marinated and braised round of sliced lamb tongue and tender beef cheeks) and "macaroni and cheese" (sweet butter-poached Maine lobster with creamy lobster broth and orzo with mascarpone cheese). But the truth is, the experience defies description, so if you absolutely love food you'll simply have to see for yourself. Portions are small, but only because Keller wants his guests to taste as many things as possible. Trust me, nobody leaves hungry.

Fun Fact **Bouchon Bakery**

Pastry lovers should make the pilgrimage to **Bouchon Bakery,** 6528 Washington St., Yountville (© **707/944-BAKE**), famous chef Thomas Keller's latest addition to Yountville's culinary landscape. The traditional country French gourmet-to-go shop sells outstanding traditional baguettes (baked twice daily), classic brioche, paper-wrapped sandwiches of butter, ham, and gruyere, and sinful éclairs, custard napoleons, and big nutter-butter cookies. In less than 6 months in existence, stopping here for provisions has already become a habit among local foodies.

The staff is well acquainted with the wide selection of regional wines; there's a $50 corkage fee if you bring your own bottle. On warm summer nights, request a table in the flower-filled garden. *Hint:* If you can't get a reservation, try walking in—on occasion folks don't keep their reservation and tables open up, especially during lunch on rainy days. Also, Auberge du Soleil reserves two tables nightly for their guests; these tables are doled out on a first-come, first-served basis. Reservations are accepted 2 months in advance to the date, starting at 10am. Anticipate hitting redial many times for the best chance. Also, insiders tell me that fewer people call on weekends, so you have a better chance at getting through the busy signal. Finally, if you can show up in person (arrive early; there's a line!) to make your reservations 2 months in advance, you're pretty much guaranteed a table.

6640 Washington St. (at Creek St.), Yountville. © **707/944-2380.** Reservations required. Vegetarian menu $80; 5-course menu $105; chef's 9-course tasting menu $120. AE, MC, V. Fri–Sun 11am–1pm; daily 5:30–9:30pm.

MODERATE

Bistro Jeanty ✹✹✹ FRENCH BISTRO   This casual, warm bistro, with muted buttercup walls, two dining rooms divided by a bar, and patio seats is where chef Phillipe Jeanty creates outstanding French comfort food for legions of fans. A few years back, the highly regarded chef left his 18-year post at Domaine Chandon to open this well-known and affordably priced gem. Jeanty was previously known for formal French cooking, but his cheery bistro is far more laid-back—and equally outstanding. The all-day menu includes legendary tomato soup in puff pastry; foie gras pâté; steak tartare; and house-smoked trout with potato slices. No meal should start without a paper cone filled with fried smelt, and none should end without the most insanely good crème brûlée, which comes with a thin layer of chocolate cream between classic vanilla custard and a caramelized sugar top. In between, I vote for decadent fall-off-the-bone coq au vin, with earthy, smoky red wine sauce or a juicy thick-cut pork chop with jus, spinach, and mashed potatoes. I'm not as excited by the too-flavorful cassoulet of white beans, fennel sausage, pork, and duck leg with an overly dry breadcrumb crust. That said, it's hard not to love this place, even if the ne'er changing menu can be too rich during summertime.

6510 Washington St., Yountville. ℰ **707/944-0103.** www.bistrojeanty.com. Reservations recommended. Appetizers $6.50–$11; most main courses $14–$23. AE, MC, V. Daily 11:30am–10:30pm. Closed Thanksgiving and Christmas.

Bouchon ℱ FRENCH BISTRO   Perhaps to appease the crowds who never get a reservation at French Laundry, Thomas Keller teamed up with his brother Joseph to open this far more casual, but still delicious, French brasserie designed by Adam Tihany, who also conceptualized New York's Le Cirque 2000. Along with a raw bar, expect superb renditions of steak frites, mussels marinières, grilled cheese sandwiches, and other heavenly French classics. My all-time favorite must orders: the bibb lettuce salad (seriously, trust me on this), french fries (perhaps the best in the valley), and roasted chicken bathing in wild mushroom ragout, which I usually consume at the locals-centric bar. Prices and atmosphere are far more down-to-earth than at French Laundry. A bonus, especially for restless residents and off-duty restaurant staff, is the late hours.

6534 Washington St. (at Humbolt), Yountville. ℰ **707/944-8037.** Reservations recommended. Main courses $14–$23. AE, MC, V. Daily 11:30am–1am.

Gordon's Cafe and Wine Bar ℱ WINE COUNTRY CUISINE If you want to escape the town's highfalutin restaurants for an intimate brush with the locals, this is the place to do it. Sally Gordon opened this adorable Yountville favorite in May 1996. Part country

---

Fun Fact **Trying a Tasting Menu**

Never heard of a tasting menu? Basically it's smaller portions and more courses, which you choose from numerous selections. It's great for people who prefer to taste lots of things without overstuffing themselves.

store, part deli, and part restaurant, one wall is lined with an intriguing collection of jams, mustards, olive oils, wines, and other gourmet goods for sale; another posts the chalkboard breakfast and lunch menu above a glass display case housing a cornucopia of deli items. The floor is scuffed hardwood, and fewer than a dozen tables are spaciously dispersed throughout the airy room. Breakfast (oatmeal, omelets, homemade pastries, and smoothies), lunch (soup, salads, and sandwiches), and real homemade flavor come from an open kitchen. Dinner, served only on Friday nights, is a fixed-price three-course feast, which changes seasonally and might include a choice of four appetizers (smoked trout salad with watercress), two main courses (marinated rack of lamb with wild mushroom and potato gratin and fresh Romano beans or pan-roasted halibut with fresh corn, diced potato, and smoked bacon, and arugula hash and a chive beurre blanc), and cabernet sorbet and vanilla gelato parfait atop lemon cake.

6770 Washington St., Yountville. ℂ 707/944-8246. Reservations necessary for Fri dinner. Breakfast $5–$7; lunch $3.75–$8; fixed-price dinner $45. AE, DC, DISC, MC, V. Breakfast daily 7:30–11am, until noon on weekends; lunch daily 11am–3pm. Coffee and wine bar open until 5pm Sun–Thurs, 9pm Fri, 6pm Sun. Dinner Fri only, 6–8:30pm.

Mustards Grill ⭐⭐ CALIFORNIA   Mustards is one of those standby restaurants that everyone seems to love because it's dependable and been around for ever and its menu has something that suits any food craving. Housed in a convivial, barn-style space, it offers an 11-page wine list and an ambitious chalkboard list of specials alongside tasty comfort foods from the wood-burning grill and oven: Think lemon and garlic chicken with garlic mashed potatoes, tea-smoked Peking duck with almond-onion sauce, and a daily-changing fish special. The menu includes something for everyone, from vegetarians to good old burger lovers (ahi, pork, *or* beef!).

7399 St. Helena Hwy. (Hwy. 29), Yountville. ℂ 707/944-2424. Reservations recommended. Main courses $11–$27. AE, DC, DISC, MC, V. Mon–Thurs 11:30am–9pm; Fri 11:30am–10pm; Sat 11am–10pm; Sun 11am–9-pm.

OAKVILLE & RUTHERFORD
EXPENSIVE
Auberge du Soleil ⭐ *Finds* WINE COUNTRY CUISINE   There is no better restaurant view than that at Auberge du Soleil. Perched on a hillside overlooking the valley, alfresco dining rises to an entirely new level here, particularly on warm summer afternoons at sunset. In fact, during warm-weather periods I recommend coming before

sundown (request terrace seating) to join the wealthy patrons, many of who have emerged from their überluxury guest rooms and are slinking to a table to dine above the vines. The kitchen, which became as celestial as the views when chef Richard Reddington arrived in late 2000, turns out superb, refined, and beautiful seasonal dishes. If the menu lists 'em, jump on the sautéed sweetbreads, venison loin with butternut squash, stuffed squab, and roasted saddle of lamb. The interior is warm, bustling, and formal enough that some folks wear ties. The only drawback: Service is unsteady and wine prices are steep.

180 Rutherford Hill Rd., Rutherford. (𝓒 707/963-1211. Reservations recommended. Main courses lunch $19–$23; main courses dinner $28–$34, 4-course pre-fixed $78. AE, DISC, MC, V. Daily 7–11am, 11:30am–2:30pm, and 6–9:30pm.

La Toque 𝓕𝓕𝓕 FRENCH   Renowned chef Ken Frank left Los Angeles's fenix at the Argyle Hotel to open one of the Wine Country's most formal dining rooms, which features a beautifully presented five-course extravaganza. Each table at the elegant restaurant adjoining Rancho Caymus Inn is well spaced, making plenty of room to showcase the chef-owner's memorable and innovative French-inspired cuisine, which changes frequently (see the restaurant's website for the latest). A recent late-summer menu included early girl tomato soup, skate wing with currants and brown butter, foie gras with fresh polenta and chanterelles, Niman Ranch rib roast, and a warm chocolate hazelnut tart with toasted hazelnut ice cream. Your big-bucks meal includes coffee, petits fours, and all the Pellegrino and Evian you can drink. Should you find room and the extra few bucks for the cheese course, try a few delicious selections, served with walnut bread. For an additional fee, you can also have well-paired wines with each course.

1140 Rutherford Rd., Rutherford. (𝓒 707/963-9770. www.latoque.com. Reservations recommended. Fixed-price menu $98. Wed–Sun 5:30–10pm. Closed Mon–Tues.

ST. HELENA
EXPENSIVE

Terra 𝓕𝓕𝓕 CONTEMPORARY AMERICAN   If you can choose only one fine dining experience, make it here. Terra is one of my all-time favorite restaurants because it manages to be humble even though it serves some of the most extraordinary food in northern California. The creation Hiro Sone, a master chef and 2003 "Best California Chef" James Beard award winner who hails from Japan, Lissa Doumani his pastry chef wife, is a culmination of talents brought together more than 15 years ago, after the duo worked at L.A.'s Spago. Today, the menu reflects Sone's full use of the region's bounty and his formal training in classic European and Japanese cuisine. Dishes—all of which are incredible and are served in the rustic-romantic stone-wall dining room—range from understated and refined (peeky toe crab salad or the famous broiled sake-marinated black cod) to rock-your-world flavorful (petit ragout of sweetbreads, prosciutto, mushroom, and white truffle oil or grilled squab with leek and bacon bread pudding with roasted garlic foie gras sauce). I cannot begin to express the importance of saving room for dessert (or forcing it even if you didn't). Doumani's recipes, which include tiramisu and an out-of-this-world, heavenly orange risotto in brandy snap with passion fruit sauce, are some of the best I've tasted.

1345 Railroad Ave. (between Adams and Hunt sts.), St. Helena. ℭ **707/963-8931.** www.terrarestaurant.com. Reservations recommended. Main courses $19–$29. DC, MC, V. Sun–Mon and Wed–Thurs 6–9:30pm; Fri–Sat 6–10pm. Closed for 2 weeks in early Jan.

MODERATE

Tra Vigne Restaurant 𝕽𝕽 ITALIAN   Tra Vigne's combination of good food, high-energy atmosphere, and gorgeous patio seating makes this restaurant a long-standing favorite among visitors and locals. Add to that plenty of seating and service running from lunch through dinner, and it's no wonder the enormous dining room packs 'em in. Whether guests are in the Tuscany-evoking courtyard (heated on cold nights) or in the center of the bustling scene, they're usually thrilled just to have a seat. Even though the wonderful bread (served with house-made flavored olive oils) is tempting, save room for the robust California dishes, cooked Italian-style. The menu features about one daily oven-roasted pizza special, tried-and-true standbys such as shortribs, frito misto, irresistible oven-roasted polenta with cheese, mushrooms, and balsamic reduction, and outstanding whole roasted fish. Equally tempting are the fresh pastas—such as spaghettini with cuttlefish bolognese and spring onions—and delicious desserts.

The adjoining **Cantinetta** (p. 119) offers a small selection of sandwiches, pizzas, and lighter meals, as well as an exciting new wine program, which features 100 by-the-glass selections.

1050 Charter Oak Ave., St. Helena. ℭ **707/963-4444.** Reservations recommended. Main courses $13–$22. DC, DISC, MC, V. Daily 11:30am–10pm.

Wine Spectator Greystone Restaurant 𝕽 WINE COUNTRY CUISINE   This place offers a visual and culinary feast that's

unparalleled in the area, if not the state. The room is an enormous stone-walled former winery, but the festive decor and heavenly aromas warm the space up. Cooking islands—complete with scurrying chefs, steaming pots, and rotating chicken—provide edible entertainment. The tastings (appetizer) menu features dishes inspired by fresh ingredients. They might include grilled mahimahi with asparagus salad, oven-roasted chicken breast with mashed potatoes, and Dungeness crab salad with avocado and grapefruit sauce. I recommend that you opt for a barrage of appetizers for your table to share. You should also order the "Flights of Fancy"—for $15 to $24, you can sample three 3-ounce pours of local wines such as white rhone, pinot, or zinfandel. While the food is serious, the atmosphere is playful—casual enough that you'll feel comfortable in jeans or shorts. If you want to ensure a meal here, reserve far in advance. I prefer to stop by, have a snack at the bar, and eat big meals elsewhere.

At the Culinary Institute of America at Greystone, 2555 Main St., St. Helena. ℂ 707/ 967-1010. Reservations recommended. Tastings $8.50; main courses $7–$27. AE, DC, MC, V. Daily 11:30am–10pm.

INEXPENSIVE

The Cantinetta ✰✰✰ WINE BAR/ITALIAN DELI   Regardless of where else I dine while in the valley, I always make a point of stopping at the Cantinetta for an espresso and a snack. Part cafe, part shop, it's a casual and hidden place with a few tables, a counter, and gorgeous garden seating. The focaccias, pasta salads, and pastries are outstanding. There's a selection of cookies and other wonderful treats, flavored oils (free tastings), wines, and an array of gourmet items, many of which were created here. You can also get great picnic grub to go. The Cantinetta is also the ultimate lifesaver when crowds are gathered elsewhere in town and I'm starving. Despite its popularity there's virtually never a line here and you can devour your feast in the same famed courtyard as diners at pricier Tra Vigne restaurant.

At Tra Vigne Restaurant, 1050 Charter Oak Ave., St. Helena. ℂ 707/963-8888. Main courses $6–$7. DC, DISC, MC, V. Daily 11:30am–6pm.

Gillwoods Café AMERICAN   In a town like this—where if you order mushrooms on your burger, the waiter's likely to ask, "What kind?"—a plain old American restaurant can be a godsend. In St. Helena, the land of snobs and broccoli rabes, Gillwoods is that place. At this homey haunt, with its wooden benches and original artwork, it's all about the basics. You'll find a breakfast of bakery goods, fruit, pancakes, omelets (with pronounceable ingredients), and a decent eggs Benedict; and a lunch menu of burgers, sand-wiches, lots of salads, veggie lasagna, chicken-fried steak, and meat-loaf. Lunch is available starting at 10:30am, but late risers can order breakfast until 3pm. A second location is in downtown Napa at 1320 Napa Town Center, © **707/253-0409.**

1313 Main St. (Hwy. 29; at Spring St.), St. Helena. © **707/963-1788.** Breakfast $5–$8; lunch $7–$9. AE, MC, V. Daily 7am–3pm.

Green Valley Cafe & Trattoria *(Value)* ITALIAN   When locals
want a casual, inexpensive night out, they convene at this small Ital-ian restaurant. Its long, green bar and row of tightly arranged tables have a casual neighborhood feel that many of the valley's restaurants lack, and chef/owner Delio's cooking is backed by big-city experi-ence at hole-in-the-wall prices. More than one St. Helena store owner simply must have the lasagna once a week. Others lean toward the eggplant topped with tomato and béchamel sauce and Parmesan, fried calamari with garlic mayo, braised lamb shank with polenta, or freshly made ravioli. Lunch offerings include spinach salad, a selection of cold and hot sandwiches (Italian sausage; burger; and grilled eggplant, tomato, cheese, peppers, onions, and olives), and of course, a few pasta dishes.

1310 Main St. (Hwy. 29; between Hunt Ave. and Adams St.), St. Helena. © **707/963-7088.** Reservations recommended. Lunch $5.75–$7; dinner $11–$19. MC, V. Tues–Sat 11:30am–3pm, 5:30–9:30pm.

Market *(★)* AMERICAN   San Francisco veterans Nick Peyton (of
Gary Danko) and Douglas Keane (chef at Jardinière) are filling a much needed niche with affordable St. Helena dining with this upscale but cheap ode to American comfort food. Mimicking its wealthy farming environs, it's a marriage of contradictions where fancy stone-wall and Brunswick bar surroundings are paired with clunky steak knives and simple white-plate presentations of meaty Dungeness crab cakes with dill-avocado mayo, barbecue sauce–glazed meatloaf over gravy, potato puree, and carrots, and toast-it-yourself s'mores with crisp homemade graham crackers. And plainly put, the burger rocks! While this is not top of my list of culinary destinations, it is the ultimate find for anyone who wants great atmosphere and a nice meal at an absurdly low price. (As of late, they've offered a three-course lunch for $12!)

1347 Main St., St. Helena. © **707-963-3799.** Most main courses $7–$15. AE, MC, V. Daily 11:30am–3:30pm (lunch), 5:30–11pm (bar menu); Sun–Thurs 5:30–9pm; Fri–Sat 5:30–11pm.

Taylor's Automatic Refresher ⚘ DINER   It isn't every day that a roadside burger shack gets a huge spread in *Food & Wine* magazine, but then again, Taylor's Refresher isn't your average fast-food stop. At this completely outdoor diner built in 1949, you order at the counter, settle at a picnic table in the front, facing Highway 29, or the more secluded back, and wait for your name to be called. When it is, you receive an excellent hamburger or ahi tuna burger on a surprisingly soft but sturdy bun, killer fries, creamy shakes, salads, and even glasses of local wine. If you're into food I seriously recommend you pay homage here. Many of the nation's culinary luminaries put it on their list of favorites.

933 Main St. (Hwy. 29), St Helena. (✆) **707/963-3486.** Main courses $2.50–$10. AE, MC, V. Daily 11am–8pm.

Pizzeria Vitte ⚘ (*Value* (*Kids* ITALIAN   After spending a week in Wine Country, I usually can't stand the thought of another decadent wine-and-foie gras meal. That's when I race to this spot for a nice, simple chopped salad. Families and locals come here for another reason: Although the menu is limited, it's a total winner for anyone in search of freshly prepared, wholesome food at atypically cheap Wine Country prices. A Caesar salad, for example, costs a mere $5.95. *Piadine*—pizzas folded like a soft taco—are the house specialty, and come filled with such delights as fresh Maine clams and oregano. Pizzas are of the build-your-own variety, with gourmet toppings such as sautéed mushrooms, fennel sausage, baby spinach, sun-dried tomatoes, and homemade pepperoni. The 26 respectable local wines come by the glass at a toast-worthy $3.75, or $18 per bottle. Dessert, at less than $4 a pop for gelato, biscotti, or pound cake, is an overall sweet deal. Everything is ordered at the counter and brought to the small or family-style tables in the very casual dining area or the outdoor patio. Kids especially like the pool table and big-screen TV.

At the Inn at Southbridge, 1016 Main St., St. Helena. (✆) **707/967-9999.** Pastas $6–$8; pizzas $8–$19. DC, DISC, MC, V. Daily 11:30am–9pm, Fri and Sat 9:30pm.

CALISTOGA
MODERATE
Alex's AMERICAN   Alex's is for non-cholesterol-counting comfort-food eaters who get excited at the sight of a big double-cut of prime rib oozing with au jus and served with the requisite side of pungent horseradish, mashed potatoes, and plenty of French bread. Whether it's breakfast, lunch, or dinner the menu aims to cure classic cravings with pancakes and eggs at breakfast and fried chicken,

spaghetti Bolognese, salads, and their famed prime rib at lunch or dinner. In an era in which the life expectancy of most restaurants is counted in months, Alex's has been around since 1969, so you know it must be doing something right. Although the doors closed for a three-year hiatus due to a loss in the family, this Art Deco standby was gussied up in 2003 by second-generation operator Sanije and her husband Niall who added fresh paint, a coffee bar, adjoining ice cream parlor (serving Double Rainbow ice cream), and new life to the joint.

1437 Lincoln Ave. (between Washington and Main sts.), Calistoga. © 707/942-6868. Main courses $9–$15. MC, V. Fri–Tues 7am–2:30pm, 4:30–9:30pm.

All Seasons Café ★★ CALIFORNIA   Wine Country devotees—including lots of restaurant pros—wend their way to the All Seasons Café in downtown Calistoga because of its extensive wine list and knowledgeable staff. The trick is to buy a bottle of wine from the cafe's wine shop, then bring it to your table; the cafe adds a corkage fee of around $10 instead of tripling the price of the bottle (as most restaurants do). The diverse menu dances through decadences such as seared main scallops with truffle scented risotto or red wine–braised short ribs. Chef Kevin Kathman saves his guests from any major faux pas by matching wines to dishes on the menu, so you know just what's right for the house-cured pork chop with braised red cabbage, ragout of apples, turnips, and potatoes.

1400 Lincoln Ave. (at Washington St.), Calistoga. © 707/942-9111. www.allseasons wineshop.com. Reservations recommended on weekends. Main courses $9–$18 at lunch, $16–$29 at dinner. MC, V. Mon–Tues and Thurs–Fri 11am–3pm; daily 5:30–9pm. Wine shop Thurs–Tues 11am–7pm.

INEXPENSIVE

Café Sarafornia AMERICAN   When Calistoga locals want a quick, inexpensive fix for breakfast or lunch, this is where they come. Café Sarafornia is pleasantly homey, a clean, bright, cheery bastion for late risers who prefer to eat their huevos rancheros or salmon and eggs at noon. (Breakfast is served all day.) The cafe consists of little more than a U-shaped counter, a few booths, wood and tile floors, and a series of bucolic wall murals. The menu is a lesson in simplicity—burgers, hot dogs, pastas, sandwiches, salads, and requisite small-town specials such as chicken-fried steak with red-eye gravy. And if you like to sweat and holler, be sure to sample the five-alarm chili. The cafe also offers kids' meals for a mere $4.25.

1413 Lincoln Ave. (at Washington St.), Calistoga. © 707/942-0555. Main courses breakfast $6–$10, lunch $6–$12. MC, V. Daily 7am–3pm.

Pacifico MEXICAN If you're in the mood for Mexican food, Pacifico is the place. The rather mundane-looking facade opens up into a surprisingly festive interior, complete with brilliantly colorful Mexican artwork and pottery, huge potted palm trees, and a south-of-the-border bar, complete with faux tile roof and waterfall. The menu is *muy grande,* covering just about every conceivable region in Mexico, from Tacos de Oaxaquenos (grilled, marinated chicken tacos topped with guajillo chile salsa) to Enchiladas del Ray (filled with Chihuahua cheese and covered with chile verde sauce).

1237 Lincoln Ave. (between Myrtle and Cedar sts.), Calistoga. © 707/942-4400. Lunch and dinner main courses $6.75–$15. MC, V. Mon–Thurs 11:30am–10pm, Fri 11am–10pm, Sat–Sun 10am–10pm.

Palisades Market 🐟🐟 DELI/MARKET Trust me, sandwiches as delicious as those served at this adorable, old-fashioned gourmet market and deli are an absolute rarity and a surefire addiction. Drop in for wine, juice, soda, cheese, tamales, green salads, lasagna, soup, picnic items, and every kind of treat you can think of, but under no circumstances should you skip the sandwiches. If they have chicken and Swiss cheese and almond butter on a toasted bun, don't hesitate! Order it heated and devour immediately. I promise you'll remember it for days. Other favorites: ham and gruyere cheese, onions, lettuce, mayo, and dijon mustard on a baguette or roast beef, cheddar cheese, grilled onions, lettuce, and roasted garlic mayo on a soft French roll. Call 2 days in advance, and Palisades will even box a lunch for you; $13 will get you a sandwich, salad, fruit, cookie, and utensils. Pay a few extra dollars for the additions of a cheese wedge, olives, and an extra cookie.

1506 Lincoln Ave., Calistoga. © 707/942-9549. Sandwiches $3.75–$7.95. AE, MC, V. Sun–Wed 7:30am–6pm; Thurs–Sat 7:30am–7pm.

Wappo Bar & Bistro 🐟🐟 GLOBAL One of the best alfresco dining experiences in the Wine Country is under Wappo's honeysuckle-and-vine-covered arbor. Unfortunately, during my last visit food and service is a very distant second. But much can be forgiven when the wine's flowing and you're surrounded by pastoral splendor. The menu offers a global selection of choices, from tandoori chicken to roast rabbit with oven tomato tagliarini. Desserts of choice are black-bottom coconut cream pie and strawberry-rhubarb pie.

1226B Washington St. (off Lincoln Ave.), Calistoga. © 707/942-4712. Main courses $14–$22. AE, MC, V. Wed–Mon 11:30am–2:30pm and 6–9:30pm.

6 Where to Stock Up for a Picnic & Where to Enjoy It

You could easily plan your whole trip around restaurant reservations. But put together one of the world's best gourmet picnics, and the valley's your oyster. There are myriad places to spread your blanket, from grassy meadows to picnic tables at the foot of the vineyards. Best of all, you don't have to count on the maitre d' for the best seat in the house. Go ahead, break out that bottle of your newfound favorite cabernet, indulge in truffle-flavored pâté, hand-feed imported chocolates to your picnic partner. The price will be a fraction of what it would cost to eat in most Wine Country restaurants, and the overall experience will be unforgettable.

One of the finest gourmet-food stores in the Wine Country, if not all of California, is the **Oakville Grocery Co.** 𝒜, 7856 St. Helena Hwy. at Oakville Cross Road (© **707/944-8802**). Here you can put together the provisions for a memorable picnic, or, if you give them at least 24 hours' notice, the staff can prepare a picnic basket for you. You'll find shelves crammed with the best breads and the choicest selection of cheeses in the northern Bay Area, as well as pâtés, cold cuts, crackers, top-quality olive oils, fresh foie gras (domestic and French, seasonally), smoked Norwegian salmon, fresh caviar (Beluga, Sevruga, Osetra), and, of course, an exceptional selection of California wines. The Oakville Grocery Co. is open daily from 9am to 6pm; it also has an espresso bar tucked in the corner (open daily 7am–6pm), offering breakfast and lunch items, and house-baked pastries.

Another of my favorite places to browse is **Dean & Deluca,** 607 S. Main St. (Hwy. 29), north of Zinfandel Lane and south of Sulphur Springs Road in St. Helena (© **707/967-9980**). This ultimate gourmet grocery store is like a world's fair of foods, where everything is beautifully displayed and usually quite pricey. As you pace the barn-wood plank floors, you'll stumble upon more high-end edibles than you've ever seen under one roof: local organic produce; 200 domestic and imported cheeses (with an on-site aging room to ensure proper ripeness and plenty of free samples once you get to the front of the line); shelves and shelves of tapenades, pastas, oils, hand-packed dried herbs and spices, chocolates, sauces, and cookware; an espresso bar; one hell of a bakery section; and more. Along the back wall you can watch the professional chefs prepare gourmet takeout—try the fresh oven-roasted salmon, grilled pork chops, or fried chicken; soups and salads are wonderful, too. Adjoining is their huge wine store with an impressive 1,200-label collection. Hours are daily from 9am to 7pm. (The espresso bar opens Mon–Sat at 7:30am and Sun at 9am.)

If you're in the northern part of the valley, go directly to down-home and downright delicious **Palisades Market,** 1506 Lincoln Ave., Calistoga (© **707/942-9549**), which is open daily from 7:30am to 7pm.

Also see p. 69 for details on **V. Sattui Winery,** 1111 White Lane (at Hwy. 29), St. Helena (© **707/963-7774**). Besides an enormous selection of wines and gourmet deli items—including 200 kinds of cheeses and desserts such as white-chocolate cheesecake—you'll also find extensive picnic facilities, making this winery one of the most popular stops along Highway 29.

If you crave a quiet, more pastoral picnic spot, head for one of the four picnic tables at **Robert Keenan Winery** in St. Helena (p. 72), located right outside the winery and surrounded by vineyards, offering stunning views. Or try the beautiful picnic grounds situated amidst 350-year-old moss-covered oak trees at **Cuvaison** in Calistoga (p. 76); the spectacular grounds at **Niebaum-Coppola** in Rutherford (p. 65); the vineyard-centric spots at **Pine Ridge** Winery (p. 59); or the Wine Country's premier picnicking site, **Rutherford Hill Winery** (p. 67), which boasts superb views of the valley.

Sonoma Valley

Sonoma Valley is often thought of as the "other" Wine Country, forever in the shadow of Napa Valley. It's true that Sonoma Valley doesn't have as much going on as Napa Valley. You won't find as many wineries, shopping outlets, or world-class restaurants here. But its less developed, more backcountry character is exactly its charm. Besides, there is more than enough to do here to fill your vacation time.

Sonoma Valley is far more rural and less traveled than its neighbor to the east, offering a more genuine away-from-it-all experience than its more commercial cousin. The roads are less crowded, the pace is slower, and the whole valley is still relatively free of slick tourist attractions and big-name hotels. Commercialization has, for the most part, not yet taken hold. Small, family-owned wineries are still Sonoma Valley's mainstay, just as in the old days of winemaking, when everyone started with the intention of going broke and loved every minute of it. (As the saying goes in these parts, "It takes a large fortune to make a small fortune.")

Unlike in Napa Valley, in Sonoma Valley you won't find palatial wineries with million-dollar art collections, aerial trams, and Hollywood ego trips (read: Niebaum-Coppola). Rather, Sonoma Valley offers a refreshing dose of reality, where modestly sized wineries are integrated into the community rather than perched on hilltops like corporate citadels. If Napa Valley feels like a fantasyland, where everything exists to service the almighty grape and the visitors it attracts, then Sonoma Valley is its antithesis, an unpretentious gaggle of ordinary towns and ranches. The result, as you wind your way through the valley, is a chance to experience what Napa Valley must have been like long before the Seagrams and Moët et Chandons of the world turned the Wine Country into a major tourist destination.

1 Orientation & Getting Around

Sonoma Valley is some 17 miles long and 7 miles wide, and it is bordered by two mountain ranges: the Mayacamas Mountains to the east and the Sonoma Mountains to the west. One major road, High-way 12 (also known as the Sonoma Hwy.), passes through the val-ley, starting at the northern edge of the Carneros District, leading though the communities of Sonoma, Glen Ellen, and Kenwood, and ending at the southern boundary, Santa Rosa. Conveniently, most of the wineries—as well as most of the hotels, shops, and restaurants—are either in the town of Sonoma, along Highway 12, or a short distance from it. Of the numerous side roads that branch off Highway 12, only Bennett Valley Road to the west and Trinity Road (aka Oakville Grade) to the east lead over the mountain ranges and out of the valley, and neither is easy to navigate. If you're com-ing from Napa, I strongly suggest that you take the leisurely south-ern route along Highway 12/121 rather than tackle Trinity Road, which is a real brake-smoker.

ALONG HIGHWAY 12: SONOMA'S TOWNS IN BRIEF

As you approach the Wine Country from the south, you must first pass through the **Carneros District,** a cool, windswept region that borders San Pablo Bay and marks the entrance to both Napa and Sonoma valleys. Until the latter part of the 20th century, this mix-ture of marsh, sloughs, and rolling hills was mainly used as sheep pasture. (*Carneros* means "sheep" in Spanish.) After experimental plantings yielded slow-growing yet high-quality grapes—particu-larly chardonnay and pinot noir—several Napa Valley and Sonoma Valley wineries expanded their plantings here, eventually establish-ing the Carneros District as an American viticultural appellation. Although about a dozen wineries are spread throughout the region, there are no major towns or attractions—just plenty of gorgeous scenery as you cruise along Highway 121, the major junction between Napa and Sonoma.

At the northern boundary of the Carneros District, along High-way 12, is the centerpiece of Sonoma Valley: the midsized town of **Sonoma,** which owes much of its appeal to Mexican general Mari-ano Guadalupe Vallejo. Vallejo fashioned this pleasant, slow-paced community after a typical Mexican village—right down to its cen-tral plaza, Sonoma's geographical and commercial center. The plaza sits at the top of a T formed by Broadway (Hwy. 12) and Napa Street. Most of the surrounding streets form a grid pattern around this axis, making Sonoma easy to navigate. The plaza's Bear Flag Monument marks the spot where the crude Bear Flag was raised in 1846, signaling the end of Mexican rule; the symbol was later adopted by the state of California and placed on its flag. The 8-acre park at the center of the plaza, complete with two ponds that are populated with ducks and geese, is perfect for an afternoon siesta in the cool shade. My favorite attraction, however, is the flock of brilliantly feathered chickens that roam unfettered through the streets of Sonoma—a sight you'll *definitely* never see in Napa.

About 7 miles north of Sonoma on Highway 12 is the town of **Glen Ellen,** which, though just a fraction of the size of Sonoma, is home to several of the valley's finest wineries, restaurants, and inns. Aside from the addition of a few new restaurants, this charming Wine Country town hasn't changed much since the days when Jack London settled on his Beauty Ranch, about a mile west. Other than the wineries, you'll find few real signs of commercialism; the shops and restaurants, located along one main winding lane, cater to a small, local clientele—that is, until the summer tourist season, when traffic nearly triples on the weekends. If you're as yet undecided about where you want to set up camp during your visit to the Wine Country, I highly recommend this lovable little town.

A few miles north of Glen Ellen along Highway 12 is the tiny town of **Kenwood,** the northernmost outpost of Sonoma Valley. Though the Kenwood Vineyards wines are well known throughout the United States, the town itself consists of little more than a few restaurants, wineries, and modest homes recessed into the wooded hillsides. The nearest lodging, the luxurious Kenwood Inn & Spa, is located about a mile south. Kenwood makes for a pleasant day trip—lunch at Café Citti, a tour of Chateau St. Jean, dinner at Kenwood Restaurant & Bar—before returning to Glen Ellen or Sonoma for the night.

A few miles beyond Kenwood is **Santa Rosa,** the county seat of Sonoma, home to more than 150,000 residents, and the gateway to northern Sonoma wine country. Historically, it's best known as the hometown of horticulturist Luther Burbank, who produced more than 800 new varieties of fruits, vegetables, and plants during his 50-year tenure here. Today it's a burgeoning city and the gateway to northern Sonoma wine country. Unless you're armed with a map, however, it's best to avoid exploring the large, sprawling area and its rural surroundings, as it's easy to get lost.

VISITOR INFORMATION

While you're in Sonoma, stop by the **Sonoma Valley Visitors Bureau,** 453 1st St. E., in the Carnegie Library Building (© **707/ 996-1090;** www.sonomavalley.com). It's open daily from 9am to 7pm in summer and from 9am to 6pm in winter. An additional **visitors**

bureau is located a few miles south of the square, at 25200 Arnold Dr. (Hwy. 121; ℂ **707/935-4747**), at the entrance to Viansa Winery; it's open daily from 9am to 4pm, and from 9am to 5pm in summer.

TOURING SONOMA VALLEY BY BIKE

Sonoma and its neighboring towns are so small, close together, and relatively flat that it's not difficult to get around on two wheels. In fact, if you're not in a great hurry, there's no better way to tour Sonoma Valley than via bicycle. You can rent a bike at the **Goodtime Bicycle Company** ℛ (ℂ **888/525-0453** or 707/938-0453; www.goodtimetouring.com). Goodtime will happily point you to easy bike trails, or you can take one of its organized excursions to Kenwood-area wineries or to southern Sonoma wineries. Not only does Goodtime provide a gourmet lunch featuring local Sonoma products, but it will also carry any wine you purchase while you ride, and it will help with shipping arrangements. Lunch rides start at 10:30am and end at around 3:30pm. The cost, including food and equipment, is $99 per person. Bike rentals cost $25 a day and include helmets, locks, and everything else you'll need (including delivery to your local hotel). Bikes are also available for rent from **Sonoma Valley Cyclery,** 20093 Broadway, Sonoma (ℂ **707/935-3377**), for $6 per hour or $25 a day.

FAST FACTS: Sonoma Valley

Hospitals The **Sonoma Valley Hospital,** 347 Andrieux St. (ℂ **707/935-5000**), in downtown Sonoma, is a district hospital that provides inpatient, outpatient, and continuing care to the public. Its emergency room is supported by state-of-the-art equipment and is staffed 24 hours a day by physicians and nurses who are specifically trained in emergency treatment. SVH also has an intensive care unit and a pediatric center, and it provides surgical services.

  Santa Rosa Memorial Hospital, 1165 Montgomery Dr. in Santa Rosa (ℂ **707/546-3210**), about a 30-minute drive north from Sonoma, offers 24-hour emergency service as well as complete inpatient and outpatient services, a cardiac center, pediatric services, and a dental clinic.

Information See "Visitor Information," above.

Newspapers/Magazines The main newspaper in Sonoma Valley is the *Press Democrat,* a *New York Times* publication that is printed daily and distributed at newsstands throughout Sonoma, Lake, Napa, and Mendocino counties. Sonoma's local paper is the *Sonoma Index Tribune;* published twice a week and available at newsstands around town, it covers regional news, events, and issues. Also available around town is the *Sonoma Valley Visitors Guide,* a slender free publication that lists just about every sightseeing, recreation, shopping, lodging, and dining option in the valley, as well as a winery map.

Pharmacy The pharmacy at **Long's Drugs,** 201 W. Napa St., Sonoma (📞 707/938-4730), is open Monday through Friday from 9am to 8pm, Saturday and Sunday from 10am to 6pm. If you prefer a more personable place to get your prescription filled, try **Adobe Drug,** 303 W. Napa St., Sonoma (📞 707/938-1144), a locally owned drugstore that claims to be Sonoma's "Prescription Specialists" and will even make deliveries; it's open Monday through Friday from 9am to 7pm, Saturday from 9am to 6pm.

Police For the local police, call 📞 707/996-3602, or in an emergency, call 📞 911.

Post Offices In **downtown Sonoma,** the post office is at 617 Broadway, at Patton Street (📞 707/996-9311). The **Glen Ellen** post office is at 13720 Arnold St., at O'Donnel Lane (📞 707/996-9233). Both branches are open Monday through Friday from 8:30am to 5pm.

Shipping Companies See "The Ins & Outs of Shipping Wine Home," in chapter 3.

Taxis Call **A-C Taxi** at 📞 707/526-4888.

2 Touring the Wineries

Sonoma Valley is currently home to more than 40 wineries (including California's first winery, Buena Vista, founded in 1857) and 13,000 acres of vineyards, which produce roughly 40 types of wine.

Unlike the rigidly structured tours at many of Napa Valley's corporate-owned wineries, tastings and tours on the Sonoma side of the Mayacamas Mountains are low-key, often free, and include plenty of friendly banter between the winemakers and their guests.

Sonoma Valley Wineries

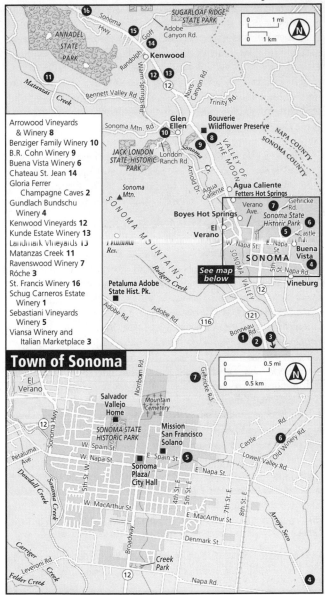

Arrowood Vineyards
    & Winery **8**
Benziger Family Winery **10**
B.R. Cohn Winery **9**
Buena Vista Winery **6**
Chateau St. Jean **14**
Gloria Ferrer
    Champagne Caves **2**
Gundlach Bundschu
    Winery **4**
Kenwood Vineyards **12**
Kunde Estate Winery **13**
Landmark Vineyards **15**
Matanzas Creek **11**
Ravenswood Winery **7**
Róche **3**
St. Francis Winery **16**
Schug Carneros Estate
    Winery **1**
Sebastiani Vineyards
    Winery **5**
Viansa Winery and
    Italian Marketplace **3**

SUGARLOAF RIDGE STATE PARK

ANNADEL STATE PARK

Kenwood

Glen Ellen

Bouverie Wildflower Preserve

JACK LONDON STATE HISTORIC PARK

VALLEY OF THE MOON

NAPA COUNTY
SONOMA COUNTY

SONOMA MOUNTAINS

Agua Caliente
Fetters Hot Springs

Boyes Hot Springs

El Verano

Sonoma State Historic Park

Castle

SONOMA

Buena Vista

Vineburg

Petaluma Adobe State Hist. Pk.

See map below

0   1 mi
0   1 km

Town of Sonoma

El Verano

Salvador Vallejo Home

Mountain Cemetery

SONOMA STATE HISTORIC PARK

Mission San Francisco Solano

Sonoma Plaza/ City Hall

Creek Park

0   0.5 mi
0   0.5 km

The towns and wineries covered below are organized geographically from south to north, starting at the intersection of Highway 37 and Highway 121 in the Carneros District and ending in Kenwood. The wineries here tend to be a little more spread out than they are in Napa Valley, but they're easy to find. Still, it's best to decide which wineries you're most interested in and devise a touring strategy before you set out so you don't find yourself doing a lot of backtracking. (For more on this, see "Strategies for Touring the Wine Country," in chapter 3; and check out the map "Sonoma Valley Wineries" on p. 131 to get your bearings.)

Below is a great selection of Sonoma Valley wineries. If you'd like a complete list of local wineries, be sure to pick up one of the free guides to the valley available at the **Sonoma Valley Visitors Bureau** (see "Visitor Information," above).

THE CARNEROS DISTRICT

Róche   The first winery you'll encounter as you enter Sonoma Valley, Róche (pronounced *rosh*) is typical of the area—a small, family-run operation that focuses on one or two varietals and has very limited distribution. (Róche wines, in fact, are sold exclusively through the tasting room.) Situated atop a gently sloping knoll, the ranch-style winery and surrounding 2,200 acres of vineyards and estate are owned by Genevieve and Joe Róche, who originally bought the property with no intention of starting a winery. But in the early 1980s, a colleague suggested that they experiment with a few vines of chardonnay—and the results were so impressive that they decided to go into business making estate-grown chardonnay, pinot noir, and syrah.

The Róches produce only about 10,000 cases per year, some of which are bought before the wine even hits the bottle. Tastings are complimentary for nonreserve wines, and prices range from $10 for a Tamarix pinot noir blanc to $36 for the unfiltered Estate reserve pinot noir. Picnic tables overlooking the valley and San Pablo Bay are available, though you'd probably prefer lunching at neighboring Viansa Winery and Italian Marketplace (see below).

28700 Arnold Dr. (Hwy. 121), Sonoma. © **800/825-9475** or 707/935-7115. www. rochewinery.com. Daily 10am–6pm (5pm in winter). No tours available.

Viansa Winery and Italian Marketplace ⊛ *Finds*   This sprawling Tuscan-style villa perches atop a knoll overlooking the entire lower Sonoma Valley. Viansa is the brainchild of Sam and Vicki Sebastiani, who left the family dynasty to create their own temple to

food and wine. (*Viansa* is a contraction of "Vicki and Sam.") While Sam, a third-generation winemaker, runs the winery, Vicki manages the marketplace, a large room crammed with a cornucopia of high-quality preserves, mustards, olive oils, pastas, salads, breads, desserts, Italian tableware, cookbooks, and wine-related gifts.

The winery, which sells its varietals exclusively at the winery and through their extensive mail-order business called the Tuscan Club, has established a favorable reputation for its Italian varietals such as muscat canelli, sangiovese, and nebbiolo. Five-dollar tastings are poured at the east end of the marketplace, and the self-guided tour includes a trip through the underground barrel-aging cellar adorned with colorful hand-painted murals. Free guided tours are held daily at 11am and 2pm.

Viansa is also one of the few wineries in Sonoma Valley that sells deli items—the focaccia sandwiches are delicious. You can dine alfresco while you admire the bucolic wetlands view.

25200 Arnold Dr. (Hwy. 121), Sonoma. © 800/995-4740 or 707/935-4700. www. viansa.com. Daily 10am–5pm. No appointment needed for the self-guided tour.

Gloria Ferrer Champagne Caves ★★ Finds

When you have had it up to here with chardonnays and pinots, it's time to pay a visit to Gloria Ferrer, the grande dame of the Wine Country's sparkling-wine producers. Who's Gloria? She's the wife of José Ferrer, whose family has made sparkling wine for 5 centuries. The family business, Freixenet, is the largest producer of sparkling wine in the world; Cordon Negro is its most popular brand. That equals big bucks, and certainly a good chunk went into building this palatial estate. Glimmering like Oz high atop a gently sloping hill, it overlooks the verdant Carneros District. On a sunny day, enjoying a glass of dry brut while soaking in the magnificent views is a must.

If you're unfamiliar with the term *méthode champenoise,* be sure to take the free 30-minute tour of the fermenting tanks, bottling line, and caves brimming with racks of yeast-laden bottles. Afterward, retire to the elegant tasting room for a flute of brut or cuvée ($4–$7 a glass, $18 and up per bottle), find an empty chair on the veranda, and say, "Ahhh. *This* is the life." There are picnic tables, but it's usually too windy for comfort, and you must buy a bottle of sparkling wine to secure a table.

23555 Carneros Hwy. (Hwy. 121), Sonoma. © 707/996-7256. www.gloriaferrer. com. Daily 10:30am–5:15pm. Tours daily; call for schedule (call © 707/933-1917 after 9:30am the day you plan to visit for an updated tour schedule for that day).

Schug Carneros Estate Winery A native of Germany's Rhine River valley, Walter Schug (pronounced *shewg*) comes from a long line of pinot noir vintners. After graduating from the prestigious German wine institute of Geisenheim in 1959, he came to California and worked as winemaker for Joseph Phelps, where he established his reputation as one of California's top cabernet sauvignon and Riesling producers. In 1980, he launched his own label from a vineyard he tended at Phelps, and he left soon afterward to build Schug Carneros Estate Winery. Since then, Schug's wines have achieved world-class status, and an astounding amount of his wine is sent overseas.

The winery is situated on top of a rise overlooking the surrounding Carneros District, a prime region for cool-climate grapes such as chardonnay and pinot noir (Schug's predominant wines). Its post-and-beam architecture reflects the Schug family's German heritage; the tasting room, however, is quite ordinary and small, designed more for practicality than pomp and circumstance (a radical contrast to neighboring Viansa and Gloria Ferrer). Typical of Sonoma wineries, there's no tasting fee for new releases (reserve tasting $5), and bottle prices are all quite reasonable, ranging from $15 for a Sonoma Valley sauvignon blanc to $50 for a Heritage reserve cabernet. The winery has new picnic facilities, but picnicking can be breezy when the winds upwell from the neighboring dairy farm. More fun: *pétanque* courts, Carneros views, and cave tours by appointment.

602 Bonneau Rd. (west of Hwy. 121), Sonoma. Ⓒ **800/966-9365** or 707/939-9363. www.schugwinery.com. Daily 10am–5pm. Tours by appointment only.

SONOMA

Gundlach Bundschu Winery ⭐⭐ If it looks like the people working here are actually enjoying themselves, that's because they are. Gundlach Bundschu (pronounced *gun*-lock *bun*-shoe) is the quintessential Sonoma winery—nonchalant in appearance but obsessed with wine: The GB clan are a nefarious lot, infamous for wild stunts such as holding up Napa's Wine Train on horseback and—egad!—serving Sonoma wines to their captives; the small tasting room looks not unlike a bomb shelter, the Talking Heads is their version of Muzak, and the "art" consists of a dozen witty black-and-white posters promoting GB wines.

This is the oldest continually family-owned and -operated winery in California, going into its sixth generation since Jacob Gundlach harvested his first crop in 1858. Drop in to sample chardonnay, pinot noir, merlot, cabernet, and more. Prices for the 15 distinct wines range from a very reasonable $14 per bottle for the Polar Bear-itage (ha, ha) white table wine to $65 for the Vintage reserve cabernet sauvignon, though most prices are in the mid-teens. Tastings are $5 and tours, which include a trip into the 430-foot cave, are held regularly on weekends and by appointment on weekdays.

Gundlach Bundschu has the best picnic grounds in the valley, though you have to walk to the top of Towles' Hill to earn the sensational view. They also have great activities (Midsummer Mozart Festival, film fests), so call or check the website if you want to join the fun.

2000 Denmark St. (off Eighth St. E.), Sonoma. (✆) 707/938-5277. www.gunbun. com. Daily 11am–4:30pm. Tours last 10–20 min. and are offered Sat–Sun; by appointment on weekdays.

Sebastiani Vineyards & Winery The name Sebastiani is practically synonymous with Sonoma. What started in 1904, when Samuele Sebastiani began producing his first wines, has in three generations grown into a small empire. After a few years of seismic retrofitting, a facelift, and a temporary tasting room, the original 1904 winery is now open to the public, with more extensive educational tours, an 80-foot S-shaped tasting bar, and lots of shopping opportunities in the gift shop. In the tasting room's mini-museum area you can see the winery's original crusher and press, as well as the world's largest collection of oak-barrel carvings, crafted by local artist Earle Brown. You can sample an extensive selection of wines for $8. Bottle prices are reasonable, ranging from $15 to $75. A picnic area adjoins the cellars, but a far more scenic spot is across the parking lot, in Sebastiani's Cherryblock Vineyards.

389 Fourth St. E., Sonoma. (✆) 800/888-5532 or 707/938-5532. www.sebastiani. com. Daily 10am–5pm. Call for tour schedules; no reservations necessary.

Buena Vista Winery Count Agoston Haraszthy, the Hungarian émigré who is universally regarded as the father of California's wine industry, founded this historic winery in 1857. A close friend of General Vallejo, Haraszthy returned from Europe in 1861 with 100,000 of the finest vine cuttings, which he made available to all growers. Although Buena Vista's winemaking now takes place at an ultramodern facility in the Carneros District, the winery maintains a tasting room inside the restored 1857 Press House. The beautiful stone-crafted room brims with wines, wine-related gifts, and accessories, as well as a small art gallery along the inner balcony.

Tastings are $5 (plus glass) and $10 for older reserve wines. You can take the self-guided tour any time during operating hours; the

Heritage Tour, offered daily by appointment at 11am and 2pm, costs $15 and includes a vertical tasting and a tour emphasizing the winery's history, viticulture, and oenology. After tasting, grab your favorite bottle, a selection of cheeses, salami, bread (fresh on weekends, crackers during the week), and pâté (all available in the tasting room), and plant yourself at one of the many picnic tables in the lush, verdant setting.

18000 Old Winery Rd. (off E. Napa St., slightly northeast of downtown), Sonoma. ℂ **800/926-1266** or 707/938-1266. www.buenavistawinery.com. Daily 10am–5pm. No appointment needed for the self-guided tour; Heritage Tour $15 by appointment only.

Ravenswood Winery   Compared to old heavies such as Sebastiani and Buena Vista, Ravenswood is a relative newcomer to the Sonoma wine scene. It has quickly established itself as the sine qua non of zinfandel, the versatile grape that's quickly gaining ground on the rapacious cabernet sauvignon. In fact, Ravenswood is the first winery in the United States to focus primarily on zins, which make up about three-quarters of its 700,000-case production; it also produces merlot, cabernet sauvignon, and a small amount of chardonnay.

The winery is smartly designed—recessed into the hillside to protect its treasures from the simmering summers. Tours follow the winemaking process from grape to glass and include a visit to the aromatic oak-barrel aging rooms. A gourmet Barbecue Overlooking the Vineyards runs from 11am to 2:30pm on weekends from Memorial Day through September; call for details and reservations. You're welcome to bring your own picnic basket to any of the tables. Tastings are $5, which is refundable with purchase.

18701 Gehricke Rd. (off Lovall Valley Rd.), Sonoma. ℂ **800/NO-WIMPY** or 707/938-1960. www.ravenswood-wine.com. Daily 10am–5pm. Tours, by reservation only, at 10:30am.

GLEN ELLEN

B. R. Cohn Winery   You may not have heard of Bruce Cohn, but you've certainly heard of the Doobie Brothers, the San Francisco band he managed to fame and fortune. He used part of his share of that fortune to purchase this wonderfully bucolic estate with its whitewashed farmhouse and groves of rare olive trees. Cohn, a native of Sonoma County, started making his own wine in 1984 and was an immediate success. The new tasting room, which opened in 2003, showcases framed gold and platinum albums and is home to the friendly and informative staff who pours $5 tastings (applied

toward purchase) of cabernet, pinot noir, chardonnay, syrah (new as of 2003) and an occasional merlot. Bottle prices range from the mid-teens to $100, and the winery often sells selections that aren't available elsewhere. Though best known for his cabernet sauvignon, it's a case of Cohn's reserve chardonnay you'll want to send back home, along with a bottle or two of his award-winning (and pricey) olive oil. There are a few picnic tables on the property, but it's not a bad idea to bring along a blanket and relax on the terraced hills of plush lawn overlooking the vineyards.

15000 Sonoma Hwy. (Hwy. 12, just north of Madrone Rd.), Glen Ellen. © **800/330-4064** or 707/938-4064. www.brcohn.com. Daily 10am–5pm. Tours by appointment.

Arrowood Vineyards & Winery   Richard Arrowood had already established a reputation as a master winemaker at Chateau St. Jean when he and his wife, Alis Demers Arrowood, set out on their own in 1986. Even though the winery was purchased by Mondavi in 2000, Arrowood still embodies Richard's winemaking vision—especially since he's still making the juice. The picturesque winery stands on a gently rising hillside lined with perfectly manicured vineyards. Tastings take place in the Hospitality House, the newer of Arrowood's two stately gray-and-white buildings, which are fashioned after New England farmhouses, complete with wraparound porches. Richard's focus is on making world-class wine with minimal intervention, and his results are impressive: More than one of his current releases has been awarded over 90 points (out of 100) from *Wine Spectator*. Mind you, excellence doesn't come cheap. Prices start at $29 for a chardonnay and quickly climb to $85 for the reserve cabernet. Arrowood charges $5 for tastings, and if you're curious about what near-perfection tastes like, it's well worth it. No picnic facilities are available.

14347 Sonoma Hwy. (Hwy. 12), Glen Ellen. © **800/938-5170** or 707/935-2600. www.arrowoodvineyards.com. Daily 10am–4:30pm. Tours, by appointment only, are at 10:30am and 2:30pm daily.

Benziger Family Winery ★★ *Finds*   When you visit here, you know you are indeed visiting a family winery. At any given time, three generations of Benzigers (pronounced *ben*-zigger) may be running around tending to chores, and they instantly make you feel as if you're part of the clan. The pastoral, user-friendly property features an exceptional self-guided tour ("The most comprehensive tour in the wine industry," according to *Wine Spectator*), gardens, a spacious tasting room staffed by amiable folks, and an art gallery.

The $10 40-minute tram tour, held six to eight times daily and pulled by a beefy tractor through the vineyards, is both informative and fun and includes wine tasting. *Tip:* Tram tickets—a hot item in the summer—are available on a first-come, first-served basis, so either arrive early or stop by in the morning to pick up afternoon tickets.

Tastings start at $5, and the winery offers several scenic picnic spots.

1883 London Ranch Rd. (off Arnold Dr., on the way to Jack London State Historic Park), Glen Ellen. © **800/989-8890** or 707/935-3000. www.benziger.com. Tasting room daily 10am–5pm. $10 tram tours daily (weather permitting) includes tasting; call for times.

KENWOOD

Kunde Estate Winery   Expect a friendly, unintimidating welcome at this scenic winery, run by four generations of the Kundes since 1904. One of the largest grape suppliers in the area, the Kunde family (pronounced *kun*-dee) has devoted 800 acres of its 2,000-acre ranch to growing ultrapremium-quality grapes, which it provides to many Sonoma and Napa wineries. This abundance allows the Kundes to make nothing but estate wines (wines made from grapes grown on the Kunde property, as opposed to also using grapes purchased from other growers).

The tasting room is located in a spiffy 17,000-square-foot winemaking facility, which features specialized crushing equipment that enables the winemaker to run whole clusters to the press—a real advantage in white-wine production. Tastings of four estate releases are $5 (refunded with purchase) and reserve tastings will set you back $10; bottle prices range from $15 for a Magnolia Lane sauvignon blanc to $50 for a Drummond Vineyards cabernet sauvignon; most labels sell in the high teens. The tasting room also has a gift shop and large windows overlooking the bottling room and tank room.

The tour of the property's extensive wine caves includes a history of the winery. Private tours are available by appointment, but most folks are happy to just stop by for some vino and to relax at one of the many picnic tables placed around the man-made pond. Animal lovers will appreciate Kunde's preservation efforts: The property has a duck estuary with more than 50 species (which can be seen by appointment only).

10155 Sonoma Hwy., Kenwood. © **707/833-5501**. www.kunde.com. Tastings daily 10:30am–4:30pm. Cave tours Tues–Thurs 11am, Fri–Mon on the hour 11am–3pm.

Kenwood Vineyards   Kenwood's history dates to 1906, when the Pagani brothers made their living selling wine straight from the barrel and into the jug. In 1970, the Lee family bought the property and dumped a ton of money into converting the aging winery into a modern, high-production facility (most of it cleverly concealed in the original barnlike buildings). Today the Korbell-Heck Estates conglomerate owns the winery with winemaker Michael Lee at the helm until his retirement at the end of 2003. Still, Kenwood keeps its solid reputation for consistent quality with each of its varietals: cabernet sauvignon, chardonnay, zinfandel, pinot noir, merlot, and most popular, sauvignon blanc—a crisp, light wine with hints of melon.

Although the winery looks rather modest in size, its output is staggering: Nearly 500,000 cases of ultra-premium wines fermented in steel tanks and French and American oak barrels. Popular with collectors is winemaker Michael Lee's Artist Series cabernet sauvignon, a limited production from the winery's best vineyards, featuring labels with original artwork by renowned artists. The tasting room, housed in one of the old barns, offers free tastings of most varieties and sells gift items. Private reserve tastings will set you back $2 per taste or three tastes for $5.

9592 Sonoma Hwy. (Hwy. 12), Kenwood. ℂ 707/833-5891. www.kenwoodvineyards. com. Daily 10am–4:30pm.

Chateau St. Jean ⊛ *Finds*   Chateau St. Jean is notable for its exceptionally beautiful buildings, expansive landscaped grounds, and gourmet market–like tasting room. Among California wineries, it's a pioneer in *vineyard designation*—the procedure of making wine from, and naming it for, a single vineyard. A private drive takes you to what was once a 250-acre country retreat built in 1920; a well-manicured lawn overlooking the meticulously maintained vineyards is now a picnic area, complete with a fountain and umbrella-shaded picnic tables. You can take a self-guided tour of the gardens or pay $25 for a private tour of the winery, gardens, and history and vineyard-designated and reserve wine tasting.

Back in the huge tasting room—where there's also a gourmet deli and plenty of housewares for sale—you can sample five featured Chateau St. Jean wines, which range from chardonnay, pinot noir, cabernet sauvignon to fumé blanc, merlot, Johannisberg Riesling, and gewürztraminer. Tastings are $5 per person. Reserve tastings, held in a more intimate old chateau, is $10 and includes three wines.

8555 Sonoma Hwy. (Hwy. 12; at the foot of Sugarloaf Ridge, just north of Kenwood), Kenwood. © **800/543-7572** or 707/833-4134. www.chateaustjean.com. Tastings and tours daily 10am–5pm.

St. Francis Winery   Although St. Francis Winery makes commendable chardonnay, zinfandel, and cabernet sauvignon, it is best known for its highly coveted merlot. Winemaker Tom Mackey, a former high-school English teacher from San Francisco, has been hailed as the Master of Merlot by *Wine Spectator,* for his uncanny ability to craft the finest merlot in California.

If you've visited this winery before but haven't been in a while, don't follow your memory to the front door. In 2001, St. Francis moved a little farther north, to new digs bordering on the Santa Rosa county line. The original property was planted in 1910 as part of a wedding gift to Alice Kunde (section of the local Kunde family) and christened St. Francis of Assisi in 1979, when Joe Martin and Lloyd Canton—two white-collar executives turned vintners—completed their long-awaited dream winery. Today the winery still owns the property, but there's a new history in development, with much larger facilities, including two tasting rooms and an upscale gift shop. Samples are $5 for current releases, and $20 for a reserve tasting and food pairing. Bottles go for $13 to $85. Now that St. Francis has special activities—holiday cooking demos—it's worth calling or checking the website for its calendar of events.

100 Pythian Rd. (Hwy. 12), Santa Rosa (at the Kenwood border). © **800/543-7713** or 707/833-4666. www.stfranciswine.com. Daily 10am–5pm.

Landmark Vineyards   One of California's oldest exclusively chardonnay estates was first founded in 1972 in the Windsor area of northern Sonoma County. When new housing development started encroaching on the winery's territory, proprietor Damaris Deere W. Ethridge (great-great-granddaughter of John Deere, the tractor baron) moved her operation to northern Sonoma Valley in 1990. The winery, which produces about 27,000 cases annually, is housed in a modest, Mission-style building set on 11 acres of vineyards. The tasting room offers complimentary samples of five current releases and pours reserve tastings for $10. (Note the wall-to-wall mural behind the tasting counter painted by noted Sonoma Co. artist Claudia Wagar.) Wine prices range from $11 for Adobe Canyon chardonnay to $45 for a reserve pinot noir.

The winery has a pond-side picnic area, as well as what is probably the only professional bocce court in the valley (yes, you can play, and yes, they provide instructions). Also available from Memorial

Day to Labor Day are free Belgian horse–drawn wagon tours through the vineyards, offered every Saturday from 11:30am to 3pm.

101 Adobe Canyon Rd. (just east of Hwy. 12), Kenwood. ℭ 800/452-6365 or 707/833-1144. www.landmarkwine.com. Daily 10am–4:30pm. Tours available by appointment.

JUST UP FROM THE VALLEY

Matanzas Creek ⚑ (Finds)   It's not technically in Sonoma Valley, but if there's one winery that's worth a detour, it's Matanzas (pronounced mah-*tan*-zas) Creek. After a scenic 20-minute drive, you'll arrive at one of the prettiest wineries in California, blanketed by fields of lavender (usually in bloom near the end of June), and surrounded by rolling hills of well-tended vineyards.

The winery has a rather unorthodox history. In 1978, Sandra and Bill MacIver, neither of whom had any previous experience in winemaking or business, set out with one goal in mind: to create the finest wines in the country. Actually, they overshot the mark. With the release of their Journey 1990 chardonnay, they were hailed by wine critics as the proud parents of the finest chardonnay ever produced in the United States, comparable to the finest white wines in the world.

This state-of-the-art, environmentally conscious winery produces chardonnay, sauvignon blanc, and cabernet, all of which you can taste for $5. Prices for current releases are, as you would imagine, at the higher end ($20–$95). Also available for purchase is culinary lavender from Matanzas Creek's own lavender field, the largest outside Provence. Purchase a full glass of wine and bring it outside to savor as you wander through these wonderfully aromatic gardens. Picnic tables hidden under groves of oak have pleasant views of the surrounding vineyards. On the return trip, be sure to take the Sonoma Mountain Road detour for a real backcountry experience.

6097 Bennett Valley Rd. (off Warm Springs Rd.), Santa Rosa. ℭ 800/590-6464 or 707/528-6464. www.matanzascreek.com. Daily 10am–4:30pm. Tours daily, by appointment only, at 10:30am, and 3pm weekdays. From Hwy. 12 in Kenwood or Glen Ellen, take Warm Springs Rd. turnoff to Bennett Valley Rd.; the drive takes 15–20 min.

3 More to See & Do

If you tire of visiting Sonoma Valley wineries, you can explore the valley's numerous other sites and attractions. The majority of activities are centered around the town of Sonoma, which is small enough to explore on foot. (The picturesque town plaza is truly worth checking out.) If the weather's warm, I strongly recommend a guided tour of Sonoma Valley via horseback or bicycle, two of the best things to do in the Wine Country (p. 145 and 129).

THE CARNEROS DISTRICT

BIPLANE RIDES   For the adrenaline junkie in your group, **Vintage Aircraft Company** 𝄢 will help you lose your lunch on one of its authentic 1940 Boeing-built Stearman biplanes. Rides range from the Scenic (a leisurely flight over Sonoma Valley) and Aerobatic (loops, rolls, and assorted maneuvers) to—drumroll, please—the Kamikaze, an intensely bowel-shaking aerobatic death wish that's (and I quote) "not for the faint of heart." For two people, prices range from $190 for the Scenic to $250 for the Kamikaze. Vintage Aircraft Company is at the Sonoma Valley Airport, 23982 Arnold Dr. (on Hwy. 121, across from Gloria Ferrer Champagne Caves), Sonoma Valley (© **707/938-2444;** www.vintageaircraft.com). Call for reservations.

SONOMA

The best way to learn about the history of Sonoma is to follow the self-guided *Sonoma Walking Tour* map, provided by the Sonoma League for Historic Preservation. Tour highlights include General Vallejo's 1852 Victorian-style home; the Sonoma Barracks, erected in 1836 to house Mexican army troops; and the Blue Wing Inn, an 1840 hostelry built to accommodate travelers—including John Fremont, Kit Carson, and Ulysses S. Grant—and new settlers while they erected homes in Sonoma. You can purchase the map for $2.75 at the **Sonoma Valley Visitors Bureau** (see "Visitor Information," earlier in this chapter) as well as at the Sonoma Barracks, which is next door to the Mission.

Also worth a look is the **Mission San Francisco Solano de Sonoma,** located on Sonoma Plaza, at the corner of 1st Street East and Spain Street (© **707/938-9560**). Founded in 1823, this was the northernmost—and last—mission built in California. It also was the only mission established on the northern coast by the Mexican government, which wanted to protect its territory from expansionist Russian fur traders. It's now part of Sonoma State Historic Park. Admission is $2 for adults, free for children 17 and under. It's open daily from 10am to 5pm except New Year's Day, Thanksgiving, and Christmas.

It may not be all bells and whistles for adults, but add steam, and that's exactly what **Train Town** is for tots. In this 10-acre

Moments   **The Super Spa**

The **Fairmont Sonoma Mission Inn & Spa,** 18140 Sonoma Hwy. (© 800/862-4945 or 707/938-9000; www.sonoma missioninn.com), has always been the most complete—and the most luxurious—spa in the whole Wine Country. With its recent $20 million, 27,000-square-foot facility, this super spa is now one of the best in the country. The Spanish Mission–style retreat offers more than 50 spa treatments, ever-popular natural mineral baths, and virtually every facility and activity imaginable. You can pamper yourself silly: Soak in mineral baths, have a facial set to music, indulge in a grape-seed body wrap, relax with a massage, take a sauna or herbal steam, go for a dip in the pool—the list goes on and on (and, alas, so will the bill). You can also work off those wicked Wine Country meals with aerobics, weights, and cardio machines; get loose in a yoga class; or just lounge and lunch by the pool. There is a catch. If you're not staying at the hotel you'll have to pay a $45 day-use fee plus extra for any spa treatment. (The $45 fee is waived if you book two or more treatments.) Plus rates here are some of the most expensive in the valley; a 50-minute massage will set you back $119.

mini amusement park the theme is locomotion—as in train rides around the wooded property, over bridges, and past doting parents. Other attractions include a petting zoo, ferris wheel, and carousel. Train Town is on Broadway, between MacArthur Street and Napa Road, Sonoma (© **707/938-3912**). The train keeps a-rolling Friday through Sunday from 10am to 4:30pm October through May and daily 10am to 5pm June through September. Rates to ride the train are $4 adults and $3.50 children and seniors; each additional ride is $1.25 to $1.75 per person.

SHOPPING   Most of Sonoma's shops, which offer everything from food and wine to clothing and books, are located around the plaza. **The Mercado,** a small shopping center at 452 1st St. E., houses several good stores that sell unusual wares. The **Arts Guild of Sonoma,** 140 E. Napa St. (© **707/996-3115**), showcases the works of local artists in a wide variety of styles and media. It's open

Monday, Wednesday and Thursday from 10am to 5pm, Friday and Saturday from 10am to 9pm, and Sunday 10am to 6pm; admission is free.

My favorite stop along the plaza is **Wine Exchange** ⚓, 452 1st St. E. (© **707/938-1794**), which carries more than 700 domestic wines, books on wine, wine paraphernalia, olive oils, and a small selection of cigars. It's a great place to begin your wine experience: You can browse though the numerous racks of bottles and ask questions of the wine-savvy staff. Even the beer connoisseur who's feeling displaced in the Wine Country will be happy at Wine Exchange, where you can find more than 300 beers from around the world. There are $1 wine and beer tastings daily at the small bar in back, which is occupied most evenings by a gaggle of friendly locals. Wine Exchange is open daily from 10am to 6pm. Shipping is available anywhere in the United States.

THE LOCAL FARMER'S MARKET   Obsessed with farm-fresh produce, Sonomans host a year-round **Sonoma Valley Farmer's Market** every Friday morning from 9am to noon at Depot Park on 1st Street West (just north of E. Spain St.). Dozens of growers offer fresh fruits, vegetables, flowers, homemade jams, honey, barbecued turkey, baked goods, and handmade crafts from local artists. It's such a popular gathering place for locals and visitors alike that they added a Tuesday-night market from 5:30pm to dusk April through October. The Tuesday market is held at the plaza in front of City Hall. (There's also a Saturday morning market from 9am to noon on the corner of Oakmont Drive and White Oak in Santa Rosa, about 5 minutes north of Kenwood.)

GLEN ELLEN

Hikers, mountain bikers, horseback riders, and picnickers will enjoy a day spent at **Jack London State Historic Park** ⚓, 2400 London Ranch Rd., off Arnold Drive (© **707/938-5216**). On its 800 acres, which were once home to the renowned writer, you'll find 10 miles of trails, the remains of London's burned-down dream house (as well as some preserved structures), and plenty of ideal picnic spots. An on-site museum, called the House of Happy Walls, was built by Jack's wife to display a collection from the author's life. The park is open daily from 9:30am to 7pm in summer, from 9:30am to 5:30pm in winter; the museum is open daily from 10am to 5pm. Admission to the park is $5 per car, $4 per car for seniors 62 and over. Pick up the $1 self-guided tour map on arrival to get acquainted with the grounds. In summer, golf-cart rides also are offered from noon to 4pm on weekends for those who don't want to hoof it.

SHOPPING   Gourmands might want to stop by **The Olive Press,** 14301 Arnold Dr., in Jack London Village (© **800/9-OLIVE-9** or 707/939-8900). With olive trees abounding in the area and the locals' penchant for gourmet foods, it's no surprise that fresh-pressed olive oil has become a lucrative business in this neck of the woods. Everyone from large commercial outfits to small-volume growers and hobbyists can pile their olives in the hopper and watch the state-of-the-art, Italian-made olive press in action, as it conveys the fruit up a belt, cleans it, and begins the pressing process. There's also a nifty gift shop, but don't expect a bargain here; even if you bring your own bottle, a gallon of oil can go for $128. (You'd be surprised how many olives it takes to make a gallon.) The Press also carries numerous varieties of olive oils, cured olives, and olive-related foods, gifts, and books. Open daily from 10am to 5:30pm.

HORSEBACK RIDING   Long before Sonoma Valley became part of the Wine Country, it was better known as cattle country— and there's no better way to explore the land's old roots than with a guided horseback tour provided by the **Triple Creek Horse Outfit** (© **707/933-1600;** www.triplecreekhorseoutfit.com), which will lead you on a leisurely stroll—with the occasional trot thrown in for thrills. April through October, when the beautiful Jack London State Historic Park is open, you can take a memorable ride through the park. The ride takes you past vineyards owned by London's descendants, across meadows blanketed with lupine, around a lake originally dammed by London, and up to enjoy Sonoma Mountain's panoramic views. Triple Creek also offers regular, sunset, and full-moon rides at Sugarloaf Ridge at the northern end of Sonoma Valley; a route that also winds through deep, shady forests and up to ridge tops with spectacular 360-degree views. Two-hour rides are $60, and it's $40 for a 1-hour ride. Call for additional information and prices.

GOLF   Thanks to the valley's mild climate, golf is a year-round pursuit. At the northern end of Sonoma Valley is the semiprivate **Oakmont Golf Club,** 7025 Oakmont Dr., off the Sonoma High-way, Santa Rosa (© **707/539-0415;** www.oakmontgc.com), which has two 18-hole championship courses, both designed by Ted Robinson, as well as a driving range, clubhouse, and locker rooms. The par 63 East course is considered the most challenging, and the par 72 West course is for higher-handicapped golfers. Greens fees are $32 Monday through Thursday, $37 Friday, and $45 weekends and holidays; carts are $26. Reservations are recommended at least a day in advance on weekdays, and at least a week in advance on weekends.

Originally designed by Sam Whiting in 1926, the **Sonoma Golf Club,** 17700 Arnold Dr., off Boyes Drive (pro shop © **707/ 996-0300**), was completely remodeled in 1991 by Robert Muir Graves, is now owned by the Fairmont Sonoma Mission Inn, and is only accessible if you're staying at the resort. Its par 72, 18-hole, 7,069-yard championship course has recently become private, which means you have to stay at the hotel to play. It's mostly flat, with several tight doglegs around an armada of redwoods and oaks. A driving range was added in the $10-million renovation; a club-house and locker rooms are also provided. Greens fees ($150 daily; packages available through the hotel) include a cart and use of the driving range. A strict dress code is enforced.

If you're a beginner or just want to bone up on your irons game, **Los Arroyos Golf Club,** 5000 Stage Gulch Rd. off Arnold Drive, a short drive from downtown Sonoma (pro shop © **707/938-8835**), is for you. The small 9-hole course is fairly flat and inexpensive— $12 on weekdays, $14 on weekends. Pull carts are an extra $2; practice greens and club rentals are also available. It's open on a first-come, first-play basis.

4 Where to Stay

When planning your trip, keep in mind that during the high season—between June and November—most hotels charge peak rates and sell out completely on weekends; many have a 2-night minimum. Always ask about discounts, particularly during mid-week, when most hotels and B&Bs drop their rates by as much as 30%. During the off-season, you will have far better bargaining power and may be able to get a room at almost half the summer rate.

The accommodations listed below are arranged first by area and then by price, using the following categories: **Very Expensive,** more than $250 per night; **Expensive,** $200 to $250 per night; **Moderate,** $150 to $200 per night; and **Inexpensive,** less than $150 per night. (Sorry, the reality is that anything less than $150 a night qualifies as inexpensive 'round these parts.)

Sonoma Valley Accommodations

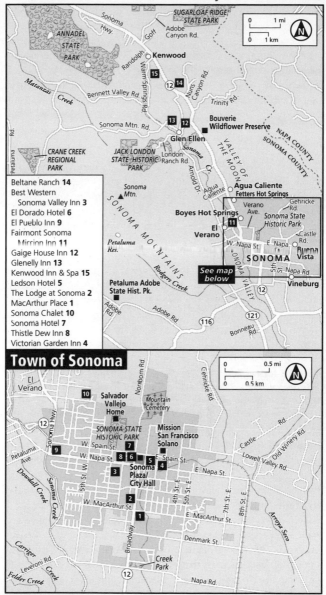

Beltane Ranch **14**
Best Western
  Sonoma Valley Inn **3**
El Dorado Hotel **6**
El Pueblo Inn **9**
Fairmont Sonoma
  Mission Inn **11**
Gaige House Inn **12**
Glenelly Inn **13**
Kenwood Inn & Spa **15**
Ledson Hotel **5**
The Lodge at Sonoma **2**
MacArthur Place **1**
Sonoma Chalet **10**
Sonoma Hotel **7**
Thistle Dew Inn **8**
Victorian Garden Inn **4**

Town of Sonoma

HELP WITH RESERVATIONS   If you are having trouble finding a room, try calling the **Sonoma Valley Visitors Bureau** (𝒞 707/996-1090), which can refer you to a lodging that has a room to spare (but won't make reservations for you). The **Bed and Breakfast Association of Sonoma Valley** (𝒞 800/969-4667 or www.sonoma bb.com) can refer you to one of its member B&Bs and can make reservations for you as well.

SONOMA
VERY EXPENSIVE

Ledson Hotel 𝒞𝒞   Sonoma's Square's hot new addition may look like a historic landmark, but this two-story six-room luxury inn is brand-spanking new. The regal brick hotel with ornate railings and an antiquated aura is the realized dream of vintner Steve Ledson who wanted to create the ultimate luxury hotel that gave a nod to the past through decor and a wink at the future with amenities. The result is six ultra-opulent rooms adorned with period furnishings, lots of rich fabrics, hardwood floors, Italian marble, fresh flowers, king-sized beds, whirlpool tubs, fireplaces, balconies, surround-sound television and digital music, and high-speed Internet access, and a welcoming of in-room wine and cheese. Alas, there are no public areas to speak of; you actually enter through a side door or its Harmony Club restaurant, which takes up the entire first floor, opens onto the plaza, and is a great wine bar and restaurant serving up small plates, Sonoma wines, and live jazz.

480 First St. E. (at the plaza), Sonoma CA 95476. 𝒞 **707/996-9779**. Fax 707/996-9776. www.ledsonhotel.com. 6 units. $350–$395. Rates include full breakfast served in the Harmony Club. AE, DISC, MC, V. **Amenities:** Restaurant and wine bar. *In room:* A/C, TV, dataport, whirlpool tub, digital music with surround sound, hair dryer, iron.

MacArthur Place 𝒞𝒞   A highly recommended alternative to the Sonoma Mission Inn is this much smaller and more intimate luxury property and spa located 4 blocks south of Sonoma's plaza. Once a 300-acre vineyard and ranch, MacArthur Place has since been whittled down to an 8-acre "Country Estate" replete with landscaped gardens and tree-lined pathways, various freestanding accommodations, and a spa and heated swimming pool and whirlpool. Most of the individually decorated guest rooms are housed within Victorian-modern cottages scattered throughout the resort; all are exceedingly well stocked with custom linens, oversized comforters, and original artwork. The newer suites come with fireplaces, porches, wet bars, six-speaker surround sound, and whirlpool tubs that often have shutters opening to the bedroom. Everyone has access to complimentary wine and cheese in the evening and the DVD library anytime. The full-service spa offers a wide array of services: fitness programs, body treatments, Indian rejuvenation treatments, skin care, astrology services, and massages. Within the resort's restored century-old barn is Saddles, Sonoma's only steakhouse specializing in mesquite-grilled prime beef and whimsically classy-western decor. There are also an array of other excellent restaurants a short walk away—as well as shops, wineries, and bars. In fact, that's where MacArthur Place has Sonoma Mission Inn beat: Once you park your car here you can *leave* it parked during a good part of your stay.

29 E. MacArthur St., Sonoma, CA 95476. ☎ **800/722-1866** or 707/938-2929. www.macarthurplace.com. 64 units. Sun–Thurs $169–$425 double; Fri–Sat $299–$525 double. Rates include continental breakfast. AE, DC, MC, V. **Amenities:** Restaurant and bar specializing in martinis; outdoor heated pool; exercise room; full service spa; co-ed steam; outdoor Jacuzzi; rental bikes; concierge; limited room service; massage; laundry service; same-day dry cleaning. *In room:* A/C, TV/DVD, dataport, wet bar and coffeemaker in suites, hair dryer, iron.

Fairmont Sonoma Mission Inn & Spa 🐾🐾🐾 As you drive through Boyes Hot Springs, you may wonder why someone decided to build a multimillion-dollar spa resort in this ordinary little town. There's no view to speak of, and it certainly isn't within walking distance of any wineries or fancy restaurants. So what's the deal? It's the naturally heated artesian mineral water, piped from directly underneath the spa into the temperature-controlled pools and whirlpools. Set on 12 meticulously groomed acres, the Sonoma Mission Inn consists of a massive three-story replica of a Spanish mission (well, aside from the pink paint job) built in 1927, an array of satellite wings housing numerous superluxury suites, and, of course, world-class spa facilities. It's a popular retreat for the wealthy and well known, so don't be surprised if you see Barbra Streisand or Harrison Ford. Big changes have occurred since the resort changed ownership a few years ago. It gained 60 suites, a $20 million spa facility (you won't even recognize the old one), and the Sonoma Golf Club.

The modern rooms have plantation-style shutters, ceiling fans, down comforters, and oversized bath towels. The Wine Country rooms feature king-size beds, desks, refrigerators, and huge limestone and marble bathrooms; some offer wood-burning fireplaces, and many have balconies. The older, slightly smaller Historic Inn rooms are sweetly appointed with homey furnishings; most have queen-size beds. For the ultimate in luxury, the opulently appointed (and brand-new) Mission Suites are the way to go.

Corner of Boyes Blvd and Calif. 12, P.O. Box 1447, Sonoma, CA 95476. © **800/441-1414** or 707/938-9000. Fax 707/938-4250. www.fairmont.com. 228 units. $199–$1000 double. AE, DC, MC, V. From central Sonoma, drive 3 miles north on Hwy. 12 and turn left on Boyes Blvd. **Amenities:** 2 restaurants; 2 large heated outdoor pools; golf course; health club and spa (see box, "The Super Spa," on p. 143 for the complete rundown); Jacuzzi; sauna; bike rental; concierge; business center; salon; room service (6am–11pm); babysitting; same-day laundry service and dry cleaning; valet parking. *In room:* A/C, TV, dataport, minibar, hair dryer, iron, safe, high speed Internet in most rooms, complimentary bottle of wine upon arrival.

EXPENSIVE

El Dorado Hotel 🍷   This 1843 Mission-revival building may look like a 19th-century Wild West relic from the outside, but inside it's all 20th-century deluxe. Each modern, handsomely appointed guest room—designed by the same folks who put together the ultra-exclusive Auberge du Soleil resort in Rutherford—has French windows and tiny terraces. Some offer lovely views of the plaza; others overlook the private courtyard and heated lap pool. All rooms (except those for guests with disabilities) are on the second floor, contain four-poster beds, plush towels, and hair dryers, and were upgraded in 2001. The two rooms on the ground floor are off the private courtyard, and each has a partially enclosed patio. The prices reflect its prime location on Sonoma Square, but this is one of the most charming options in its price range. Breakfast, served inside or out in the courtyard, includes coffee, fruits, and freshly baked breads and pastries.

405 First St. W., Sonoma, CA 95476. © **800/289-3031** or 707/996-3030. Fax 707/996-3148. www.hoteleldorado.com. 27 units. Summer $170–$190 double; winter $135–$155 double. Rates include continental breakfast and bottle of wine. AE, MC, V. **Amenities:** Restaurant; heated outdoor pool; access to nearby health club; bike rental; concierge; room service (11:30am–10pm); laundry service; dry cleaning. *In room:* A/C, TV/DVD, dataport, hair dryer, iron, fridge, CD player.

The Lodge at Sonoma 🍷🍷   Not surprisingly, a large-scale hotel finally made its way to downtown Sonoma. The good news is that this one, which is privately owned and operated by Marriott, takes into account its surroundings, offering some country charm in its 182 rooms. At the center of this resort is a U-shaped building with a classic big-hotel lobby, a Carneros restaurant with fine food and city-slick ambience, and a large courtyard swimming pool with plenty of lounge chairs. The very tasteful and spacious accommodations in the main building are decorated in various shades of earth tones and come complete with prints by local artists, artistic lighting fixtures, balconies or patios, and some fireplaces and tubs with shutters that open from the lovely bathroom to the bedroom. The two-story cottages along the property are especially appealing because they're surrounded by trees, flowers, and shrubs and offer a sense of seclusion. All rooms have great robes and bath amenities. The full-service spa, where I've twice had one of the best massages of my life, makes excellent use of its outdoor public space, with a number of small pools surrounded by lush plants.

1325 Broadway, Sonoma, CA 95476. ℂ **888/710-8008** or 707/935-6600. Fax 707/ 935-6829. www.thelodgeatsonoma.com. 182 units. $159–$349 double. AE, MC, V. **Amenities:** Restaurant; large heated outdoor pool; health club and spa; Jacuzzi; concierge; business center; limited room service; in-room massage. *In room:* A/C, TV w/pay movies, dataport, wet bar in suites, coffeemaker, hair dryer, iron.

MODERATE

Best Western Sonoma Valley Inn *(Kids)*   There are just two reasons to stay at the Sonoma Valley Inn: It's the only place left with a vacancy, or you're bringing the kids along. Otherwise, unless you don't mind staying in a rather drab room with thin walls and small bathrooms, you're probably going to be a little disappointed. Kids, on the other hand, will love the place: There's plenty of room to run around, plus a large heated outdoor pool, a gazebo-covered spa, and a sauna to play in. The rooms *do* have a lot of perks, however, such as continental breakfast delivered to your room each morning, a gift bottle of white table wine from Buena Vista Vineyards chilling in the fridge, and satellite TV with HBO. Most rooms have either a balcony or a deck overlooking the inner courtyard. It's also in a good location, just a block from Sonoma's plaza.

550 Second St. W. (1 block from the plaza), Sonoma, CA 95476. ℂ **800/334-5784** or 707/938-9200. Fax 707/938-0935. www.sonomavalleyinn.com. 82 units. $109– $349 double. Rates include continental breakfast. AE, DC, MC, V. **Amenities:** Heated outdoor pool; Jacuzzi; sauna; steam room; exercise room. *In room:* A/C, TV, dataport, fridge, coffeemaker, hair dryer, iron.

Thistle Dew Inn   Innkeepers Larry and Norma Barnett will be the first to admit that they don't run the fanciest B&B in town, but they'll just as quickly tell you that you'd be hard-pressed to find a better deal in Sonoma. Six rooms—all with private baths, queen beds, and phones with voice mail—are split between two homes, one built in 1869 and the other 1910. Both are handsomely furnished with an impressive collection of original Arts and Crafts furniture. If you're looking to save a few bucks, opt for a room in the main house; otherwise, you'll want one of the four larger and quieter rooms in the rear house. Each of the rooms in the rear house has its own deck overlooking Larry's cactus garden and is furnished

with either a gas fireplace, a two-person whirlpool tub, or both. A second-floor two-room suite was added in 2000.

Luxury perks at Thistle Dew Inn include breakfast (most popular are the Dutch babies—German pancakes with ricotta cheese and jams), which can be delivered to your room for an additional fee; afternoon hors d'oeuvres; free use of bicycles and utensil-filled picnic baskets; passes to the nearby health club; and use of the garden hot tub. You're bound to like the location—just half a block from Sonoma's plaza—as well as your hosts Larry and Norma and their very low-key, help-yourself approach toward innkeeping.

171 W. Spain St., Sonoma, CA 95476. ✆ **800/382-7895** or 707/938-2909. Fax 707/ 996-8413. www.thistledew.com. 6 units. $140–$275 double; ask about winter weekday specials. Rates include full breakfast and afternoon hors d'oeuvres. AE, DISC, MC, V. **Amenities:** Passes to nearby health club; free bikes; hot tub. *In room:* A/C, 1 room with TV.

INEXPENSIVE

El Pueblo Inn   Located on Sonoma's main east-west street, 8 blocks from the center of town, this isn't Sonoma's fanciest hotel, but it did just undergo renovations, is well cared for, and offers some of the best-priced accommodations around. The rooms here are pleasant enough, with individual entrances, post-and-beam construction, exposed brick walls, light-wood furniture, and geometric prints. A new addition in 2002 resulted in 20 new larger rooms with high ceilings, DVDs, and fireplaces in some rooms. They also recently made each room open to a courtyard with a fountain. Their new reception area doubles as a breakfast room for their continental breakfast and leads to a small meeting room. Reservations should be made at least a month in advance for the spring and summer months.

896 W. Napa St., Sonoma, CA 95476. ✆ **800/900-8844** or 707/996-3651. Fax 707/ 935-5988. www.elpebloinn.com. 53 units. May–Oct $108–$255 double; Nov–Apr $90–$195 double. AE, DISC, MC, V. Corporate, AAA, and senior discounts are available. **Amenities:** Heated outdoor pool; Jacuzzi; in-room massage. *In room:* A/C, TV, DVD (newer rooms only), dataport, fridge, coffeemaker and biscotti, hair dryer, iron.

Sonoma Chalet 🌟   This is one of the few accommodations in Sonoma that's truly secluded; it's on the outskirts of town, in a peaceful country setting overlooking a 200-acre ranch. The accommodations, housed in a Swiss-style farmhouse and several cottages, have all been delightfully decorated by someone with an eye for color and a concern for comfort. You'll find claw-foot tubs, country quilts, Oriental carpets, comfortable furnishings, and private decks; some units have wood stoves or fireplaces. The two least expensive rooms share a bathroom, and the cottages offer the most privacy. A breakfast of fruit, yogurt, pastries, and cereal is served either in the country kitchen or in your room. If you like country rustic, you'll like the Sonoma Chalet.

18935 5th St. W., Sonoma, CA 95476. (C) **800/938-3129** or 707/938-3129. www.sonomachalet.com. 7 units including 3 cottages. Apr–Oct $110–$225 double; Nov–Mar $110–$195 double. Rates include continental breakfast. AE, MC, V. **Amenities:** Hot tub. *In room:* A/C, coffeemaker in cottages, hair dryer, iron on request, no phone.

Sonoma Hotel 🐾🐾   This cute little historic hotel on Sonoma's tree-lined town plaza emphasizes 19th-century elegance and comfort. Built in 1880 by German immigrant Henry Weyl, it has attractive guest rooms decorated in early California style, with French country furnishings, antique beds, and period decorations. In a bow to modern luxuries, recent additions include private bathrooms, cable TV, phones with dataports, and (and this is crucial) air-conditioning. Perks include fresh coffee and pastries in the morning and wine and cheese in the evening. The lovely restaurant The Girl & the Fig (see "Where to Dine," later in this chapter) is now located right next to the hotel.

110 W. Spain St., Sonoma, CA 95476. (C) **800/468-6016** or 707/996-2996. Fax 707/996-7014. www.sonomahotel.com. 16 units. Summer $110–$245 double. Winter Sun–Thurs $95–$170 double; Fri–Sat $115–$195 double. Rates include continental breakfast and evening wine. AE, DC, MC, V. *In room:* A/C, TV, dataport.

Victorian Garden Inn 🐾🐾   Proprietor Donna Lewis runs what is easily the cutest B&B in Sonoma Valley. A small picket fence and a wall of trees enclose an adorable Victorian garden brimming with violets, roses, camellias, and peonies, all shaded under flowering fruit trees. It's truly a marvelous sight in the springtime. The guest rooms—three in the century-old water tower and one in the main building, an 1870s Greek revival farmhouse—continue the Victorian theme, with white wicker furniture, floral prints, padded armchairs, and claw-foot tubs. The most popular rooms are the Top o' the Tower and the Woodcutter's Cottage. Each has its own entrance and a garden view; the cottage boasts a sofa and armchairs set in front of the fireplace. After a hard day's wine tasting, spend the afternoon cooling off in the pool or on the shaded wraparound porch, enjoying a mellow merlot while soaking in the sweet garden smells.

316 E. Napa St., Sonoma, CA 95476. (C) **800/543-5339** or 707/996-5339. Fax 707/996-1689. www.victoriangardeninn.com. 4 units. $125–$240 double. Rates include continental breakfast. AE, DC, MC, V. **Amenities:** Outdoor pool; concierge; business center; room service (8am–5pm); laundry service; dry cleaning, hot tub. *In room:* A/C, fireplaces in some rooms.

GLEN ELLEN
VERY EXPENSIVE

Gaige House Inn ⭐⭐⭐ *Finds*   Owners Ken Burnet Jr. and Greg Nemrow have managed to turn what was already a fine B&B into *the* finest in the Wine Country. They've done it by offering a level of service, amenities, and decor normally associated with outrageously expensive resorts—but without the snobbery. Every nook and cranny of the 1890 Queen Anne–Italianate building and Garden Annex is swathed with fashionable articles found during the owners' world travels. Spacious rooms offer everything one could want—firm mattresses, wondrously silk-soft linens, and premium down comforters grace the beds, and even the furniture and artwork are the kind you'd like to take home with you. Breakfast is a momentous event, accented with herbs from the inn's garden and prepared by a chef who cooked at the James Beard House in 2001. Bathrooms are equally luxe, range in size, and are stocked with Aveda products. Attention to detail means you'll be treated to the best robe I've ever worn and evening appetizers at wine hour that might include freshly shucked oysters or a sautéed scallop served ready-to-slurp on a Chinese soupspoon.

But wait, it gets better. Behind the inn is a 1½-acre oasis with perfectly manicured lawns, a 40-foot-long pool, and an achingly inviting creek-side hammock shaded by a majestic Heritage oak. All 15 rooms, each artistically decorated in a plantation theme with Asian and Indonesian influences (trust me, they're beautiful), have king- or queen-size beds; four rooms have Jacuzzi tubs, one has a Japanese soaking tub, and several have fireplaces. For the ultimate retreat reserve one of the suites, which have patios overlooking a stream. On sunny days, breakfast is served at individual tables on the large terrace. Evenings are best spent in the reading parlor, sipping premium wines. Greg and Ken also manage four long-term rentals (private guesthouses on private estates) for those who want more privacy and fewer services.

13540 Arnold Dr., Glen Ellen, CA 95442. © **800/935-0237** or 707/935-0237. Fax 707/935-6411. www.gaige.com. 15 units. Summer $250–$375 double, $375–$525 suite; winter $175–$325 double, $325–$525 suite. Rates include full breakfast and evening wines. AE, DC, DISC, MC, V. **Amenities:** Large heated pool; in-room massage. *In room:* A/C, TV, fax, dataport, hair dryer, iron, safe.

INEXPENSIVE

Beltane Ranch ⭐ *Finds*   The word "ranch" conjures up a big ol' two-story house in the middle of hundreds of rolling acres, the kind of place where you laze away the day in a hammock watching the grass grow or pitching horseshoes in the garden. Well, friend, you can have all that and more at the Beltane Ranch, a century-old buttercup-yellow manor that's been everything from a bunkhouse to a brothel to a turkey farm. You simply can't help but feel your tensions ease away as you prop your feet up on the shady wraparound porch overlooking the vineyards, sipping a cool, fruity chardonnay while reading *Lonesome Dove* for the third time. Each room is uniquely decorated with American and European antiques; all have sitting areas and separate entrances. A big country breakfast is served in the garden or on the porch overlooking the vineyards. For exercise, you can play tennis on the private court or hike the trails meandering through the 1,600-acre estate. *Tip:* Request one of the upstairs rooms, which have the best views.

11775 Sonoma Hwy. (Hwy. 12), Glen Ellen, CA 95442. © 707/996-6501. www. beltaneranch.com. 5 units, 1 cottage. $130–$180 double; $220 cottage. Rates include full breakfast. No credit cards; personal checks accepted. **Amenities:** Tennis court *In room:* No phone

Glenelly Inn ☆   This former 1916 railroad inn is positively drenched in serenity. Located well off the main highway on an oak-studded hillside, the inn comes with everything you would expect from a country retreat: long verandas with comfy wicker chairs and views of the verdant Sonoma hillsides; a hearty country breakfast served beside a large cobblestone fireplace; and bright, immaculate rooms with private entrances, authentic antiques, old-fashioned claw-foot tubs, Scandinavian down comforters, firm mattresses, and ceiling fans. The simmering hot tub is ensconced within a grapevine- and rose-covered arbor. As this book goes to press, new garden cottages are slated to open.

5131 Warm Springs Rd. (off Arnold Dr.), Glen Ellen, CA 95442. © 707/996-6720. Fax 707/996-5227. www.glenelly.com. 10 units. $150–$250 double. Rates include full breakfast. AE, DISC, MC, V. **Amenities:** Hot tub, spa services, massage.

KENWOOD
VERY EXPENSIVE
Kenwood Inn & Spa ☆☆ *Finds*   Inspired by the villas of Tuscany, the Kenwood Inn's honey-colored Italian-style buildings, flower-filled flagstone courtyard, and pastoral views of vineyard-covered hills are enough to make any Northern Italian homesick. But the friendly staff and luxuriously restful surrounds made this California girl feel right at home. What's not to like about a spacious room lavishly and exquisitely decorated with imported tapestries, velvets, and antiques plus a fireplace, balcony (except on the ground floor),

feather bed, CD player, and down comforter? With no TV in the rooms, relaxation is inevitable—especially if you book treatments at the spa, which gets creative with its rejuvenating program. A minor caveat is road noise, which you're unlikely to hear from your room, but can be slightly audible over the tranquil pumped-in music around the courtyard and decent-size pool. Longtime guests will be surprised to find more bodies around the pool—18 new guestrooms on a neighboring property joined this slice of pastoral heaven in June 2003. But anyone with a hefty credit card limit can buy complete seclusion by renting the inn's new nearby two-bedroom house.

An impressive three-course gourmet breakfast is served poolside or in the Mediterranean-style dining room. Mine consisted of a poached egg accompanied by light, flavorful potatoes, red bell peppers, and other roasted vegetables, all artfully arranged, followed by a delicious homemade scone with fresh berries, and a small lemon tart.

10400 Sonoma Hwy., Kenwood, CA 95452. © **800/353-6966** or 707/833-1293. Fax 707/833-1247. www.kenwoodinn.com. 30 units. Apr–Oct $400–$725 double; Nov–Mar $375–$675 double. Rates include gourmet breakfast and bottle of wine. 2-night minimum on weekends. AE, MC, V. **Amenities:** Heated outdoor pool; full-service spa; concierge. *In room:* CD player, hair dryer, iron.

5 Where to Dine

In the past decade, Sonoma Valley has experienced a culinary revolution. In response to the saturation of restaurants in the Bay Area, both budding and renowned chefs and restaurateurs have pulled out their San Francisco stakes and resettled in Sonoma Valley to craft culinary art from the region's bounty of organic produce and meats. The result is something longtime locals never dared to dream of when it came to fine dining in Sonoma: a choice.

Granted, the restaurants in Sonoma Valley—both in quality and quantity—pales in comparison to those found in Napa Valley, but the overall dining experience is splendid regardless. Even the big players are forced to concede to Sonoma's small-town code by keeping their restaurants simple and unpretentious, hence the absence of ostentatious eateries such as Napa's Tra Vigne and Pinot Blanc.

As you travel through the valley, you'll find a few dozen modestly sized and privately owned cafes, often run by husband-and-wife teams who pour their hearts and bank accounts into keeping their businesses thriving during the off-season. In fact, don't be surprised if the person waiting your table is also the owner, chef, host,

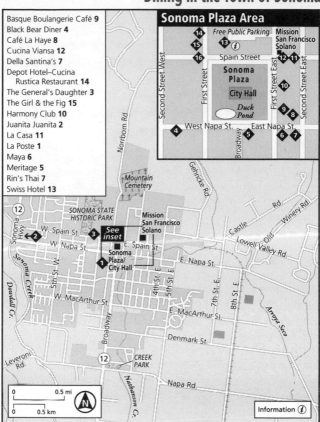

Dining in the Town of Sonoma

Sonoma Plaza Area

Basque Boulangerie Café **9**
Black Bear Diner **4**
Café La Haye **8**
Cucina Viansa **12**
Della Santina's **7**
Depot Hotel–Cucina
  Rustica Restaurant **14**
The General's Daughter **3**
The Girl & the Fig **15**
Harmony Club **10**
Juanita Juanita **2**
La Casa **11**
La Poste **1**
Maya **6**
Meritage **5**
Rin's Thai **7**
Swiss Hotel **13**

sommelier, and retired professor from Yale. It's this sort of combination that often makes dining in Sonoma a very personable experience and one that you'll relish long after you leave the Wine Country.

The restaurants listed below are classified first by town, then by price, using the following categories: **Expensive,** dinner from $50 per person; **Moderate,** dinner from $35 to $50 per person; and **Inexpensive,** dinner less than $35 per person. These categories reflect prices for an appetizer, a main course, and a dessert.

Note: Though Sonoma Valley has far fewer visitors than Napa Valley, its restaurants are often equally crowded, so be sure to make reservations as far in advance as possible. Also bear in mind that the food in the Wine Country is usually served in large portions and washed down with copious amounts of wine—enough so that I make a point of eating at only one restaurant a day, lest I explode.

SONOMA
EXPENSIVE

Santé Restaurant ⊛ CALIFORNIA/SPA   One of the fanciest restaurants in the Wine Country, Santé Restaurant has long suffered from a solid reputation for serving high-caliber spa cuisine. But in 2003 they moved away from "spa" and their old chef and into the luxury food realm with chef Rod Williams at the helm. Selections from the seasonally changing menu might include clay oven specials (think herb-infused prawns with papaya and jicama salad with cilantro crème fraîche); seared Thai snapper on arugula with citrus habanero chile vinaigrette; butternut and acorn squash ravioli with sautéed arugula, anjou pear emulsion, and candied pecans; and grilled Niman Ranch pork chop with caramelized onion mashed potatoes, and apple-balsamic glaze. Service is professional yet friendly, and the wine list is extensive and expensive.

At Sonoma Mission Inn, 18140 Sonoma Hwy., Sonoma. ⓒ 707/938-9000. Reservations recommended. Main courses $23–$29, fixed-price menu $55. AE, DC, MC, V. Daily 6–9:30pm.

MODERATE

Café La Haye ⊛⊛ (Value) ECLECTIC   Well-prepared, wholesome food, an experienced waitstaff, friendly owners, a soothing atmosphere, and reasonable prices—including a modestly priced wine list—make La Haye a favorite. In truth, everything about this place is charming. The small split-level dining room is smart, intimate and pleasantly decorated with hardwood floors, an exposed-beam ceiling, and revolving contemporary artwork. The vibe is small-business—a welcome departure from Napa Valley's big-business restaurants. The straightforward seasonally inspired cuisine, which chefs bring forth from the tiny open kitchen, is delicious and wonderfully well priced. Although the menu is concise, it offers just enough options. Expect a risotto special, pasta such as fresh tagliarini with butternut squash, prosciutto, sage, and garlic cream and pan-roasted chicken breast, perhaps with goat cheese–herb stuffing, caramelized shallot jus, and fennel mashed potatoes. Meat-eaters are sure to be pleased with filet of beef seared with black pepper–lavender sauce and served with gorgonzola-potato gratin, and no one can resist the beautiful salads. Sunday brunch includes a handful of creative breakfast dishes, such as white cheddar grits with grilled ham, poached egg, and cracked pepper hollandaise, as well as salads and sandwiches.

140 E. Napa St., Sonoma. © 707/935-5994. Reservations recommended. Main courses $14–$24. MC, V. Tues–Sat 5:30–9pm; Sun brunch 9:30am–2pm.

Depot Hotel—Cucina Rustica Restaurant NORTHERN ITALIAN   Michael Ghilarducci has been the chef and owner here for nearly 2 decades, which means he's either independently wealthy or a darned good cook. Fortunately, it's the latter. A block north of the plaza in a handsome 1870 stone building, the Depot Hotel offers pleasant outdoor dining in an Italian garden, complete with a reflecting pool and cascading Roman fountain. The menu is unwaveringly Italian, featuring classic dishes such as spaghetti bolognese and veal alla parmigiana. Start with the bounteous antipasto misto, and end the feast with a dish of Michael's handmade Italian ice cream and fresh-fruit sorbets.

241 1st St. W. (off Spain St.), Sonoma. © 707/938-2980. www.depothotel.com. Reservations recommended. Main courses lunch $10–$16; dinner $14–$22. AE, DISC, MC, V. Wed–Fri 11:30am–5pm; Wed–Sun 5–9pm.

The Girl & the Fig 🐖🐖 COUNTRY FRENCH   Already well established in its downtown Sonoma digs (it used to be in Glen Ellen), this modern, attractive, and cozy eatery, with lovely patio seating, is home to Sondra Bernstein's (The Girl) beloved restaurant. Here the cuisine, orchestrated by executive chef John Toulze, is nouveau country with French nuances, and yes, figs are sure to be on the menu in one form or another. The wonderful winter fig salad contains arugula, pecans, dried figs, Laura Chenel goat cheese, and fig-and-port vinaigrette. Toulze uses garden-fresh produce and local meats, poultry, and fish whenever possible, in dishes such as pork tenderloin with a potato-leek pancake and roasted beets, and sea scallops with lobster-scented risotto. For dessert, try the warm pear galette topped with gingered crème fraîche, a glass of Quady Essensia Orange Muscat, and a sliver of raclette from the cheese cart. Sondra knows her wines and will be happy to choose the best accompaniment to your meal.

110 W. Spain St., Sonoma. © 707/938-3634. www.thegirlandthefig.com. Reservations recommended. Main courses $18–$21. AE, MC, V. Daily 11:30am–11pm.

La Poste 🐖 FRENCH BISTRO   It's a gastronome's game of sardines at shoebox-size French bistro. The original Williams-Sonoma storefront is now downtown Sonoma's tiniest dining room with 26 chairs and maple banquettes strategically squeezed amidst brass sconces, mahogany wainscoting, a whitewashed press tin ceiling, and just enough space on the French concrete-tiled floor for staff to refill wine glasses. The ever-changing chalkboard menu announces chef Rob Larman's complete U-turn from the more casual fare he served at his recently closed restaurant Rob's Rib Shack. The menu changes faster than you can say "Pass the profiteroles," but recent winners included seared scallops seasoned with tomato-herb vinaigrette over truffled mashed potatoes; braised veal cheeks with cream, Calvados, English peas, and chanterelles; and quail stuffed with foie gras and sweetbreads on a warm salad of fingerling potatoes. Finish the eve with chocolate mousse and take a stroll around the plaza. Oh, and when weather permits you'll find 14 more seats on the sidewalk.

599 Broadway (just south of the plaza), Sonoma. ℂ **707/939-3663.** Reservations recommended. Main courses $16–$25. AE, MC, V. Sun and Wed–Thurs 5:30–9pm, Fri–Sat 5:30–10pm.

Harmony Club ⭐⭐ *(Finds* CONTINENTAL   The most welcome addition in 2003, The Harmony Club is not only a looker with its elegant Italianate dining room with dark woods, high ceilings, marble flooring, a wall of giant doors opening to sidewalk seating and Sonoma's plaza. It also delivers in great food and live entertainment. Drop in anytime after their gourmet breakfast for fantastic "small plates" such as tender Moroccan spiced lamb loin with saffron couscous, grapes, and mint; french fries with tarragon aioli; seared scallops with vegetable ragout and truffle beurre blanc; and Scharffen Berger chocolate and orange Muscat tort. Go for sidewalk seating during warmer weather (they also have heat lamps), sit inside, or hang at the carved wood bar. Either way you'll want to face the piano when the nightly performer is tinkling the keys and singing jazz standards. Alas, the only bummer is the wine list, which leaves little in the way of options since this spot, owned by Steve Ledson of Ledson Winery, naturally features only Ledson wines.

480 First St. E. (at the plaza), Sonoma. ℂ **707/996-9779.** No reservations. Small plates $6–$14. AE, MC, V. Sun–Thurs 11:30am–10pm, Fri–Sat 11:30am–11:30pm.

Maya MEXICAN   Gourmet Mexican might be the best way to describe the food at this lively grill-and-rotisserie restaurant on the southeast corner of Sonoma's plaza. I'm not talking top-shelf enchiladas here—rather, it's a winning combination of traditional Yucatán dishes prepared with ultrafresh ingredients. Take salmon for instance: a thick cut of fresh fish, perfectly cooked with pasilla pesto, chervil and tarragon risotto, and a medley of root vegetables. The commendable Maya pollo rostizado—a spit-roasted half chicken with a Yucatán spice rub—could easily feed two. Other menu items I considered seriously included smoked duck salad with goat cheese, seasoned walnuts, and blood orange vinaigrette and grilled pork loin with apple chutney, chive potato cake, and Swiss chard. Yes, you're probably going to pay a bit more than you planned to pay for Mexican food, but it's worth the extra few dollars. You are likely to enjoy the faux Mayan village ambience as well: desert earth tones with bright splashes of colorful art and thick, hand-carved wood furnishings. The only caveat is the *muy fuerte* noise level, but a couple of fantastic margaritas on the rocks, and you'll soon be in fiesta mode yourself.

101 E. Napa St., Sonoma. ℂ 707/935-3500. Reservations recommended. Main courses $9–$20. MC, V. Tues–Sun 11:45am–9:30pm; Mon 4–9:30pm. Jan–Apr closed Mon.

Meritage SOUTHERN FRENCH/NORTHERN ITALIAN

Learning from the previous occupants' mistakes—that Sonoma ain't New York City and shouldn't treat its customers that way—chef/owner Carlo Cavallo eliminated the big-city attitude and prices at his new restaurant, without diminishing style, service, and quality. The former executive chef for Giorgio Armani, Cavallo combines the best of southern French and northern Italian cuisines (hence "Meritage," after a blend made with traditional Bordeaux varieties), giving Sonomans yet another reason to eat out. The menu, which changes twice daily, is a good read: handmade roasted pumpkin tortellini in Parmesan cheese sauce; napoleon of escargot in champagne–and–wild thyme sauce; organic greens, strawberries, corn, and French feta salad; wild boar chops in white truffle sauce with mashed potatoes. Shellfish fans can't help but love the oyster raw bar and options of live crab and lobster. A lovely garden patio is prime positioning for sunny breakfasts and lunches and summer dinners. Such edible enticement—combined with reasonable prices, excellent service, a stellar wine list, cozy booth seating, a handsome dining room, and Carlo's practiced charm—make Meritage a trustworthy option.

522 Broadway, Sonoma. ℂ 707/938-9430. www.sonomameritage.com. Reservations recommended. Main courses $13–$30. AE, MC, V. Wed–Sun 8am–9pm. Mon 11:30am–9pm.

Swiss Hotel CONTINENTAL/NORTHERN ITALIAN

With its slanting floors and beamed ceilings, the historic Swiss Hotel, located right in the town center, is a Sonoma landmark and very much the local favorite for fine food served at reasonable prices.

The oak bar at the left of the entrance is adorned with black-and-white photos of pioneering Sonomans. The bright white dining room and rear dining patio are pleasant spots to enjoy lunch specials such as penne with chicken, mushrooms, and tomato cream; hot sandwiches; and California-style pizzas fired in a wood-burning oven. But the secret spot is the back garden patio, a secluded oasis shaded by a wisteria-covered trellis and adorned with plants, a fountain, gingham tablecloths, and a fireplace. Dinner might start with a warm winter salad of radicchio and frisée with pears, walnuts, and bleu cheese. Main courses run the gamut; I like the linguine and prawns with garlic, hot pepper, and tomatoes; the filet mignon wrapped in bleu cheese crust; and roasted rosemary chicken. It's all very traditional and satisfying, a style of cuisine that's becoming increasingly rare in Sonoma Valley.

18 W. Spain St., Sonoma. ℂ **707/938-2884.** Reservations recommended. Main courses lunch $8.50–$16, dinner $10–$24. AE, MC, V. Daily 11:30am–2:30pm and 5–9:30pm. (Bar, daily 11:30am–2am.)

INEXPENSIVE

Basque Boulangerie Café BAKERY/DELI If you prefer a lighter morning meal and strong coffee, stand in line with the locals at the Basque Boulangerie Café, the most popular gathering spot in Sonoma Valley. Most everything—sourdough Basque breads, pastries, quiche, soups, salads, desserts, sandwiches, cookies—is made in-house and made well. Daily lunch specials, such as a grilled-veggie sandwich with smoked mozzarella cheese ($4.95), are listed on the chalkboard out front. Seating is scarce, and if you can score a sidewalk table on a sunny day, consider yourself one lucky person. A popular option is ordering to go and eating in the shady plaza across the street. The cafe also sells wine by the glass, as well as a wonderful cinnamon bread by the loaf that's ideal for making French toast.

460 1st St. E., Sonoma. ℂ **707/935-7687.** Menu items $3–$7. No credit cards. Daily 7am–6pm.

Black Bear Diner DINER When you're craving a classic Americana breakfast, lunch, or dinner with all the cholesterol and the fixin's, bee-line to this old-fashioned diner. First, it's fun with its over-the-top bear paraphernalia, gazette-style menu listing local news from 1961 and every possible diner favorite, and absurdly friendly wait staff. Second, it's darned cheap. Third, helpings are huge. What more could you want? Kids get a kick out of coloring books, old-timers reminisce over Sinatra playing on the jukebox, and everyone leaves stuffed on omelets, scrambles, pancakes, steak sandwiches and other classics, salads, and comfort food faves like barbecued pork ribs, roast beef, fish and chips, and spaghetti and meat sauce. Whatever you want, it's almost guaranteed to part of Black Bear's extensive selection. Dinners come with salad or soup, bread, and two sides and seniors are buffed out with a special-priced menu.

201 W. Napa St. (at Second St.), Sonoma. © **707/935-6800.** Main courses breakfast $5–$8.50, lunch and dinner $5.50–$17. AE, DISC, MC, V. Sun–Thurs 6am–10pm, Fri–Sat 6am–midnight.

Cucina Viansa ITALIAN DELI   When it comes to straightforward fresh, contemporary Italian fare, Cucina Viansa is the sexiest thing going in Sonoma. Lines out the door inspired Sam and Vicki Sebastiani, who also run Viansa Winery and own the suave restaurant and wine bar, to make the place double as a full-service restaurant as well as a mecca for to-go items and gourmet condiments. A visual masterpiece with shiny black-and-white-checked flooring, long counters of Italian marble, tables 'round back, and track lighting, it's a very casual place to drop in for cured meats, cheese, fruit, pastas, salads, breads, focaccia sandwiches, and specialties from the centerpiece wood-burning oven at the deli. Or park yourself at one of the window-front tables or tall cocktail tables in the back and enjoy rigatoni Bolognese with artichokes; roasted chicken with thyme, orange, garlic mashed potatoes, sugar snap peas and sherry sauce; and roasted fennel-spiced pork with mashed potatoes and fava bean sauce. Opposite the deli is the wine bar, featuring all of Viansa's current releases for both tasting and purchase, as well as a small selection of microbrewed beers on tap. On your way out, stop at the gelateria and treat yourself to some intense Italian ice cream.

400 First St. E., Sonoma. © **707/935-5656.** Deli items $5–$9. AE, DISC, MC, V. Daily 11am–9pm; Fri–Sat until 10pm.

Della Santina's ITALIAN   Those of you who just can't swallow another expensive, chi-chi, California meal should follow the locals to this friendly, traditional Italian restaurant. How traditional? Just ask father-and-son team Dan and Robert who preside over Signora Santina's Tuscan recipes. (Heck, even the dining room looks like an old-fashioned, elegant Italian living room—and their patio is great!) Dishes tend to be pure and well flavored, without overbearing sauces or one *hint* of California pretentiousness. Be sure to start with traditional antipasti, especially sliced mozzarella and tomatoes, or delicious white beans. The pasta dishes are wonderfully authentic (gnocchi lovers, rejoice!). The spit-roasted meat dishes are a local favorite (although I found them a bit overcooked); for those who can't choose between chicken, pork, turkey, rabbit, or duck, there's a selection that offers a choice of three. Don't worry about breaking your bank on a bottle of wine, because most of the choices go for under $40. Portions are huge, but save room for a wonderful dessert.

133 E. Napa St. (just east of the square), Sonoma. © **707/935-0576.** Reservations recommended. Main courses $9–$15. AE, DISC, MC, V. Daily 11:30am–3pm and 5–9:30pm.

Juanita Juanita MEXICAN   Everyone loves this roadside shack hawking fresh Mexican specialties and hearty sides of who-gives-a-heck attitude. Lines out the door during weekends prove the point. But if you've gotta have a killer quesadilla, nachos, enchiladas, tacos, and their very fabulous "plate" specials (think grilled chicken with chipotle cream sauce on a bed of spinach and avocado with rice, beans, and tortillas) it's worth the wait. Besides, the place is fun. Here the decor and vibe is about as casual as you can get. Plop down at the counter or pull up a chair at one of the mix-and-match tables, kick up your heels, dig into the plastic bucket of tortilla chips and side o' salsa, sip on an ice cold beer, and revel in the oh-so-Sonoma-casual vibe as you fill up on the huge portions. Kids dig the place, too, and have their own specialties offered at pint-sized prices of $3.75.

19114 Arnold Dr. (just north of W. Napa St.), Sonoma. © **707/935-3981.** www.juanitajuanita.com. No reservations. Main courses $5.95–$12. No credit cards. Daily 11am–8pm.

Rin's Thai 🐸 THAI   When valley residents or visitors get a hankering for Pad Thai, curry chicken, or *tom yam* (classic spicy soup) they head to this adorable little restaurant just off Sonoma Plaza. The atmosphere itself—contemporary, sparse, yet warm environs within an old house—is tasty and the staff is extremely accommodating. After you settle into one of the well-spaced tables within or on the outside patio (weather permitting), go for your favorites—from satay with peanut sauce and cucumber salad or salmon with grilled veggies to yummy *gai kraprao* (minced chicken, chiles, basil, and garlic sauce) or char-broiled ribs with chile-garlic dipping sauce they've got it covered, including that oh-so-sweet Thai iced tea, fried bananas with coconut ice cream, and fresh mango with sticky rice (seasonal).

139 E. Napa St. (just east of the plaza), Sonoma. © **707/938-1462.** Reservations recommended. Main courses lunch $7.50–$9.25; dinner $8.25–$11. MC, V. Daily 11:30am–9:30pm.

GLEN ELLEN
MODERATE

Wolf House 🌟 ECLECTIC   The most polished-looking dining room in Glen Ellen is elegant yet relaxed, and under its new name and ownership as of 2003 it's also a trustworthy place to eat. Whether you're seated in the handsome dining room—smartly adorned with maple floors, gold walls, dark-wood wainscoting, and a corner fireplace—or outside on the multilevel terrace under the canopy of trees with serene views of the adjacent Sonoma Creek, you can lunch on standards like an excellent chicken Caesar salad, grilled ahi tuna nicoise sandwich, or a juicy half-pound burger with Point Reyes Original Blue cheese. During dinner the kitchen antes up with sparkling wine battered prawns with upland cress salad; seared Sonoma lamb sirloin with roasted eggplant, chickpea ragout, and tomato confit; and pan-seared day boat scallops with heirloom tomatoes and avocado-cucumber emulsion. The reasonably priced wine list offers many by-the-glass options as well as a fine selection of Sonoma wines. Oh! And locals love the brunch complete with huevos rancheros, steak and eggs, omelets, and brioche French toast. During my visit service was rather languid, but well meaning.

13740 Arnold Dr., Glen Ellen. © **707/996-4401.** Reservations recommended. Main courses brunch and lunch $8–$12, dinner $18–$20. AE, DISC, MC, V. Brunch Sat–Sun 10:30am–3pm; lunch Mon–Fri 11am–3pm; dinner nightly 5:30–9:30pm.

Glen Ellen Inn Restaurant 🌟 CALIFORNIA   Christian and Karen Bertrand have made this restaurant so quaint and cozy that you feel as if you're dining in their home, and that's exactly the place's charm. Garden seating is the favored choice on sunny days, but the covered, heated patio is always welcoming. First courses from Christian's open kitchen might include a poached pear, spinach, and arugula salad with blue cheese, pecans, and blackberry honey-mustard vinaigrette or Dungeness crab pot stickers with leek cream sauce. Main courses, which change with the seasons, range from sesame-seared ahi tuna on a creamy potato cake with pickled ginger, wasabi, and port reduction to grilled pork tenderloin with pineapple-mango chutney and smoked Sonoma jack cheese polenta. The 350-selection wine list offers numerous bottles from Sonoma, as well as more than a dozen wines by the glass. *Tip:* There's a small parking lot behind the restaurant.

13670 Arnold Dr., Glen Ellen. 🕐 **707/996-6409**. www.glenelleninn.com. Reservations recommended. Main courses $18–$25. AE, MC, V. Fri–Tues 11:30am–2:30pm and 5:30–9:30pm; Wed–Thurs 5:30–9:30pm. Closed Mon–Thurs last week in Jan.

KENWOOD
MODERATE
Kenwood Restaurant & Bar 🕭 CALIFORNIA/CONTINEN-
TAL   From the terrace of the Kenwood Restaurant, diners enjoy a view of the vineyards set against Sugarloaf Ridge as they imbibe Sonoma's finest at umbrella-covered tables. On nippy days, you can retreat inside to the Sonoma-style roadhouse, with shiny wood floors, pine ceiling, vibrant artwork, and cushioned rattan chairs at white-cloth-covered tables. Regardless of where you pull up a chair, expect first-rate cuisine, perfectly balanced between tradition and innovation, and complemented by a reasonably priced wine list. Great starters are Dungeness crab cake with herb mayonnaise; superfresh sashimi with ginger, soy, and wasabi; and a solid Caesar salad. Main-dish choices might include poached salmon in creamy caper sauce, prawns with saffron Pernod sauce, or braised Sonoma rabbit with grilled polenta. But the Kenwood doesn't take itself too seriously: Great sandwiches and burgers are available.

9900 Sonoma Hwy., Kenwood. 🕐 **707/833-6326**. Reservations recommended. Main courses lunch and dinner $11–$27. MC, V. Tues–Sun 11:30am–9pm.

INEXPENSIVE
Café Citti NORTHERN ITALIAN   If you're this far north into
the Wine Country, then you're probably doing some serious wine tasting. If that's the case, then you don't want to spend half the day at a fancy, high-priced restaurant. What you need is Café Citti (pro-nounced *cheat*-ee), a roadside do-it-yourself Italian trattoria that is both good and cheap. You order from the huge menu board dis-played above the open kitchen. Afterward, you grab a table (the ones on the patio, shaded by umbrellas, are the best on warm after-noons), and a server will bring your meal. It's all hearty, home-cooked Italian. Standout dishes are the green-bean salad, tangy Caesar salad, focaccia sandwiches, and roasted rotisserie chicken stuffed with rosemary and garlic. The freshly made pastas come with a variety of sauces; try the zesty marinara. Wine is available by the bottle, and the espresso is plenty strong. Everything on the menu board is available to go, which makes Café Citti an excellent resource for picnic supplies.

9900 Sonoma Hwy., Kenwood. 🕐 **707/833-6326**. Reservations recommended. Main courses $13–$26. MC, V. Wed–Sun 11:30am–9pm.

Café Citti **4**
Glen Ellen Inn
  Restaurant **2**
Kenwood
  Restaurant & Bar **3**
Santé Restaurant **1**
Wolf House **2**

---

6 Where to Stock Up for a Picnic & Where to Enjoy It

Sure, Sonoma has plenty of restaurants, but when the weather's warm there's no better way to have lunch in the Wine Country than by toting a picnic basket to your favorite winery and basking in the sweet Sonoma sunshine. Even Sonoma's central plaza, with its many picnic tables, is a good spot to set up a gourmet picnic. But first you need grub, so for your picnicking pleasure, check out Sonoma's top spots for stocking up for an alfresco fete.

If you want to pick up some specialty fare on your way into town, stop at **Angelo's Wine Country Deli,** 23400 Arnold Dr. (© 707/ 938-3688), where you'll find all types of smoked meats, special salsas, and homemade mustards. The deli is known for its half-dozen types of homemade beef jerky. It's open in summer daily from 9am to 6pm; off-season, daily from 9am to 5pm.

The venerable **Sonoma Cheese Factory** ☆, on the plaza at 2 Spain St. (© 707/996-1931), offers award-winning house-made cheeses and an extraordinary variety of imported meats and cheeses; a few are set out for tasting every day. The factory also sells caviar, gourmet salads, pâté, and homemade Sonoma Jack cheese. Good, inexpensive sandwiches are also available, such as fire-roasted pork loin or New York steak. While you're there, you can watch a narrated slide show about cheese making. The factory is open Monday through Friday from 8:30am to 6pm and Saturday and Sunday 8:30am to 6:30pm.

At 315 2nd St. E., a block north of East Spain Street, is the **Vella Cheese Company** ℛ (℅ **800/848-0505** or 707/938-3232), established in 1931. The folks at Vella pride themselves on making cheese into an award-winning science, and their best-known beauty, the Monterey Dry Jack, continues to garner blue ribbons. Other cheeses range from flavorful High Moisture Jack to a razor-sharp Raw Milk Cheddar. Vella has also become famous for its Oregon Blue, made at its southern Oregon factory—it's rich, buttery, and even spreadable, one of the few premier bleues produced in this country. Any of these fine handmade, all-natural cheeses can be shipped directly from the store. Hours are Monday through Saturday from 9am to 6pm.

Other highly recommended picnic outfitters include **Cucina Viansa** and **Basque Boulangerie Cafe** in Sonoma; **Café Citti** in Kenwood (see "Where to Dine," above); and **Viansa Winery & Italian Marketplace,** which makes fabulous focaccia sandwiches— and has a lovely picnic area for noshing on them, too (p. 132).

Gundlach Bundschu (p. 134), located on the outskirts of Sonoma, also has a wonderful picnic area perched on the side of a small hill overlooking the Sonoma countryside (though you'll have to earn the sensational view by making the trek to the top). On the opposite side of the valley, my favorite picnic picks are **Chateau St. Jean's** (p. 139) big, beautiful lawn overlooking the vineyards (bring a blanket) and the blissfully quiet pond-side picnic area at **Landmark Vineyards** (p. 140), which also sports a bocce court.

If you'd rather have someone else provide the picnic grub for you, check out **Ravenswood Winery** (p. 136), which offers the gourmet Barbecue Overlooking the Vineyards, held each weekend from 11am to 4:40pm, Memorial Day through the end of September. It's a great time for not much money; items range from $7 to $10, and sides cost a few bucks.

Appendix: Grape Varietals in the Wine Country

by Erika Lenkert & Matthew R. Poole

1 Major Grape Varietals

Below is a list of the most prevalent grape varietals found in California Wine Country and abroad.

CABERNET SAUVIGNON   This transplant from Bordeaux has become California's most well-known varietal. The small, deep-colored, thick-skinned berry is a complex grape, yielding medium- to full-bodied red wines that are highly tannic when young and usually require a long aging period to achieve their greatest potential. Cabernet is often blended with other related red varietals, such as merlot and cabernet franc (see below), into full-flavored red table wines. Cabernet is often matched with red-meat dishes and strong cheeses. If you're looking to invest in several cases of wine, cabernet sauvignon is always a good long-term bet.

CHARDONNAY   Chardonnay is the most widely planted grape variety in the Wine Country, and it produces exceptional medium- to full-bodied dry white wines. In fact, it was a California chardonnay that revolutionized the world of wine when it won the legendary Paris tasting test of 1976, beating out France's top white burgundies. You'll find a range of chardonnays in the Wine Country, from delicate, crisp wines that are clear and light in color to buttery, fruity, and oaky (no other wine benefits more from the oak aging process) wines that tend to have deeper golden hues as they increase in richness. This highly complex and aromatic grape is one of the few grapes in the world that doesn't require blending; it's also the principal grape for making sparkling wine. Chardonnay goes well with a variety of dishes, from seafood to poultry, pork, veal, and pastas made with cream and/or butter.

MERLOT   Traditionally used as a blending wine to smooth out the rough edges of other grapes, merlot has gained popularity in California since the early 1970s—enough so that wineries such as Sonoma's St. Francis are best known for producing masterful merlots. The merlot grape is a relative of cabernet sauvignon, but it's fruitier and softer, with a pleasant black-cherry bouquet. Merlots tend to be simpler and less tannic than most cabernets, and they are drinkable at an earlier age, though these wines, too, gain complexity with age. Serve this medium- to full-bodied red with any dish you'd normally pair with a cabernet. (It's great with pizza.)

PINOT NOIR   It has taken California vintners decades to make relatively few great wines from pinot noir grapes, which are difficult to grow and vinify. Even in their native Burgundy, the wines are excellent only a few years out of every decade, and they are a challenge for winemakers to master. Recent attempts to grow the finicky grape in the cooler climes of the Carneros District have met with promising results. During banner harvest years, California's pinot grapes produce complex, light- to medium-bodied red wines with such low tannins and such silky textures that they're comparable to the finest reds in the world. Pinots are fuller and softer than cabernets and can be drinkable at 2 to 5 years of age, though the best improve with additional aging. Pinot noir is versatile at the dinner table, but it goes best with lamb, duck, turkey, game birds, semisoft cheeses, and even fish.

RIESLING   Also called Johannisberg Riesling or white Riesling, this is the grape from which most of the great wines of Germany are made. It was introduced to California in the mid–19th century by immigrant vintners and is now used mainly to produce floral and fruity white wines of light to medium body, ranging from dry to very sweet. (It's often used to make late-harvest dessert wine.) Well-made Rieslings, of which California has produced few, have a vivid fruitiness and lively balancing acidity, as well as a potential to age for many years. Suggested food pairings include crab, pork, sweet-and-sour foods, and anything with a strong citrus flavor. Asian-influenced foods also pair well with Riesling.

SAUVIGNON BLANC   Also labeled as fumé blanc, sauvignon blanc grapes are used to make crisp, dry whites of medium to light body that vary in flavor from slightly grassy to tart or fruity. The grape grows very well in the Wine Country and has become increasingly popular due to its distinctive character and pleasant acidity; indeed, it has recently become a contender to the almighty chardonnay. Because of their acidity, sauvignon blancs pair well with shellfish, seafood, and salads.

ZINFANDEL   Zinfandel is often called the "mystery" grape because its origins are uncertain. "Zinfandel" first appeared on California labels in the late 1800s; hence, it has come to be known as California's grape. In fact, most of the world's zinfandel acreage is planted in Northern California, and some of the best zinfandel grapes grow in cool coastal locations and on century-old vines up in California's Gold Country. Zinfandel is by far the Wine Country's most versatile grape, popular as blush wine (the ever-quaffable white zinfandel: a light, fruity wine, usually served chilled); as dark, spicy, and fruity red wines; and even as a port. Premium zins, such as those crafted by Ravenswood winery in Sonoma (the Wine Country's Zeus of zins), are rich and peppery, with a lush texture and nuances of raspberries, licorice, and spice. Food-wise it's a free-for-all, although premium zins go well with beef, lamb, venison, hearty pastas, pizza, and stews.

2 Lesser-Known Grape Varietals

Here are a few lesser-known grape varietals that you may encounter as you explore the Wine Country. In addition to these, California's winemakers are beginning to experiment with a number of French varietals from the Rhône region and the Italian sangiovese grape with some success.

CABERNET FRANC   A French black grape variety that's often blended with and overshadowed by the more widely planted cabernet sauvignon, cabernet franc was actually recently discovered to be one of the parent grape species that gave rise to cabernet sauvignon. The grape grows best in cool, damp climatic conditions and tends to be lighter in color and tannins than cabernet sauvignon; therefore, it matures earlier in the bottle. These wines have a deep purple color with an herbaceous aroma.

CHENIN BLANC   Planted mainly in France, chenin blanc runs the gamut from cheap, dry whites with little discernible character to some of the most subtle, fragrant, and complex whites in the world. In the Wine Country, the grape is mostly used to create fruity, light-to medium-bodied, and slightly sweet wines. Chenin blanc lags far behind chardonnay and sauvignon blanc in popularity in the Wine Country, though in good years it's known for developing a lovely and complex bouquet, particularly when aged in oak. It's often served with pork and poultry, Asian dishes with soy-based sauces, mild cheeses, and vegetable and fruit salads.

GEWÜRZTRAMINER   The gewürztraminer grape produces white wines with a strong floral aroma and litchi nutlike flavor.

Slightly sweet yet spicy, it's somewhat similar in style to Johannisberg Riesling, and it is occasionally used to make late-harvest, dessert-style wine. The grape grows well in the cooler coastal regions of California, particularly Mendocino County. The varietal is particularly appreciated for its ability to complement Asian foods; its sweet character stands up to flavors that would diminish a drier wine's flavors and make it seem more tart.

PETITE SIRAH Widely grown throughout the warmer regions of California, petite sirah's origins are a mystery. The grape, which produces rich red wines that are high in tannins, serves mainly as the backbone for Central Valley "jug" wines. Very old vines still exist in cooler northern regions, where the grapes are often made into a robust and well-balanced red wine of considerable popularity.

PINOT BLANC A mutation of the pinot gris vine, the pinot blanc grape is generally grown in France's Alsace region to make dry, crisp white wines. In California, pinot blanc is used to make a fruity wine similar to the simpler versions of chardonnay. It's also blended with champagne-style sparkling wines, thanks to its acid content and clean flavor.

SANGIOVESE The primary grape used in Italy's Tuscany region and northern and central Italy is used to make everything from chianti and Brunello di Montalcino to "Super Tuscan" blends. As of late, it's also making a name for itself in California. Its style varies depending on where it's grown, but it's commonly described as anything from "fruity," "smooth," "spicy," "good acidity," and "medium-bodied" to "structured" and "full-bodied."

SYRAH This red varietal is best known for producing France's noble and age-worthy Rhône Valley reds such as côte-rôtie and hermitage. Syrah vines produce dark, blackish berries with thick skins, resulting in typically dark, rich, dense, medium- to full-bodied wines with distinctive pepper, spice, and fruit flavors (particularly cherry, black currant, and blackberry).

Index

See also Accommodations and Restaurants indexes, below.

RESTAURANTS

180   INDEX

FROMMER'S® COMPLETE TRAVEL GUIDES

Alaska
Alaska Cruises & Ports of Call
Amsterdam
Argentina & Chile
Arizona
Atlanta
Australia
Austria
Bahamas
Barcelona, Madrid & Seville
Beijing
Belgium, Holland & Luxembourg
Bermuda
Boston
Brazil
British Columbia & the Canadian Rockies
Brussels & Bruges
Budapest & the Best of Hungary
California
Canada
Cancún, Cozumel & the Yucatán
Cape Cod, Nantucket & Martha's Vineyard
Caribbean
Caribbean Cruises & Ports of Call
Caribbean Ports of Call
Carolinas & Georgia
Chicago
China
Colorado
Costa Rica
Cuba
Denmark
Denver, Boulder & Colorado Springs
England
Europe
European Cruises & Ports of Call

Florida
France
Germany
Great Britain
Greece
Greek Islands
Hawaii
Hong Kong
Honolulu, Waikiki & Oahu
Ireland
Israel
Italy
Jamaica
Japan
Las Vegas
London
Los Angeles
Maryland & Delaware
Maui
Mexico
Montana & Wyoming
Montréal & Québec City
Munich & the Bavarian Alps
Nashville & Memphis
New England
New Mexico
New Orleans
New York City
New Zealand
Northern Italy
Norway
Nova Scotia, New Brunswick & Prince Edward Island
Oregon
Paris
Peru
Philadelphia & the Amish Country
Portugal

Prague & the Best of the Czech Republic
Provence & the Riviera
Puerto Rico
Rome
San Antonio & Austin
San Diego
San Francisco
Santa Fe, Taos & Albuquerque
Scandinavia
Scotland
Seattle & Portland
Shanghai
Sicily
Singapore & Malaysia
South Africa
South America
South Florida
South Pacific
Southeast Asia
Spain
Sweden
Switzerland
Texas
Thailand
Tokyo
Toronto
Tuscany & Umbria
USA
Utah
Vancouver & Victoria
Vermont, New Hampshire & Maine
Vienna & the Danube Valley
Virgin Islands
Virginia
Walt Disney World® & Orlando
Washington, D.C.
Washington State

FROMMER'S® DOLLAR-A-DAY GUIDES

Australia from $50 a Day
California from $70 a Day
England from $75 a Day
Europe from $70 a Day
Florida from $70 a Day
Hawaii from $80 a Day

Ireland from $60 a Day
Italy from $70 a Day
London from $85 a Day
New York from $90 a Day
Paris from $80 a Day

San Francisco from $70 a Day
Washington, D.C. from $80 a Day
Portable London from $85 a Day
Portable New York City from $90 a Day

FROMMER'S® PORTABLE GUIDES

Acapulco, Ixtapa & Zihuatanejo
Amsterdam
Aruba
Australia's Great Barrier Reef
Bahamas
Berlin
Big Island of Hawaii
Boston
California Wine Country
Cancún
Cayman Islands
Charleston
Chicago
Disneyland®
Dublin
Florence

Frankfurt
Hong Kong
Houston
Las Vegas
Las Vegas for Non-Gamblers
London
Los Angeles
Los Cabos & Baja
Maine Coast
Maui
Miami
Nantucket & Martha's Vineyard
New Orleans
New York City
Paris
Phoenix & Scottsdale

Portland
Puerto Rico
Puerto Vallarta, Manzanillo & Guadalajara
Rio de Janeiro
San Diego
San Francisco
Savannah
Seattle
Sydney
Tampa & St. Petersburg
Vancouver
Venice
Virgin Islands
Washington, D.C.

FROMMER'S® NATIONAL PARK GUIDES

Banff & Jasper
Family Vacations in the National Parks

Grand Canyon
National Parks of the American West
Rocky Mountain

Yellowstone & Grand Teton
Yosemite & Sequoia/Kings Canyon
Zion & Bryce Canyon

Frommer's® Memorable Walks

Chicago
London

New York
Paris

San Francisco

Frommer's® With Kids Guides

Chicago
Las Vegas
New York City

Ottawa
San Francisco
Toronto

Vancouver
Washington, D.C.

Suzy Gershman's Born to Shop Guides

Born to Shop: France
Born to Shop: Hong Kong,
  Shanghai & Beijing

Born to Shop: Italy
Born to Shop: London

Born to Shop: New York
Born to Shop: Paris

Frommer's® Irreverent Guides

Amsterdam
Boston
Chicago
Las Vegas
London

Los Angeles
Manhattan
New Orleans
Paris
Rome

San Francisco
Seattle & Portland
Vancouver
Walt Disney World®
Washington, D.C.

Frommer's® Best-Loved Driving Tours

Britain
California
Florida
France

Germany
Ireland
Italy
New England

Northern Italy
Scotland
Spain
Tuscany & Umbria

Hanging Out™ Guides

Hanging Out in England
Hanging Out in Europe

Hanging Out in France
Hanging Out in Ireland

Hanging Out in Italy
Hanging Out in Spain

The Unofficial Guides®

Bed & Breakfasts and Country
  Inns in:
  California
  Great Lakes States
  Mid-Atlantic
  New England
  Northwest
  Rockies
  Southeast
  Southwest
Best RV & Tent Campgrounds in:
  California & the West
  Florida & the Southeast
  Great Lakes States
  Mid-Atlantic
  Northeast
  Northwest & Central Plains

Southwest & South Central
  Plains
  U.S.A.
Beyond Disney
Branson, Missouri
California with Kids
Central Italy
Chicago
Cruises
Disneyland®
Florida with Kids
Golf Vacations in the Eastern U.S.
Great Smoky & Blue Ridge Region
Inside Disney
Hawaii
Las Vegas
London
Maui

Mexio's Best Beach Resorts
Mid-Atlantic with Kids
Mini Las Vegas
Mini-Mickey
New England & New York with
  Kids
New Orleans
New York City
Paris
San Francisco
Skiing & Snowboarding in the West
Southeast with Kids
Walt Disney World®
Walt Disney World® for
  Grown-ups
Walt Disney World® with Kids
Washington, D.C.
World's Best Diving Vacations

Special-Interest Titles

Frommer's Adventure Guide to Australia &
  New Zealand
Frommer's Adventure Guide to Central America
Frommer's Adventure Guide to India & Pakistan
Frommer's Adventure Guide to South America
Frommer's Adventure Guide to Southeast Asia
Frommer's Adventure Guide to Southern Africa
Frommer's Britain's Best Bed & Breakfasts and
  Country Inns
Frommer's Caribbean Hideaways
Frommer's Exploring America by RV
Frommer's Fly Safe, Fly Smart

Frommer's France's Best Bed & Breakfasts and
  Country Inns
Frommer's Gay & Lesbian Europe
Frommer's Italy's Best Bed & Breakfasts and
  Country Inns
Frommer's Road Atlas Britain
Frommer's Road Atlas Europe
Frommer's Road Atlas France
The New York Times' Guide to Unforgettable
  Weekends
Places Rated Almanac
Retirement Places Rated
Rome Past & Present

Fly.
Sleep.
Save.

Now you can book your flights and
hotels together, so you can get even better deals
than if you booked them separately.

Travelocity

**Visit www.travelocity.com
or call 1-888-TRAVELOCITY**